Winning!

Using Lawyers' Courtroom Techniques
To Get Your Way In Everyday Situations

NOELLE C. NELSON Ph.D.

PRENTICE HALL
Paramus, New Jersey 07652

Library of Congress Cataloging-in-Publication Data

Nelson, Noelle C.
   Winning! : using lawyer's courtroom techniques to get your way in
everyday situations / Noelle C. Nelson.
     p. cm.
   ISBN 0-13-287129-7 (case)
   1. Trial practice—Psychological aspects. 2. Forensic oratory—
Popular works. 3. Persuasion (Psychology)—Popular works.
I. Title.
   KF8915.Z9N45   1997
   303.3'42—dc21
                                           97-2433
                                         CIP

© 1997 by
Prentice Hall, Inc.
Paramus, NJ

This publication is designed to provide accurate and authoritative information in regard to the
subject matter covered. It is sold with the understanding that the publisher is not engaged in
rendering legal, accounting, or other professional service. If legal advice or other expert
assistance is required, the services of a competent professional person should be sought.

*—From a Declaration of Principles jointly adopted by a Committee of the American Bar Association
and a Committee of Publishers and Associations.*

Printed in the United States of America

10 9 8 7 6 5 4 3 2 1

ISBN 0-13-287129-7

ATTENTION: CORPORATIONS AND SCHOOLS

Prentice Hall Books are available at quantity discounts with bulk purchase for
educational, business, or sales promotional use. For information, please write to:
Prentice Hall Career & Personal Development Special Sales, 240 Frisch Court,
Paramus, NJ 07652. Please supply: title of book, ISBN number, quantity, how the
book will be used, date needed.

PRENTICE HALL
Career & Personal Development
Paramus, NJ 07652
A Simon & Schuster Company

On the World Wide Web at http://www.phdirect.com

Prentice Hall International (UK) Limited, *London*
Prentice Hall of Australia Pty. Limited, *Sydney*
Prentice Hall Canada, Inc., *Toronto*
Prentice Hall Hispanoamericana, S.A., *Mexico*
Prentice Hall of India Private Limited, *New Delhi*
Prentice Hall of Japan, Inc., *Tokyo*
Simon & Schuster Asia Pte. Ltd., *Singapore*
Editora Prentice Hall do Brasil, Ltda., *Rio de Janeiro*

"Dr. Noelle Nelson has provided invaluable strategies to help me negotiate more effectively in both my professional work and my personal life. Her book will be an essential resource for anyone who wants to more successfully deal with conflict and achieve their goals."

Wendy Brickman
Brickman Marketing

"Dr. Nelson's exceptional insight into human nature has helped me improve my communicative and interactive skills, which has dramatically increased my success in business and personal relationships.

Felicia R. Meyers Esq.
Attorney at Law

"With Dr. Nelson's techniques, I learned how to successfully get what I want from the work place without negative manipulation."

Kimberly Olivo
TV Production Manager

"Dr. Nelson provided me within valuable life-skills . . . she gently, but firmly guided me to use practical techniques that affirm who I am and what I need and want."

Nina Mora
Educational Consultant

"Over the years I have witnessed the compelling transformations . . . this written guide will prove to be an invaluable tool for any individual who wants to utilize persuasive communication to get what they want out of life."

Tamme Hansen
President, See It All
Legal Video Services

"Dr. Noelle Nelson has given me some basic, easy to understand skills that allow me to handle problems whether personal or business . . . I'm in a better place financially and personally since I have known her."

Erica Jordan
Director, Total Body Studio

"In a variety of situations ranging from intensely personal issues to business and professional relationships . . . Dr. Nelson provides a startling effective method of getting from here to there."

Richard Houser
Richard Houser and Associates

"Dr. Nelson has many pearls of wisdom which have helped my personal relationships as well as my professional ones . . . I've learned more effective ways to communicate with people, and as a result, my business is growing."

Betsy L. Cohen
Independent Representative
Excel Telecommunications

"Dr. Nelson's techniques will increase anyone's abilities to achieve what they want from work, relationships and life."

Mimi Gramatky
Motion Picture & Television
Production Design

"Dr. Nelson brings astounding insight and clarity to every situation, sharing with us practical tools and lifelong skills for success in all facets of life."

Karyne Cutler
Entrepreneur

"Dr. Nelson's brilliance is evident in both her revealing insights into the courtroom drama, and her ability to effectively translate those insights into workable ideas for greater success in daily life."

Marcia G. Lamm, Ph.D.
Director, West Valley Psychological Clinic

"Dr. Nelson, in elegant and illuminating fashion, offers a rare combination of the practical and the profound. She not only improves skills but enhances lives.

Mitchell Taubman, Ph.D.
Director, Center for Professional Education

"Dr. Noelle Nelson has demystified the negotiation process! Like never before, I feel I have the home court advantage in the corporate world."

J. Alan Graham, Ph.D.
Corporate Consultant

"The skills I've learned have not only helped me in my professional career, they have worked wonders in my personal life. Thanks to those skills I get the results I want."

Geoffrey L. Rivas
Professional Actor

About the Author

Noelle C. Nelson, Ph.D. is a nationally respected psychologist, author, seminar leader, and consultant. Dr. Nelson gives trial attorneys the necessary tools to present a persuasive and credible case before a judge and jury, works with CEOs, professionals of all kinds and business people to better their communication and presentational skills, and facilitates individuals' successful handling of life's many challenges.

As part of her work with the legal community, Dr. Nelson, is the author of *A Winning Case* (Prentice Hall, 1991) and *Connecting with Your Client* (American Bar Association, 1996), and has published more than 75 articles in legal publications on trial strategies, witness preparation, mock trials, and the use of psychological and communication skills by attorneys. Dr. Nelson, an approved continuing legal education provider, conducts in-house seminars and often speaks before legal organizations including bar associations, the Los Angeles Trial Lawyers Association, the Practicing Law Institute and the Southern California Defense Counsel. She produced the highly acclaimed five-part video series "*A Winning Case*," and "*How to Give a Good Deposition and How to Testify Well in Court.*" Dr. Nelson's column, *A Winning Case* appears regularly in the *Daily Journal*, the legal newspaper for California. She has been interviewed in connection with legal matters by the *Los Angeles Times* and has appeared as a commentator on CNN and the E! Network during the O. J. Simpson trials.

Dr. Nelson holds advanced degrees in clinical psychology from the United States International University (M.A., Ph.D.), and sociology degrees from the University of California at Los Angeles (B.A.) and the Sorbonne, Paris (Maitrise, Doctorat 3eme Cycle). She is a Staff Therapist at the West Valley Psychological Clinic and a continuing psychological education provider with the Center for Professional Education.

Dr. Nelson is a member of the American Society of Trial Consultants, the American Psychological Association and Psy Chi, the national honors society in psychology.

Dr. Nelson welcomes your questions, thoughts and comments either by Voice Mail at 310-859-4604, E-mail (dr.noelle.c.nelson@worldnet. att.net), or by mail c/o the West Valley Psychological Clinic, 5435 Balboa Blvd., Suite 214, Encino, California 91316.

Acknowledgments

Writing a book is an exciting and challenging adventure. It starts out as a solitary journey, yet only comes to a satisfying and fulfilling end with the participation and active support of many good people. I feel privileged and honored to be once again published by Prentice Hall. I am deeply grateful to the wonderful editing, production and marketing staff at Prentice Hall (Sally Hertz, Joan-Ellen Messina, Yvette Romero, Nancy Kahan and Mariann Hutlak, among others) for their constant and tireless efforts to make this the best book possible. In particular, I would like to thank Susan McDermott, my editor, for her enthusiasm, persistence, and unswavering commitment to seeing this book through from mere idea to finished manuscript.

For permission to quote copyrighted materials, I am grateful for the excerpts as follows: from Outrage: The Five Reasons Why O. J. Simpson Got Away with Murder by Vincent Bugliosi. Copyright © 1996 by Vincent Bugliosi. Reprinted by permission of W. W. Norton & Company, Inc.; from Hung Jury: The Diary of a Menendez Juror by Hazel Thornton. Copyright © 1995 by Hazel Thornton. Reprinted by permission of Temple University Press; from Madam Foreman: A Rush to Judgment? by Armanda Cooley, Carrie Bess, and Marsha Rubin-Jackson. Copyright © 1995 by Dove Audio, Inc. Reprinted with permission by Dove Books; from How To Argue and Win Every Time by Gerry Spence. Copyright © 1995 by Gerry Spence. Reprinted by permission of St. Martin's Press Incorporated; from With Justice For None by Gerry Spence. Copyright © 1989 by Gerry Spence. Reprinted by permission of Times Books, a division of Random House, Inc.; Copied from *Trial Communication Skills* by Aron, Fast & Klein with permission of the Publisher: Clark Boardman Callaghan, 155 Pfingsten Road, Deerfield, IL, 60615. For additional information, please contact Clark Boardman Callaghan at (800) 221-9428.

My heartfelt thanks to all those who so generously gave of their opinions and comments on "Winning!" and the techniques contained therein. A special note of gratitude to Diane Rumbaugh, Erica Jordan-Anka, Erwin Pearlman, Suzy and Frank Cross for their constant patience, encouragement and love.

Preface

What if . . . every time you wanted something from your boss you had a successful strategy to go about getting it?

What if . . . every time you wanted to convince your spouse of something, you had a set of techniques that would help you succeed?

What if . . . every time you wanted to persuade a client or customer you had the steps to get you there?

Most of us go about getting our way by latching onto whatever seems workable at the time: reasoning, threatening, pleading, bargaining, crying, yelling, arguing, getting hysterical. Sometimes you give up after your first attempt, sometimes you try again and again and again. Sometimes you get what you want and sometimes you don't.

Trial lawyers don't have that luxury. Every time a trial lawyer stands in front of a jury, someone's life, honor, well-being, or pocketbook is on the line. Lawyers have to get their way—every time. Lawyers who want to succeed can't afford to leave persuasion up to chance, and successful lawyers don't.

For the past twelve years I have worked actively with lawyers as a trial consultant, advising them on strategy and courtroom techniques, and at the same time have had a thriving practice with (so-called) "ordinary" people as a psychologist. Being above all a practical person, I have long helped the ordinary people who consulted me in my private practice get what they want in their lives by sharing with them the very techniques I was teaching trial lawyers to succeed with in the courtroom. It certainly made sense to me to do so: Persuasion is persuasion, and who better to use as models of persuasive talents than those men and women whose persuasive ability is on the line every day of their career.

These techniques, which help my lawyer clients win cases and my private-practice clients get what they want in their lives, are the techniques I now share with you in this book. These techniques *work*, both in and out of the courtroom.

Successful trial lawyers are masters of persuasion, continually honing and developing their persuasive skills, because as times change, ways to convince people change. "Winning by intimidation," for example, doesn't work much anymore. "My way or the highway" is more likely to get you sued for harassment or wrongful termination rather than to enlist someone's cooperation. Clients, employees, co-workers, customers, spouses, friends, and family all expect more than that. They increasingly expect to be treated with respect, dignity, and consideration.

"Well, that all sounds very nice," you say, "but how do I get what I want in such an environment? I have things to do! I can't just sit around babying people all day." You're right. You can't. And you don't have to. What you do need to do is be willing to look at a different way of approaching getting your way, of interacting with people.

Top trial lawyers succeed not because they are better at law, but because they are better at *people*. However they have come to it, successful trial lawyers understand what people need in order to be convinced, and that's what they play to. If winning a case were just about "the facts," you'd never need a courtroom; all you'd have to do is hand each juror a book listing all the "facts." As we all witnessed in the O. J. Simpson trial and continue to witness daily on *Court TV,* the facts are just the beginning—they must then be presented in a certain way to persuade the jurors of the rightness of a particular cause. Similarly, the idea you have in mind, the product you sell, the service you provide, and the information you want to convey are the beginning—the raw material that you then must present in a certain way for people to want it.

Part I of *Winning* takes you through the seven steps to success that trial lawyers use to win, showing you in very practical, concrete terms 110 techniques lawyers use to ensure their success and how you can use those techniques. In Chapter 1, for example, you'll learn about credibility, the "believability factor." Credibility determines whether or not someone will believe something you say is true just because you said it. It is the foundation of a lawyer's success as a persuasive advocate. You'll learn the techniques lawyers use to establish "instant credibility" with the jurors and how you can use these same techniques to establish yours.

In Chapter 2, you'll find out that what you have to say and how you say it are two entirely different things. You'll see how the way facts are communicated makes the difference between winning and losing. Chapter 2 shows you how successful trial lawyers use body language to communicate their interpretation of the facts powerfully and how you can use the same techniques to communicate your facts powerfully.

In Chapter 3, you'll discover there is a world of difference between *presenting* and *persuading*. Successful trial lawyers, whose main thrust is persuasion, use the full range of their voices, varying the volume, pitch, and pace to keep the jury listening with both ears, ready and willing to hear more. They use vocal techniques and skills to make sure the jury is truly convinced. Chapter 3 gives you these vocal techniques and skills lawyers use to persuade juries and shows you how to apply those skills practically.

Chapter 4 deals with the important issue of trust. Without trust, there can be no persuasion. A trial lawyer's first task is to create the kind of relationship with the jurors that will, in turn, engender their trust. Chapter 4 brings you lawyers' key rapport-producing techniques, such as "mirroring," "perceptual modes," and "pace and lead," and shows you how to make these work for you.

In Chapter 5, you'll learn that persuasion is not a one-way street. The successful trial lawyer is always listening to how others receive what he/she is saying and adjusts his/her approach, argument, and strategy in function of that feedback. Chapter 5 shows you how lawyers listen, with both eyes and ears, in a way that helps them win their case and gives you techniques to enable you to listen with discernment to your advantage.

In Chapter 6, you'll discover how successful trial lawyers get the jurors to see the case the way the lawyer does, to interpret the facts the way the *lawyer* wants the facts of the case interpreted, not haphazardly or according to opposing counsel's point of view. Chapter 6 shows you the techniques lawyers use to appeal to the jurors' need for logic and how you can use logic to guide those you want to convince to your point of view.

Chapter 7 addresses the all-important issue of emotions. Successful trial lawyers are those who know best how to stir up jurors' emotions, to touch their hearts and souls. Chapter 7 shows you how lawyers use emotions purposefully and effectively to sway jurors and how you can use the same to win over those you want to persuade.

At the end of each chapter are several worksheets that will help you apply the techniques discussed in practical, everyday situations. The worksheets make the narrative a reality and can be used again and again as you increase your confidence.

As should be clear from the first seven chapters, persuasion is not about arguing, at least not in the sense most people think of arguing: two people pitted against each other, each trying to impose his/her differing point of view. Persuasion is about carefully designing and expressing your point of view in a way that wins people over without "arguing" in the traditional sense of the term. Persuasion is a strategy. The seven steps provide you with a clear and easy way to determine the strategy that will be most effective in getting you what you want in each particular situation.

Part II is devoted to practical application of these techniques, showing you how to use them in real-life situations, at work, at home, and in the world. For example, you'll see how to

- Negotiate with your employer to give you better raises and more fulfilling work conditions.
- Convince your family members to do things your way.
- Persuade your co-workers, employees, and bosses to go along with your ideas and projects.
- Win voters, contractors, in-laws, and others over to your point of view and get what YOU want.

These are the strategies and techniques I want to share with you, because with them you can persuade people of the worth of your idea, of the benefit of your service or product, of the rightness of your cause; you can get your way just as successful trial lawyers do. No, it won't happen every time. Even great lawyers lose occasionally. But with these techniques and their application, you will surprise yourself at how often and how wonderfully easy it will be to get your way. Learn, practice, and apply the techniques that have made trial attorneys rich and famous and get more of what you want—every time!

Contents

six

THE SIXTH STEP: 225
Persuade with Logic and Reason

seven

THE SEVENTH STEP: 257
Win with Emotion

eight _____

OUT OF THE COURTROOM, INTO YOUR LIFE   311

CHECKLIST OF STEPS AND TECHNIQUES TO USE IN DESIGNING YOUR SPECIFIC PERSUASIVE STRATEGIES

REFERENCES

INDEX

Techniques Highlighted in this Book

The First Step:
Create a Sure Foundation With Credibility

"One can stand as the greatest orator the world has known, possess the quickest mind, employ the cleverest psychology, and have mastered all the technical devices of argument, but if one is not credible, one might just as well preach to the pelicans."[1] So says one of the premier trial lawyers, Gerry Spence, in describing the absolute rock-bottom importance of credibility. Credibility is something a successful trial lawyer pays attention to from day one of a trial.

WHAT LAWYERS KNOW ABOUT HOW PEOPLE CREATE FIRST IMPRESSIONS AND HOW YOU CAN USE IT TO YOUR ADVANTAGE

First impressions are critical to a lawyer's success in the courtroom. From the moment a lawyer walks through the courtroom door, the jurors are already determining whether that lawyer is believable or not. The lawyer's initial physical presentation determines how the jurors view the lawyer, what they think of the lawyer and his/her client, and how the jurors will assess whatever is said or done by that lawyer from then on: Initial physical presentation is the background against which the lawyer's every deed and word is evaluated.

Why is this first impression so important? Because lawyers know that unless the jurors believe that he/she is a credible human being, the jurors will not allow themselves to be persuaded by him/her. Credibility is your believability factor. Credibility is what inspires confidence and influences decisions. Credibility determines whether or not someone will believe something you say is true just because you said it. Credibility is absolutely critical. It is the foundation of a lawyer's success as a persuasive advocate, as it will be the foundation of your success, and as such it must be carefully established.

JOHNNIE COCHRAN: HIS CREDIBILITY PRECEDED HIM

Choosing Johnnie Cochran as a highly visible key member of the team of lawyers defending O. J. Simpson in his criminal trial was a very smart move. Mr. Cochran had great credibility within the black community and with his colleagues. He walked into the courtroom already positioned as someone who could be trusted, someone the jurors were predisposed to believe.

"Cochran was one of those people who [prior to the Simpson case] it had always been hard not to like. He has a ready smile and warm, jovial manner with everyone, rolls with the punches, and doesn't project arrogance or pomposity. Cochran's motto seems to be 'Live and let live.' He has always been very well liked and respected in the legal community and is particularly known and respected in the black community."[2]

District Attorney Robert Morgenthau sums up the informed opinion of many outstanding trial lawyers when he states, "A lot of jurors make their decision not only on the evidence but on whether the lawyer is believable."[3] The worthiness of the client's cause is intimately related to the perceived worthiness of the lawyer. If the jury believes the lawyer is credible, it is willing to extend that credibility to the client and to the case. The lawyer is every bit as much on trial as is the client.

So too, if you are believable, others will extend your credibility to whatever it is you are trying to convince them of. They will be willing to listen seriously to what you have to say, just because you impress them as someone worth listening to.

"Gee," you say to yourself, "I am who I am. How do I know if I'm 'credible' or not? Certainly I know when I'm lying—I probably don't do it very well and people can tell, but beyond being honest, I don't know what else to do." There is a great deal you can do to assure your credibility once you understand, as lawyers do, how first impressions are formed.

Jurors assess what they see by a process called "stereotyping," which then becomes the basis of their initial impression of a lawyer or a witness.

A CATHOLIC SCHOOLGIRL'S PURITY RUBS OFF: THE WOODY ALLEN/MIA FARROW TRIAL

In the Woody Allen/Mia Farrow trial, *The New York Times* referred to Mia Farrow during her questioning (cross-examination) by Elkon Abromowitz in the following terms:

"The woman who calmly answered Mr. Abromowitz's questioning during a long, tedious day looked like a Roman Catholic schoolgirl, the kind who earns straight A's for deportment and penmanship. Dressed in a pleated teal skirt, a navy blazer and a white shirt buttoned to the throat, Ms. Farrow politely responded to a seemingly unending series of questions."[4]

The "Catholic schoolgirl look" described by *The New York Times* grounded Ms. Farrow's credibility in dress and body language, which conveyed honesty, innocence, and trust. Who could be more truthful than a polite, demure Catholic schoolgirl?

Stereotyping is the process that allows us to conduct our daily affairs with the speed and efficiency dictated by modern life. Stereotyping helps people figure out what to do with complex information by organizing and simplifying it; it enables us to categorize information virtually instantaneously so that we may react or respond appropriately.

LT. COL. OLIVER NORTH: THE VIRTUOUS WORKING MAN UP AGAINST THE PAMPERED FAT CATS

In commenting on Lt. Col. North's credibility, a participant in the chat line bulletin board, undertaken by Judge Richard B. Klein (Judge of Court of Common Pleas, Pennsylvania) to assess the impact of North on the average juror, said: "I think it helped that he was tall, thin and good looking. He didn't look like a pampered fat cat, like Poindexter. He didn't *look* like he was after power, or prestige, or wealth. He was a working man."[5]

People knew what to think of Lt. Col. North by placing what he had to say within the context of what he looked like. He seemed to be "a working man." This greatly colored how people heard and interpreted what North had to say.

CASE IN POINT

Here are some examples of how people use stereotyping in daily life:

Situation #1

A worried-looking middle-aged woman, wearing a plain but clean housedress and carrying a crying child in her arms asks you for help.

Stereotyped Interpretation: Your instant stereotyped interpretation of the situation is: "Here is a concerned mother, the child is crying, he/she's probably sick."

Appropriate Response Based on Stereotyped Interpretation: You respond to her plea with compassion, and try to help her.

Situation #2

A young man, long greasy-looking hair flapping in the wind, dressed in torn leather with metal studs, tattoos adorning his naked chest, roars up on a motorcycle and asks you for help.

Stereotyped Interpretation: Your instant stereotyped interpretation of the situation is: "This man looks like a Hell's Angel; his plea for help is undoubtedly just a way of getting me close enough to him so he can steal my wallet or knife me."

Appropriate Response Based on Stereotyped Interpretation: You pretend you never heard the man's plea and duck into the nearest shop to avoid him.

Stereotyping helps us interpret and evaluate new information on the basis of what we already know and thus helps us to make potentially meaningless situations meaningful. Once an individual has made sense of a situation, he/she can anticipate future behavior or events based on the stereotype and so is free to go on to deal with other matters. Given how stereotyping works generally, how does stereotyping impact a lawyer's credibility with the jurors?

A lawyer fidgets and keeps chewing on his mustache during opposing counsel's cross-examination of his witness. The fidgeting and chewing are stereotyped as evidence of worry and anxiety. The jurors' assessment of such worry and anxiety is that the lawyer must be ill prepared and therefore unprofessional. With this frame of reference in mind, the jurors now know how to interpret anything the attorney does and so are free to attend to other events occurring in the courtroom.

You create an impression of yourself whether you do it on purpose or not. It doesn't make a bit of difference if you spend hours of thought, creativity, and effort to create a given impression or if you don't spend a moment on it, the result is the same: People will respond to you on the basis of their perception of who you are.

Let me repeat that last statement because it is critical: You will be responded to in function of how people *perceive* you, not in terms of who you really are. This is an important distinction. The worried woman in the example cited earlier could have been a kidnapper; the motorcycle rider could have been honestly in need of help. Most certainly, attractive-looking men have been known to rape. These are realities. But the response to all these people is a function of how they are *perceived*, not as a function of who they really are.

WOULD THE REAL SMUGGLER PLEASE STEP FORWARD?

In a study by Kraut & Poe,[6] observers tried to determine, during the course of a Customs interview, which airline travelers were smuggling contraband goods and which were not. Observers shared such a clear consensus about the stereotype of how a smuggler behaves that they agreed to a striking degree as to which travelers were smugglers and which were not, yet in reality, the observers were almost always wrong in their perceptions. *Regardless of the fact that the stereotype did not conform to the real behavior of smugglers, it was maintained as the guiding principle in "how to discern a smuggler"!*

The problem, then, is not whether you are credible, but whether that is what comes across? If you don't express yourself to the people you are addressing in ways that are stereotypically recognizable as credible, you will not be perceived as such.

Using First Impressions to Establish Your Credibility the Way Lawyers Do

A lawyer's credibility is composed of two basic elements: expertness, the lawyer's ability to make valid statements; and trustworthiness, how fair and sincere is the lawyer in making these statements.

Technique #1: Establish credibility with expertness

Expertness relates to how well the lawyer has prepared his/her case, how thorough he/she has been, how "professional" he/she is. "Professional" is defined by jurors as "careful presentation of the evidence": the prototypical lawyer is one who is "meticulous and incisive."[7] If you are to be believed, you not only must *be* well prepared and know your subject thoroughly, you must also look and sound as if you are well prepared to those who are listening to you.

Technique #2: Follow through with trustworthiness

Trustworthiness includes "authoritative presentation" and the juror's perception of the lawyer's "demonstrated allegiance and zeal for his client's cause."[8]

The great trial lawyers truly believe in their client or their client's cause, and this belief shines through and informs their every word and action.

Case in Point

"It is the magic of *caring* for one's clients, because caring is the secret of winning. Juries feel its irresistible power and respond to it. . . How can you expect a jury to care for your client if you do not? Caring is contagious. . ." exclaims Gerry Spence in talking with young lawyers.[9] It is this caring that convinces the jurors of lawyers' true worth; of their credibility.

You may have the same intense belief in your cause, but if you do not express that belief both verbally and nonverbally in a way that others *perceive* as sincere, you will not be believed.

Successful trial lawyers learn to leave their habitual ways of expressing themselves at the door of the courtroom and attend to how they want to be perceived in that courtroom. What matters to the successful presentation of his/her case is not the lawyer's private self, but the self the jurors perceive the lawyer to be. Hopefully, the lawyer's public and private selves will end up being one and the same.

A word of caution: Sincerity cannot truly be faked. It can perhaps be imitated for awhile, but it cannot be pretended for any length of time. Therefore, it goes without saying that if you are not sincere in what you are saying, no amount of communication skills training will somehow "give" you that sincerity. It is your first consideration to be genuinely trustworthy and expert, to be well prepared and willing to pursue your cause with "passion and zeal." The inner sense you have of your honesty, sincerity, and worth can then be translated into observable behaviors reflecting those qualities.

In forming their initial impression of a lawyer's credibility, jurors rely on the basic decision-making processes: gathering information, then assessing it. Scrutinizing the lawyer, client, and witnesses for outward signs of worthiness and sincerity are significant parts of the information-gathering process; right from the start of trial, jurors often keep extensive notes of what lawyers do, including their personal grooming, habits, and gestures.

CAPTIVES IN THE COURTROOM: THE MENENDEZ BROTHERS' TRIAL

The trial of the Menendez brothers was widely publicized. Although the brothers admitted to killing their parents, the trial resulted in a hung jury. A juror who participated in the trial of one of the brothers, Erik Galen Menendez, remarked: "Since we are held captive in the courtroom, we have little else to do besides pay attention. We attach great significance to things that a nonjuror might not even notice: a snide remark by one of the attorneys, a subtle reprimand by the judge, a glance exchanged by the defendants, a third or fourth reference to something that has evidently been ruled off-limits."[10]

Consequently many behaviors that would, in the course of daily life, go unnoticed, and certainly unjudged, suddenly assume new and critical proportions.

Situation #1

A lawyer gropes in his briefcase for a document.

Jurors' Reaction: Jury takes this observed behavior as evidence that the lawyer is unprepared and therefore probably incompetent.

Situation #2

A lawyer twists his/her wedding ring back and forth.

Jurors' Reaction: Jurors interpret this as nervousness and judge the lawyer to be incompetent: If the lawyer is nervous, he/she must be worried, so the lawyer must not be doing well, and he/she must be losing the case.

In sum, your perfectly innocuous personal habits and mannerisms are read as meaningful clues to your credibility and take on a life of their own. Whether we like it or not, appearances do matter. They directly influence what people think of us and therefore how they respond to us.

Not only is a first impression created almost instantaneously, but it is difficult to alter once it has been created. Research demonstrates that people hold tenaciously to their first opinion and will attempt to deny or devalue information that appears to contradict that first opinion.

WHY GOOD-LOOKING RAPISTS RARELY GO TO JAIL

In rape cases in which the defendant is good looking or handsome, female jurors often ignore the facts pointing toward the guilt of the defendant, claiming that anyone who is that attractive has no need to rape in order to be sexually satisfied. The women prefer to trust their first opinion, based on the initial impression, "attractive, therefore not a rapist," to the facts of the case. A sobering thought.

Although it is important that you maintain your credibility with the people you want to persuade at all times, the establishment of your first impression as a credible person is the most important of all. If you establish a credible impression from the start, it will carry you through many mistakes and problems. If you fail to do so, you will have one heck of a time getting others to believe you; they will have no foundation for their belief.

Wʜᴀᴛ Gᴏᴇꜱ ɪɴᴛᴏ ᴀ Lᴀᴡʏᴇʀ'ꜱ Wɪɴɴɪɴɢ Fɪʀꜱᴛ Iᴍᴘʀᴇꜱꜱɪᴏɴ Cᴀɴ Gᴏ ɪɴᴛᴏ Yᴏᴜʀ Cʀᴇᴀᴛɪɴɢ ᴀ Wɪɴɴɪɴɢ Iᴍᴘʀᴇꜱꜱɪᴏɴ Aʟʟ ᴛʜᴇ Tɪᴍᴇ

To establish credibility, somehow the lawyer has to convey two intangible qualities—expertness and trustworthiness—from the moment he/she enters the courtroom, long before uttering a single word. This is not as mysterious as it sounds. Successful trial lawyers know there are three cardinal rules to creating a winning first impression with the jurors:

1. Look credible in appearance.
2. Appear self-assured and in control.
3. Respect the judge, court process, and courtroom personnel.

PORTRAIT OF A PERENNIAL WINNER

"Walk into any courtroom and you can immediately pick out the insurance company lawyer. He is stately in his appearance, always immaculate with a proper haircut. He usually wears a white shirt, and his tie complements his navy-blue pinstriped suit perfectly. And he seems quite unimposing, quite humble, quite kind, quite gentle, quite to-the-toenails right. People inevitably look to him and listen to him, and because they tend to believe nice people, he usually wins."[11] Such a lawyer is eminently credible, both in appearance and demeanor. His credibility is a sure stepping stone to his success.

How does this translate into your life and your ability to persuade?

Look Credible by Enhancing Your Attractiveness

Social psychologists have demonstrated time and again that attractive people are viewed more favorably and are automatically granted more credibility than those perceived as less attractive. Does this mean you must undergo extensive plastic surgery in order to be successful if you weren't born looking like Mel Gibson or Demi Moore? Certainly not.

"Attractive" is a much broader concept than "beautiful" or "handsome." To be attractive means to have the power to attract; to be able to draw people to you, to be pleasing and inviting to others. "Attractive" has a great deal more to do with how you present your physical person than it does with the sheer beauty of your person. A clean, well-groomed individual, for example, with a healthy, fit body, whose hair style is properly cut to set off his or her features to their best advantage, whose clothes fit well and are of good cloth, free of spots or wrinkles, whose nails are clean and well tended, whose smile is wholesome because he or she takes good care of their teeth is enormously attractive, able to draw people easily, regardless of the actual beauty of his or her features or body. In contrast, a person who is devastatingly handsome or beautiful but who has ill-kempt hair, whose clothes are ill fitting and soiled, who smells like yesterday's fish, and whose nails are dirty and jagged will not be attractive regardless of the incomparable beauty of his or her face.

CHIEF JUSTICE TWESME: ON THE MERIT OF BEING A WELL-DRESSED THIEF

Albert L. Twesme, Chief Justice of the Seventh Judicial District of the State of Virginia, after spending over thirty years as a trial judge in Wisconsin, observed that "anyone connected with a thief, including the attorney, does better if he appears in proper clothing and with proper grooming."[12] Some truths are short, simple, and to the point. This is one of them.

Technique #3: Cleanliness counts

Cleanliness may or may not be next to godliness, but it is certainly next to successfulness. Cleanliness means clean hair, body, face, and hands and well-taken-care-of teeth. Be aware of your personal odor. People equate body odor with poverty and ill health, neither of which are linked to success. People recoil from bad breath. It is difficult to attend to someone's words when you're fighting off their breath. Don't allow something so truly inconsequential to get in the way of your credibility.

It is easy to forget the impact your hands may have on others, yet clean nails are important. What is your instant opinion of someone with dirty nails? How unfortunate if your credibility were undercut by something so simply remedied. Cleanliness also means clean clothes with no spots on ties or blouses; wrinkle-free clothes, freshly pressed.

As lawyers well know, when people are putting together their first impressions, they notice everything about you. What seems like an insignificant spot to you may assume gigantic proportions to an individual trying to ascertain who you really are.

Technique #4: Be well-groomed

Good grooming means that your choices of what you wear, how you cut your hair and nails, and how your makeup is applied are all predicated on what fits and suits you well. This means you choose clothes which fit you well, are of good quality, and are appropriate to the occasion. Good quality does not necessarily mean "outrageously expensive." Good quality means decently made, with seams that don't fall apart and buttons that don't fall off. You cannot "get away" with slightly frayed cuffs, an outdated tie, or a scraggly hem when you are seeking to create a winning first impression. Your shoes must be clean or shined, your stockings run-free, and your socks matching your shoes.

HOW A $20 HAIRCUT COULD HAVE TURNED THE TIDE OF HISTORY: THE SENATE INVESTIGATION COMMITTEE ON THE IRAN-CONTRA AFFAIR

Bendan V. Sullivan, who was the legal counsel for Oliver North as he testified before Congress, was keenly aware of the importance of credibility. Every detail was attended to: "Sullivan's appearance also contrasted with that of the House and Senate attorneys. His greying hair was cropped close, and he wore horn-rimmed glasses. This conservative, almost scholarly look enabled him to be very aggressive and outspoken and still have the visual look of the professor being reasonable.

"Many people noted problems in the television personality of House counsel John W. Nields, Jr. and Senate counsel Arthur L. Liman. If there ever was false economy, it was the $20 or so that Nields and Liman saved by not getting first-rate haircuts prior to the hearings. Many people commented on the fact that both were trying to hide their baldness, and many took the next step to consider this 'deceit.' "[13]

You can't afford to have people interpreting your haircut as a sign of "deceit" when you're trying to be persuasive. Genius has often been called "attention to detail," and certainly such attention is part and parcel of success.

Appropriateness is part of good grooming. Choose clothes appropriate to the occasion. If you are attending a business meeting, for example, wear clothes appropriate to a business situation. If you are seeking to persuade a youth group at your local Y, dress more casually. Your hair and makeup should also be appropriate to the occasion, as well as carefully chosen to best suit your face, not according to what is the latest fad.

There are many excellent consultants who can help you groom yourself: color consultants, hair stylists, personal wardrobe consultants, and so forth. Shop around, find out who is good, and consult. It will be worth the fee to look really well groomed and thereby enhance your credibility.

Technique #5: Choose appropriate accessories

The rule of thumb is, less is more. When in doubt, underaccessorize rather than over. We tend to dress and accessorize to express our personalities. When your primary purpose is to create a winning first impression, pay attention to what nonverbal message your accessories are conveying. You may have a special fondness for earrings, for example, but it would be highly inadvisable to wear your favorite razzmatazz-and-all-that-jazz earrings to a business meeting for the simple reason that more attention will be paid to your ears than to what you are saying.

Accessories such as jewelry, glasses, hair clips, and so forth, are so much a part of us we forget to take a look and see what function they may or may not be performing. As we will see in Chapter 2, good eye focus is critical to persuasiveness. Your glasses may obscure your look: Is the frame too heavy or too dark? Might you be better off with contact lenses? On the contrary, do your contact lenses make you blink all the time and tear? Might you be better off with glasses?

Ask yourself: Is your jewelry (and other accessories) consistent with the way you want to present yourself? What is the stereotyped message of a large heavy pinky ring on a man? What is the stereotyped message of a simple string of pearls on a woman? You will know what those messages are because within a common culture, we share the same stereotyped understandings. Advertisers have long taken advantage of our stereotypes; notice how advertisers portray successful men and women. Take a good look at yourself in the mirror and start questioning every one of your ordinary accessories; be sure they enhance and support your credibility rather than detract from it.

Technique #6: Be in shape

An out-of-shape, tired body is not attractive. No, you don't need to turn into a fitness buff, but you do need to recognize that you're hardly going to project a confident, credible image if you're drastically out of shape.

Being in shape doesn't necessarily mean going on a diet. Weight isn't everything. People can be somewhat overweight, but if they keep up a decent regimen of exercise, their bodies will be toned and thus an impression of positive self-assurance will radiate forth. If you're reasonably in shape you'll stand straighter more easily, your movements will be more fluid, and your gestures will have more life to them, all of which enhance credibility.

Appear Self-Assured and in Control

The second way in which successful trial lawyers convey their expertness and trustworthiness is by appearing self-assured and in control. Use the following three techniques to establish an impression of yourself as someone self-assured and in control, in other words as someone who knows what he/she is doing, someone who is therefore trustworthy.

Technique #7: Do things one thing at a time

The first technique of appearing in control is based on doing things one thing at a time. Whenever you do two (or three or four . . .) things at the same time, you are splitting your focus. In other words, you are giving only a portion of your focus to each item. Some people are perfectly capable of doing five things at once and accomplishing each well, but since few people are capable of this, the stereotyped reaction to someone doing five things at once is that some of those things are going to be done poorly. When people do things one thing at a time, the assumption is that they are attending to each thing carefully and that each will therefore be properly accomplished.

Most rituals are executed with this principle in mind. An example is the Japanese ritual of the tea ceremony. Each step of the ritual is carefully performed, with great attention given to every detail. Nothing is rushed, and the focus is total on whichever part of the ceremony is being performed at that moment. The impression conveyed is one of absolute mastery. Absolute mastery is power. So, for you to convey an impression of mastery, you must look as if you are in complete control of what is going on, and one of the basic elements of that control is doing things one thing at a time.

No matter how pressed for time or impatient a lawyer is, for example, you will not see a successful trial attorney rushing into the courtroom without looking where he/she is going or surveying what is going on and slamming him/herself into a seat without further ado. To convey mastery, the lawyer will attend fully to each part of his/her entrance, albeit only for a moment. For most successful lawyers, this is a completely unconscious process, yet it is part and parcel of how his/her credibility is established. Professionalism, the meticulous attention brought to each point, the careful and thorough preparation of the case, is a trait highly valued by jurors. This impression is conveyed by a calm and confident manner, easily achieved by the simple physical expression of doing things one thing at a time.

Regardless of how rushed you are, take a breath before you make your entrance, wherever that is, make sure your clothes are in order, your hair is in place, your papers or other equipment are neatly tucked away in your briefcase or other carrying case, and that nothing is spilling out of your case, pockets, or hands. Then walk in as if you had nothing more on your mind than going through that door (Illustration 1–1). At the door,

1-1

take a moment to notice who is where, then walk into the room. If, for example, you are joining others for a meeting at a table, look at the table, determine where you want to sit, walk over there, greeting others on the way as is appropriate, put your briefcase down, and then, sit. Once you've calmly seated yourself, open your briefcase, take out what you need, and only what you need. Then shut your case and put it aside on the floor, or wherever it won't be in the way.

Contrast the calm, self-assured impression conveyed by this entrance with the impression conveyed by a hurried entrance, where you rush in, papers and equipment in hand, slightly out of breath, hair mussed (Illustration 1–2). How much expertness do you think you convey with

1-2

such an entrance? It literally takes only a few moments longer to complete a calm, doing-things-one-thing-at-a-time-type entrance than it does to effect a "rushed" approach, yet in those few moments you will have projected an image of self-assuredness and of confidence that, properly maintained, provides the solid foundation your persuasiveness requires.

Doing things one thing at a time in such a fashion also gives you the appearance of being well organized. Jury studies have demonstrated that the lawyer who appears to be well organized impresses the jurors as being thorough and well prepared and thereby increases his/her credibility, and by extension, his/her ability to persuade.

Be sure you take out whatever needed papers, files, or other equipment you have with you to show others carefully, one at a time, putting them in specific places on the table, attending carefully to what goes where. These are all behavioral expressions of the quality "well-organized." Neatness or tidiness are also stereotypically read as manifestations of "well organized." Lawyers who frenetically search through a disorganized pile of papers are considered unprofessional. If you are not sure, for example, of where something is in your files, it is better to take a little longer to look for it in systemized fashion by going through one file at a time, deliberately, than to try to speed up the process by rifling through your files. You lose credibility in the process.

Doing things one thing at a time is a principle that is applied in more general fashion throughout a trial whenever a lawyer wants to convey mastery over a situation. Whenever you want to give an impression of authority, of competence, slow yourself down and do things one thing at a time.

For example, in making a point regarding a piece of evidence, a lawyer will walk over to the evidence, stop, look at it, pick it up if appropriate, and only then look up at the jury or witness to say whatever it is he/she has to say. Apply the same technique, for example, in making a point about an item. Do one thing at a time: Look over at the item, then pick it up or point to it, then look at the person you are addressing, and only then say whatever it is you want to say.

In asking an important question of a witness, for example, a trial lawyer will walk over to the witness, stop, look at the witness, and only then ask the question. The lawyer's unflustered approach conveys an attitude of self-assurance and authority. Apply the same principle when you have something important to say or ask of someone. Take the time to stop and look at the person before you speak or ask your question. You will appear confident and therefore credible.

It is said that Ernest Hemingway defined poise as "grace under pressure." The more hassled and harried you are in any given situation and the less you let it show by trying to do five things at once, the less reactive you seem to be to the situation. The impression created is one of ability to cope in situations that would drive others mad, of not losing your control just because the *situation* is out of control. What you are feeling inside is irrelevant to your perceived credibility. You may be feeling awful: panicked, scared, unsure. But people cannot crawl into your emotions and feel what is going on inside you, and they will not find out unless you let your insecure feelings show. So if you do things one thing at a time, which projects self-assurance and being in charge, people will assume that is how you feel and who you are *regardless* of your inner reality, and your credibility is thereby enhanced.

No one likes to be guided by a fool. When jurors observe an attorney who is trying to do three things at once—take notes, whisper to co-counsel, and ask a question of the witness all at the same time—they report having the distinct impression that this lawyer is ill-prepared, and the question becomes: Does this lawyer know what he/she's doing? How can I rely on him/her to show me what's going on in this case, when he/she doesn't seem to know what to do right now—take notes, whisper, or question? Make up your mind!

Whatever you focus on is automatically what those observing you will focus on. What you give importance to, by virtue of your attention, is what those listening to you will attend to. If you attend to three things at once, people get confused, and confused people are difficult to persuade.

Technique #8: Know when to be still

The second technique of appearing self-assured and in control is being still. When powerful people have something important to say, they start by holding perfectly still. Holding perfectly still is a great way of getting attention. It is also an important factor in the creation of focus. A soldier listening for the enemy doesn't move a muscle, his/her focus is completely on that not-yet-heard sound on which his/her life depends. In a football game, no one moves until the ball has gone into play, then all heck breaks loose. Focus consists of keeping everything else still so you can give all your attention to what is going on in the present moment. Focus is what gives you the appearance of self-assurance.

Successful trial lawyers who must appear self-assured and in control if they are to win have developed the art (naturally or otherwise) of standing and sitting perfectly still, not twitching or itching or anything else when either saying something important or listening to something important. More aptly stated, successful trial lawyers make it *seem* as if they are listening to something important. You may be thinking of a thousand other things, but if you look as if you are totally attentive, you will be effective.

Have you ever noticed how when you're talking to someone and they're scribbling a note, drinking coffee, and tapping their feet under the desk or table all at the same time that you hardly feel listened to? That person may indeed have been listening to you and may be able to repeat the conversation verbatim, but you didn't *perceive* the person as listening to you, and "perceive" is the operative word here. This principle, however, is not to be interpreted as just don't move and people will think you're in control. No, not quite. Just don't move and people are likely to think there's something wrong with you. Being still works specifically in two instances:

- You want to get other people's attention, for example, before you say something particularly important, or to be sure they heard something you deem important.
- You want to give an impression of complete and undivided attention; letting someone know by your stillness that he/she has your complete attention at that moment.

In both instances, the result is that you seem to be totally self-assured and in complete control of the situation.

CASE IN POINT

A successful lawyer, when called to the bench, will display utter self-assurance by simply walking up there and being still. Judges have remarked that they are less than impressed when an attorney fidgets or scratches an earlobe or other body parts. None of these actions conveys focus.

When you have something important to say or hear, be still. By your physical attitude, you are literally sending the nonverbal message, I am ready to hear whatever you have to say. It is the single most important thing in my life at this moment. I therefore give you my undiluted, undivided, complete attention. That's power. And it is respected as such.

Stillness is equally useful when you want to ask someone a particularly important question. When a trial lawyer, for example, gets ready to ask that one devastating question of the witness, he/she will first be completely still and will only then ask the question: "Did you kill your wife, Mr. Jones?" The lawyer's stillness alerts the jury to pay attention, something of importance is about to happen.

Although we did not witness the use of this technique much during the O. J. Simpson trial, frequently, trial lawyers will also use stillness to establish control of an unpleasant situation. If opposing counsel, for example, has just made a particularly inappropriate or inept remark, the lawyer disapproving of the remark will be still for a moment, thereby effectively signaling by his/her stillness to the jury that something of consequence has just happened and will only then proceed to make whatever comment is deemed appropriate.

CASE IN POINT

The following illustration is a classic example of a lawyer successfully taking control of an unpleasant situation.

An eminent trial lawyer, who happens to be Jewish, was cross-examining a witness. During the course of the cross-examination, the witness made a noticeable anti-Semitic comment. Rather than say anything, the lawyer simply kept silent, stayed perfectly still, and allowed the jury to digest the full import of what had just happened. It worked. The lawyer won his case, and post-trial interviews with the jurors revealed that the way the lawyer dealt with this unpleasant situation convinced the jurors of his integrity and that the perception of the lawyer as having integrity significantly influenced their favorable evaluation of his case.

Should you find yourself in a similar circumstance, remember that silence often is louder than words, and the moment of silence you impose by being still can be compelling.

Technique #9: Develop direct and steady eye focus

Eye focus is tremendously powerful. With eye focus, we nonverbally tell people whether they are important or unimportant, to be respected or cast aside, to be valued or neglected. We are susceptible to each other's eye focus: Jurors frequently comment on lawyer and witness use of eye focus.

DON'T BELIEVE UNTIL YOU SEE THE WHITES OF THEIR EYES: THE O. J. SIMPSON TRIAL

Jurors in the O. J. Simpson criminal trial commented frequently on the lack of eye focus demonstrated by attorneys and witnesses for the prosecution.

"He [Chris Darden] never could look you in the eye . . . Because when I would look at him some days, his eyes would sort of look the other way. I have a problem with people who can't look me in the eye."[14]

"Vannatter [a key witness] never looked at the jury. Vannatter didn't do no looking. Vannatter always stared out straight ahead . . . You're looking at all these people. You're waiting. You can watch their mannerisms, their expressions. You got eye-to-eye contact. You're waiting for them to tell you and look at you."[15] The ability of others to look us straight in the eye when speaking is highly correlated with perceived truthfulness.

When I work with witnesses, preparing them for trial, I spend a great deal of time helping them correct their eye focus so that their credibility will not be damaged.

When people are unsure of themselves, their eyes wander and the focus is unsteady. How many times were you told as a child, "Look at me when I talk to you!" An unsteady gaze is considered indicative of deception, lying, or insincerity. It is crucial to your credibility that you be perceived as sincere. Good eye focus is associated with calm, sanity, and forthrightness. In credible people, eye focus is direct, steady, and level.

WHAT MADE OLIVER NORTH LOOK SO CANDID?

"The way North maintained eye contact also helped his cause. He did not avoid his questioners' gaze, and seldom relied on notes. While he might look at a document, he looked at the questioner when answering the questions. This strengthened the impression that he was being candid."[16]

But how do you do it? When instructed to "maintain good eye focus," witnesses will often stare, which doesn't look right, or will keep their eyes rigidly open. I have found that steady eye focus is most effectively achieved by a technique called the "fishhook." It is very difficult to look steadily into a person's eyes when you have two eyes to deal with; what usually ends up happening is a fixed stare. So rather than deal with two eyes, I suggest you deal with only one.

To do a fishhook, send out your look just as a fisher sends out a line and "hook" the other person's diagonal eye with your look. In other words, look with your right eye at the person's right eye close to the bridge of the nose, not toward the temple, or with your left eye at the person's left eye (as in Illustration 1–3, but of course, facing each other). When you get tired of looking at one eye, simply switch to the other. If you are doing this properly:

- Your look will be a gaze, not a stare, and therefore will be respectful, not rude.
- It is much easier on you to maintain your gaze for long periods of time on one eye only.
- The other individual will have no idea that you are looking at only one eye.

The fishhook may sound extremely artificial and will indeed take some practice before it feels natural, but remember, the only reason you are so comfortable with your present eye focus is that you've been using it for years and years. Any new behavior is going to feel foreign and artificial, especially one as personal as eye focus. Be patient; comfort will come in time.

1-3

Bear in mind that the purpose of the fishhook is to establish initial contact, or reestablish contact at important moments; it is not necessary to do it all the time. The discomfort the use of the fishhook may occasion when you first start using it is more than made up for by the rewards in terms of the self-assurance and control it will enable you to project.

A trial lawyer has a particular challenge in terms of eye focus when addressing the whole jury. When I've debriefed jurors after a trial, they have often commented on how impressed they were when a lawyer looked directly at each of them while conducting his/her opening statement and how uninvolved they felt when a lawyer failed to do so. Your ability to connect with eye focus when addressing a group is very important to group members' perception of you as a trustworthy individual.

When addressing a group, look first at one member of the group for a sentence or two, then at another for another couple of sentences, then focus on another member, and so on. Do not "pan" the group with your eyes, letting the eyes just sweep over the members, this does not establish contact, and it is vital that you connect with the group in order to establish your credibility.

Avoid a pattern of looking first at one group member, then at the person directly next to the first person you looked at, then at the person directly next to the second person, and so on down the line. This is very unnatural and feels phony to people. Instead, follow the example of successful trial lawyers, who allow their eyes to skip around and select jurors in different parts of the jury box, making sure to look specifically and directly at each member of the jury in turn. Each member of the group you are addressing is important and must be made to feel verbally and nonverbally that he/she is of value. Your calm gaze at the different members of the group as you speak gives an unbeatable impression of self-assurance.

If looking at jurors is important, maintaining good eye focus when addressing the judge is even more so. Successful trial lawyers know to first look at the judge before speaking. When you address someone important to you, make sure your look actually connects with that individual before opening your mouth, even if it is only for a split second. This is a sign of respect.

Trial lawyers use eye focus differently for different purposes in questioning a witness. If a lawyer wants to put a witness on the spot, during cross-examination for example, an easy way to do that is to look steadily at the witness, refusing to let his/her gaze wander the whole time the lawyer asks the question, waits for the witness's answer, and then listens to that answer. The witness will literally feel skewered by such a steady look. If you wish to let someone know you are most definitely in charge and in control, use this approach.

If, on the other hand, a lawyer is questioning a friendly witness, the lawyer might use an entirely different type of eye focus. The lawyer might start by looking directly at the witness during the actual question, then might look at the witness during some of his/her answer, but might take his/her eyes off the witness and look thoughtfully a little to the side and down, still attentively listening, during some other parts of the witness's answer. At the end of the witness's answer, however, the lawyer would make sure to look directly at the witness when he/she finishes. This is a more casual or interactive style; it allows the person you are questioning to relax, as it were, when your eyes are off him/her. The impression you create with this approach is one of attentive warmth, self-assurance combined with friendliness.

Observe, in your daily life, how people use eye focus and what it feels like to you when people look at you attentively or fail to do so. Experiment with taking your eye focus on and off people and observe their reactions. Observation is a great teacher.

Convey Respect

Technique #10: Get respect by giving it

Jury studies have shown, time and again, that jurors have high regard both for the court process and for the judge. Successful trial lawyers enhance their credibility with the jurors by honoring that regard with unfailing respect and politeness.

In studies and reports of how the great trial lawyers work, the words "polite" and "respectful" are repeatedly mentioned. If you want people to

A JUDGE SPEAKS UP: RESPECT TIPS THE SCALES

Given the high regard jurors have for the judge, "It is beyond me," says Justice Patrick E. Higginbotham, "how, in the face of this reality, lawyers do other than treat judges with reverence in the presence of the jury. While I think that lawyers should be courteous to judges out of respect for the law, my point is the very practical one that you must do so to be successful."[17]

respect you and what you have to say, be respectful of them. Be courteous at all times, whether you are in the situation where you are attempting to convince others or outside it. Good trial lawyers do not blow their credibility by being rude to the courthouse cafeteria attendant or pushing past others to get into an elevator. Trial lawyers are aware of the jurors' silent observation of them at all times.

Being respectful and polite does not mean rolling over and playing dead; it means being ever mindful of others and treating them as you would like to be treated. It means being appropriate to the situation and to your objective. It's not a good idea to act out your negative feelings on people you are trying to persuade. If angered, don't blow up on the spot; respond with firm words, but wait until you're in a private place to vent your feelings. If you become annoyed, don't show it by tapping your pencil or rolling your eyes; hear the person through, acknowledge him/her, and move on. People are not persuaded by rude, overbearing individuals. People are persuaded by competent, self-confident people. Being polite and respectful is a trademark of successful lawyers.

COMMUNICATE YOUR CREDIBILITY WITH THE ATTITUDE LAWYERS USE TO WIN

Good trial lawyers don't just have credibility, they communicate it actively to the jurors with their attitude. It is that winning attitude that transforms the lawyer's credibility from an asset into a tool of persuasion. People are persuaded most easily by others who are "extroverted, involved, positive, and moderately relaxed."[18]

Technique #11: Focus Out Toward People

Contrary to popular belief, "extroverted" does not mean "ebullient" or "flamboyant." Extroverted means: "One whose attention and interest are directed chiefly towards other people and the external world rather than towards himself."[19] A trial lawyer must have a genuine liking of people, a willingness to go toward them, in order to succeed. Anyone who seeks to persuade others is in the "people business." As obvious as it may sound, people often ignore this important factor to the detriment of their persuasive efforts.

You may say to yourself: But I'm shy; it's hard for me to go toward others. People who are shy are in fact preoccupied with what others will think of them: Learning to go toward other people is often learning to switch your focus from what *others think of you* to how *you can help them*. Trial lawyers who are by nature shy will remind themselves of their competence as attorneys and what they have to offer others to help them overcome their shyness. Remind yourself of your competence and what you have to offer to those you seek to convince; it will help you take your focus off yourself.

Technique #12: Be Dedicated and Committed

"Involved" means dedicated and committed to your cause.

CONVICTION IS CONVINCING: LT. COL. OLIVER NORTH AS A PRINCIPLED MAN

A participant in the chat line bulletin board commented on Lt. Col. North's attitude: "People love someone who seems to believe in what he is doing, who is a man of principle. It doesn't seem to matter what the principle is, as long as he holds to it against all odds, expresses himself clearly, does not get defensive, and sticks to his story."[20] In and of itself, conviction is convincing. People are inevitably more persuaded when you yourself are visibly involved in your cause.

You cannot remain distant. Good trial lawyers allow themselves to become intrigued, fascinated, wrapped up in their cases. Their passionate conviction is greatly appreciated by jurors and is key to their success. Why should anyone be persuaded by you of the rightness of your cause if you are not already profoundly convinced of its merit? Be passionate in your dedication to your cause.

AN ACADEMY AWARD FOR LYLE MENENDEZ?

"All I can say is either that boy [Lyle] is the best actor I've ever seen in my life or he's telling the utter truth, because he's sticking to his story like glue. Either way, he held up extremely well under X-exam, in my opinion. He appears to be polite and humble, yet dignified. He brings every accusation successfully back to his version of the truth. . . ."[21] Lyle's passionate conviction was very instrumental in swaying the jurors to his version of the facts.

Technique #13: Have a Positive Focus

"Positive" means you see the upside, look for the pluses, look for the way forward. Successful trial lawyers do not indulge in disappointment or disheartened feelings, they do not give up. Good trial lawyers always look for a way to turn even the most disastrous events to their advantage. They may not always succeed, but they will always be thinking in terms of, and looking for, a positive way out.

Jurors do not appreciate a negative or downbeat approach. Regardless of how a lawyer's case is going, jurors expect a lawyer to keep a positive attitude toward his/her cause.

LOOKING DOWN MAY KEEP YOU DOWN: HOW CHRIS DARDEN'S MOODINESS AFFECTED THE JURORS

"I thought all the attorneys were great in their own way. I really did. But I sort of felt that Chris [Darden] was a little down. Maybe he was playing down. I don't know. He did not have that upbeat mentality. I thought he was very moody."[22]

Certainly, you may feel disappointed and disheartened from time to time; just do not wallow in such feelings. Feel them and release them. *Expect* that you will be persuasive, and you are more likely to *be* persuasive.

Expectation of success is not to be confused with arrogance. Arrogance has no basis in fact. An arrogant person assumes he/she will be victorious just by virtue of being. Arrogant individuals make no efforts to support that conviction by dealing with reality. Good trial lawyers succeed not because they are overinflated with their existence, but because they strive to create a winning case with their facts, evidence, witnesses, and arguments at all times, and they keep working to make their expectation of victory real.

Technique #14: Be Moderately Relaxed

"Moderately relaxed" means you are comfortable with yourself and your cause; you are not overly anxious. You are relaxed, but not so relaxed that you are casual or asleep. A certain degree of tension is necessary in the maintenance of alert attention. A certain degree of relaxation reassures those you are trying to persuade that you know what you are doing. Too much relaxation makes them think you don't care.

Successful trial lawyers are at home with themselves, have come to terms and accepted themselves for who they are, and thus appear relaxed and comfortable. They are well prepared and confident of their skills, which further contributes to their relaxed appearance. Good trial lawyers are excited by the challenge of trial and thus display good energy along with their relaxation. "Focused attention" is a good way of characterizing the energy state common to successful trial lawyers. As you come to terms with who you are, feel confident and prepared, excited about that which you want to persuade others of, your energy state will also be one of focused attention.

Summary

In the first four minutes people see you, they form an initial lasting impression of you. Be in control of those first four minutes—use the trial lawyer's knowledge of stereotyping to your advantage. Be aware of how you want to be perceived and do not confuse reality with the perception of reality. Credible presence is a combination of different factors that all create focus: doing things one thing at a time, being still, creating and maintaining good eye focus. A well-groomed appearance and an attitude of respect and politeness toward those you seek to persuade reinforces that presence and underscores your professionalism. Communicate your credibility by being involved, positive, and focused. A winning first impression is crucial to your ability to persuade others to your point of view.

WORKSHEETS
STEREOTYPES

Increase your understanding of stereotypes by observing your own stereotyped and nonstereotyped interpretations of the following situations:

You see a person who is:	Your stereotyped interpretation of the situation is:	Other possible interpretations are:
flustered	_____	_____
	_____	_____
	_____	_____
	_____	_____
anxious	_____	_____
	_____	_____
	_____	_____
neat	_____	_____
	_____	_____
	_____	_____
unhurried	_____	_____
	_____	_____
	_____	_____
giggly	_____	_____
	_____	_____
	_____	_____
calm	_____	_____
	_____	_____
	_____	_____
	_____	_____

running away   _____   _____

                _____   _____

                _____   _____

                _____   _____

dressed in rags _____   _____

                _____   _____

                _____   _____

                _____   _____

dressed in tails _____   _____

                _____   _____

                _____   _____

                _____   _____

smiling   _____   _____

                _____   _____

                _____   _____

serious   _____   _____

                _____   _____

                _____   _____

frowning   _____   _____

                _____   _____

                _____   _____

gesticulating   _____   _____

                _____   _____

                _____   _____

swearing

coughing

standing stiffly

smiling pleasantly

muttering to
   him/herself

crying

wearing unmatched
   socks

staring off into space _____   _____

                      _____   _____

                      _____   _____

                      _____   _____

Observe how characters are interpreted on television programs and commercials. Many of these are stereotyped interpretations. Study them and use both these and your observations of your own interpretations to better your understanding of how the jurors perceive you and others.

Television Characters	Stereotyped Interpretation
1. _____	_____
_____	_____
_____	_____
2. _____	_____
_____	_____
_____	_____
3. _____	_____
_____	_____
_____	_____
4. _____	_____
_____	_____
_____	_____
5. _____	_____
_____	_____
_____	_____
6. _____	_____
_____	_____
_____	_____
7. _____	_____
_____	_____

8. _____

9. _____

DOING THINGS ONE THING AT A TIME

Practice doing things one thing at a time. If you have access to a video-recorder, by all means, use it. Videotape provides excellent feedback that makes learning easy and quick.

Place a table and chair some distance in front of a doorway, roughly where you'd expect them to be if you were to walk into a room where you were to attend a meeting or give a talk. Put the videocamera on a tripod in front of the table so it faces you as you come in the door. Once you have recorded the sequences described here, watch the playback of what you have done, being sure to take note of what you are doing *well*, before taking note of what needs to be corrected. If you don't have access to a videocamera, ask a friend to watch you in order to give you feedback.

Practice the following sequences, noting any problems as you see the playbacks, and repeating the sequences until you are able to execute them fluidly and easily.

1. Open the door, walk in, stop, look at who is in the room (who you expect to be in the room when you are in the real situation), go to your table, put down your briefcase or whatever else you might carry in with you, and sit.

   Problems: Too rushed _____

   One part of the sequence overlapping another

   _____

   Unnaturally slow pace _____

   Uneven pace _____

   Other _____

   _____

2. From your seated position, open your briefcase, take out what you need, close your briefcase, put it aside.

   Problems: Too rushed _____

   One part of the sequence overlapping another

   _____

   Unnaturally slow pace _____

   Uneven pace _____

Other   _____

_____

3. From your seated position, arrange what you took out of your brief-case (that is, notes, files) in organized fashion on the table.

Problems: Too rushed   _____

One part of the sequence overlapping another

_____

Unnaturally slow pace   _____

Uneven pace   _____

Other   _____

_____

4. From your seated position, practice finding something in your papers and files in unhurried systematic fashion.

Problems: Too rushed   _____

One part of the sequence overlapping another

_____

Unnaturally slow pace   _____

Uneven pace   _____

Other   _____

_____

BEING STILL

Learn how to be still when it will really count for you by practicing keeping your body perfectly still at different moments in your daily life. Note whatever problems you are having and work toward correcting them as you repeatedly practice being still.

1. Be still when listening to a friend or co-worker. Keep your body totally quiet and really focus on what you are listening to.

   Problems: Body swaying _____

   Shifting weight from one foot to the other

   _____

   Head bobbing _____

   Hands moving _____

   Other _____

2. Practice stilling your body before making an important point or a statement. Let the quiet of your body provide an effective backdrop to the importance of your words.

   Problems: Body swaying _____

   Shifting weight from one foot to the other

   _____

   Head bobbing _____

   Hands moving _____

   Other _____

EYE FOCUS

Practice good eye focus as much as possible. When you speak with your spouse, your friends, or your co-workers, deliberately train yourself to use the fishhook. Notice whatever problems you are having. Being aware of the problems you have in maintaining good eye focus enables you to correct them. Repeat whichever part of the sequence is difficult for you until it becomes easy. Then integrate the formerly problematic part back into the whole sequence and repeat the sequence until the whole is fluid. Practice the fishhook until it is easy for you to do, but do not expect it ever to become totally comfortable.

1. Practice looking diagonally into one eye of the person you are inter-acting with, hold for a while, then look into his/her other eye. Hold for a moment.

   Problems: Difficulty in establishing original eye contact

   _____

   Difficulty in maintaining eye contact

   _____

   Eyes seem to have a life of their own, you can't keep
   them still   _____

   Eyes glaze; focus is unnaturally held too long   _____

   Other _____

   _____

2. Practice looking into someone's eye, then looking away bringing your eyes slightly to the side and down (see Illustration 1–3 on page 21), then bringing your eyes back to the person's eyes and reestablishing a fishhook. Practice this until you begin to feel a natural flow to look-ing, looking away, and looking back.

   Problems: Difficulty in establishing original eye contact

   _____

   Difficulty in maintaining eye contact

   _____

   Difficulty in leaving initial point of focus

   _____

Difficulty in returning to original point of focus

Eyes seem to have a life of their own, you can't keep
them still   _____

Eyes glaze; focus is unnaturally held too long   _____

Other _____

RESPECT

Observe your own behavior toward family, friends, co-workers, and others. Be honest in your assessment. Only by accurately evaluating your behavior are you in a position to correct it.

		Degree of respect shown	
Family	minimal:	some of the time	_____
		most of the time	_____
		hardly ever	_____
	moderate:	some of the time	_____
		most of the time	_____
		hardly ever	_____
	100% respect:	some of the time	_____
		most of the time	_____
		hardly ever	_____
Friends	minimal:	some of the time	_____
		most of the time	_____
		hardly ever	_____
	moderate:	some of the time	_____
		most of the time	_____
		hardly ever	_____
	100% respect:	some of the time	_____
		most of the time	_____
		hardly ever	_____
Co-workers and others	minimal:	some of the time	_____
		most of the time	_____
		hardly ever	_____
	moderate:	some of the time	_____
		most of the time	_____
		hardly ever	_____

100% respect: some of the time   _____

most of the time   _____

hardly ever   _____

The Second Step:
Engage The Power Of Your Body

"[A] trial lawyer *has to* be confident in front of the jury. If he's not, then he has to be a good actor and at least appear to be confident. It's one of the most important ingredients of a successful trial lawyer. If he's not confident, the jury will pick it up just like that—*in the way he talks, the way he walks, the expression on his face, the inflection in his voice.*"[1] Thus does Vincent Bugliosi—who, among the many outstanding trials he prosecuted successfully prosecuted Charles Manson for murder—succinctly sum up the power of body language.

What you have to say and how you say it are two entirely different things. If trials were won on the basis of the facts alone, jurors could read a list of facts, make their determination, and be on their way. The facts are what brings a case to court, but how those facts are communicated will make the difference between winning and losing.

WHAT LAWYERS KNOW ABOUT THE POWER OF BODY LANGUAGE

Successful trial lawyers don't rely on the facts to carry the day. Successful trial lawyers know that there are three fundamental aspects to communication:

- The actual words they say.
- The way they say those words.
- Their body language.

To a lot of people, "body language" conveys images of "if she crosses her legs, it's a come-hither sign" or "if he crosses his arms in front of his chest, he's angry," and that may be so; however, trial lawyers know there is much more to body language, and they are adept at using it.

Body language is the single most powerful communication channel. Communication research has demonstrated time and again that when body language and the content of a communication are in disagreement, body language will *always* be believed over words.

CASE IN POINT

A lawyer concludes his opening statement. His words are: "And the evidence will show, ladies and gentlemen of the jury, that my client, Mr. Jones, is not guilty of negligence."

His body language is: He stands slump shouldered, both hands jammed in his pockets, his eyes darting about the jurors. Result: The jurors believe his client is guilty.

Discussion: Why? When polled, the jurors said their belief had nothing to do with the client, but with how the lawyer presented himself. The jurors said "It didn't have to do with what he said or how he said it. He said it fine. We just didn't believe him; there was something about how that lawyer was that made us think he was lying."

The "how that lawyer was" had to do with the lawyer's body language. His body language belied his words. His body language clearly stated:

- Slumped shoulders, eyes darting: "I'm nervous, insecure, and unsure of myself."
- Eyes darting, hands jammed in pockets: "Maybe I'm even hiding something."

In this example, it hardly mattered what the lawyer actually said; his body language was so strongly in contradiction to the content of his statement that it completely overrode the effect of his words.

Your body language is used by people as a constant check on the truthfulness of your words. If your body language is consistent with what you are saying, your words will be believed; if it is inconsistent with what you are saying, your words will not be believed.

THE TELLTALE SQUIRM:
HOW JURORS KNEW MARK FUHRMAN WAS LYING

"When he [Mark Fuhrman, a witness for the prosecution in the O. J. Simpson trial] was being examined by the prosecution, he was cool, calm, and collected. But when the defense started to interview him, his whole demeanor changed. His breathing patterns shifted and, from where I was sitting, you could see him squirming. You could see the tension in his hands. . . . Fuhrman kept pushing his feet up against the back board of the stand. You could tell there was just a little anger building in him. I'm thinking, 'This man is lying.' You could see it right there. I thought I was the only one who saw it until we got into the deliberation room and I found that other people saw it, too."[2]

Successful trial lawyers use this awareness to their advantage. They do not take their body language for granted—far from it—consciously or unconsciously they use their body language deliberately to support and enhance their interpretation of the facts.

CASE IN POINT

A lawyer cross-examines a witness she is sure is lying. She doesn't want to say flat out "You're lying," but she does want to let the jurors know she isn't buying this witness's story at all. She therefore adjusts her body language to communicate the real message she wants to convey to the jurors, that this witness is lying.

1. She says: ". . . and so you were simply out for a stroll, when you happened to see the gun and pick it up."
2. As she says this, the lawyer's body language is: She stands, arms crossed in front of her, her head level (Illustration 2–1). This body posture states: I am defending myself against what you said are the facts, I am not receptive to it, I do not believe it.
3. The witness says: "Yes."
4. The lawyer responds nonverbally to the witness's "yes" by dropping her head down just a little and cocking it to one side just a bit (Illustration 2–2). Her body language states: "Now I'm really closing off to you (head dropped slightly down); I'm curious, I wonder what you're up to. I'm not sure I trust it (head a little cocked to one side).

2-1   **2-2**

Without saying a word, the lawyer has effectively communicated her distrust of the witness's testimony. The jurors will invariably read the lawyer's body language, recognize the statement it makes, and believe the lawyer's body language regardless of the words said. This is a striking way trial lawyers can make important points in subtle yet highly persuasive fashion.

There is no such thing as the "right" body language. There is only the body language that will effectively enhance or support what you want to communicate. Knowing this, you can use your body to say what your mouth cannot. The bottom line is, if you want your words to be believed, align your body language so that it is consistent with and supports those words. If you do want to convey something other than what you are saying with your words, shape your body language so that it is in contradiction with, or to some degree invalidates, what you are saying. How you use your body language will depend entirely on your purpose at any given point in time.

How do trial lawyers know how people will interpret body language? Trial lawyers have a keen understanding of stereotypes, the ways in which specific body postures and gestures are commonly interpreted by people within a given culture.

A HIGH-FLYING, LIP-SMACKING KATO KAELIN CRASHES WITH THE JURORS

"Kato Kaelin came to court [as a witness in the O. J. Simpson trial] just as high as he wanted to be. I think he was on some type of speed. That's the impression he gave me . . . I truly believe he was high. Smacking his lips—I know that from just being exposed to people who are high."[3] Mr. Kaelin's lip smacking could just as easily have been a sign of anxiety, but the common cultural stereotype the jurors used in assessing his behavior was that of a drug addict. Mr. Kaelin's credibility suffered from such an evaluation and with it, the prosecution's case. It is possible that the prosecution either was unaware of how Mr. Kaelin's lip-smacking would be "read" or that they dismissed it as unimportant. When it comes to body language, nothing is unimportant.

For you to use your body language successfully you must first learn what are the common body language stereotypes used to convince others, then how to actually use those common body language stereotypes to persuade.

A trial lawyer's first job is to get the jurors to trust him/her. Body language is extremely useful in creating this foundation. As mentioned in Chapter 1, do not confuse reality with the perception of reality. It is irrelevant, for example, that you cross your arms only because it is more comfortable for you, and in no way expresses defensiveness. Crossed arms are stereotypically read as indicative of defensiveness and will be read as such regardless. As with the stereotypes connoting credibility, an awareness of body language stereotypes can be used entirely to your advantage.

How You Can Use Lawyers' Techniques to Gain People's Confidence with Effective Body Language

Technique #15: Your posture: Confidence-maker or confidence-breaker?

All good trial lawyers are self-confident or, put more accurately, exude self-confidence. Good posture is critical in expressing the self-confidence that encourages others to trust you. Good posture implies strength and energy.

When your posture is good, those around you sense that the world can literally sit on your square shoulders. You seem able to handle whatever may come your way; your back is strong and will not yield to every knock and blow. It is hardly coincidental that armies all over the world demand that their soldiers demonstrate erect posture: It symbolizes force and resilience in the face of adversity.

A trial attorney's good posture is the mark of an energized person, someone who not only can but *wants* to take on responsibilities, one who is not only willing but *eager* to demonstrate his/her competence. Good posture signals readiness and the energy to get things done now, rather than put them off to another day.

How do you do it then? How do you encourage others to trust you with your posture? Stand straight! Good posture is basically erect posture. Stand with your spine straight, not curved in either direction (Illustration 2–3). If your spine is curved forward, you seem old and without energy (Illustration 2–4). If you stand so erect that your back is arched, curving backwards, your posture suggests a military background or rigidity (Illustration 2–5).

I have taught many an attorney to use this dancer's trick to help you stand erect: Stand with your feet about eight inches apart, hands at your side. In your imagination, run a cord from the base of your spine, through your spine, up through your neck, and out the top of your head (Illustration 2–6). Then pull the imaginary cord upwards. Feel your spine

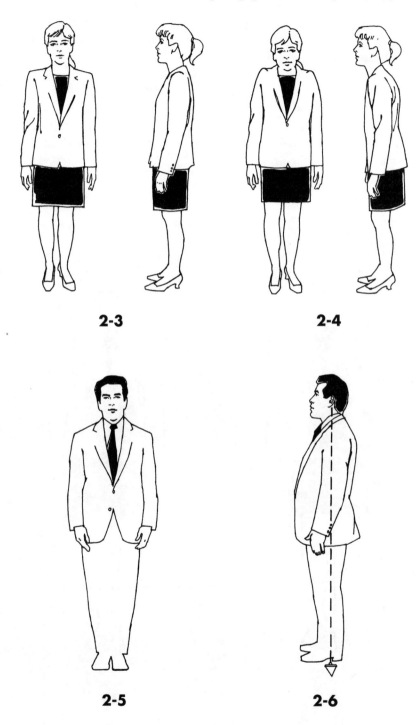

2-3

2-4

2-5

2-6

straighten as you do this. If you are unsure as to whether or not you are achieving good posture, consult a trainer in a gym, a physical therapist, or another qualified professional.

In good posture, the shoulders are "square," that is to say, level (Illustration 2–7). Stand with your shoulders comfortably in line with your straight spine. Do not slump your shoulders forward; this makes you seem weak or insipid. Do not tilt your shoulders downwards either to the right or to the left; this makes you seem unwilling to carry your load (Illustration 2–8). It should not cause you any pain to achieve good posture. If it does, or if any of the other body language positions described are painful, discontinue them at once and consult your physician.

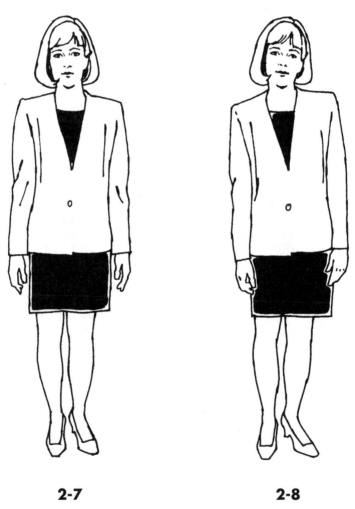

2-7   **2-8**

Technique #16: Your Stance: Create a Sure Foundation

If a trial lawyers' posture symbolically represents their ability to carry the weight of the world—or their portion thereof—on their shoulders, trial lawyers' stance is the foundation that enables them to carry that weight. How you stand lets the observer know whether or not you have what it takes to fulfill your responsibilities.

Use the trial lawyers' "neutral stance" to express solid confidence and reliability, without appearing aggressive or belligerent. Start by standing with your feet slightly apart. "Slightly" means the following: Stand with your feet apart and find the top of your pelvic bone, just under your waist and in front of your hip (Illustration 2–9). If you were to drop an imaginary plumb line from the top of your pelvic bone on either side straight down, it should hit the top of your toes (Illustration 2–10). Your knees should be straight but not stiff, and your arms should hang loosely by your sides, hands relaxed and easy.

2-9

2-10

When you first try the neutral stance, you will probably find it quite awkward and uncomfortable. Yet the neutral stance looks terrific: It gives you an appearance of easy self-confidence, energy, and readiness, as well as sure-footed dependability. The neutral stance feels awkward to you when you first try it simply because you are not used to standing that way. Most of us have very sloppy standing habits and have had these habits for many years. Changing anything as intimate as personal stance is undoubtedly uncomfortable, but the rewards in presentational effectiveness are well worth it.

The neutral stance is effective by virtue of its balanced nature. Be sure your feet are equidistant and only the distance apart described in the previous paragraph. Do not stand with your feet close together; you can be pushed over quite easily, both physically and symbolically. If your feet are farther apart, you are certainly solid and cannot be pushed over easily, but the width of your stance conveys belligerence, an attitude that is usually too strong for the courtroom (Illustration 2–11a and 2–11b)

2-11a   **2-11b**

and to be used with caution elsewhere. The neutral stance is "balanced"; you're not a pushover, but you're not pushing for war, either.

Use a wide neutral stance to show determination

There are probably no situations in which a trial lawyer wishes to be seen as a "pushover," but there are many occasions on which a trial lawyer, without giving verbal utterance to his/her willingness to do battle, wants to transmit that message clearly with body language. If you find yourself in a similar position, adopt a wide neutral stance (just a little wider than "balanced"), which is the nonverbal equivalent of "Don't mess with me, I won't let you push me or my client around." People will easily read your message regardless of how gently and calmly you speak your words. There is no one "right" way to design your body language; the right way is whichever suits your purpose.

Use the neutral stance as a safety mechanism when in trouble or in doubt

The neutral stance is your "safe stance." Anytime you want to project an image of self-confidence and reliability, go to your neutral stance. Anytime you've been thrown for a loop, but don't want it to show, resume your neutral stance. When in doubt as to how to communicate a point effectively nonverbally, go back to your neutral stance. At the worst, you'll be expressing poise and self-assuredness. This, of course, is assuming your posture is erect, as discussed previously. If you lack good posture, your stance is meaningless. If the foundation is excellent, but the house is shoddy and collapsing, who cares? Build a good foundation and have it support a solid structure.

"Sitting on a hip": Appear confident even when you're casual and relaxed

A trial lawyer doesn't stand around "at attention" all the time. As terrific as the neutral stance is, it is not the only way to appear confident. "Sitting on a hip" is a more casual, yet energized and confident stance, which may be assumed as a relaxed alternative to the neutral stance. In this stance, your weight is slightly more on one leg, with your hip jutting out in the direction of the leg you're standing on, and the other leg somewhat bent (Illustration 2–12). There are several variations on this stance, but they all share a more relaxed, more intimate feel than the neutral stance.

For that reason, you won't see most trial lawyers adopt a sitting-on-a-hip stance when addressing the judge, as it is less formal (and by extension, less respectful), nor with the jury until the lawyer has had a chance to get to know the jurors. Even when the trial lawyer knows the jury well, however, he/she won't sit on a hip when the lawyer has something important to say, as the casualness of that stance would negate the seriousness of the lawyer's message.

The variations on the sitting on a hip stance have to do with the degree to which the hip is jutted out and the way the feet are placed. The rule of thumb is, the more your hip is jutted out, the more the nonverbal message is one of indifference or cockiness (Illustration 2–13). If

2-12   **2-13**

your feet are very close together, the message is of snobbiness; if your feet are very far apart, you appear arrogant. In general, therefore, in order to convey simple relaxation, only moderately jut your hip out and keep your feet slightly apart. For most people, this is a very comfortable and easy position.

In other variations of sitting on a hip, your foot may be crossed in front of your supporting foot or behind it (Illustration 2–14). These are somewhat ambivalent foot positions, which are read by some people as denoting irritation or restlessness, an unwillingness to "stand one's own ground," and by others as indifference or boredom. Be mindful of these stereotyped interpretations if you choose to use these variations.

Sitting on a hip is *not* a good position to use when you are establishing a first impression, as it does not convey self-confidence and relia-

2-14a   **2-14b**

bility in the same unmistakable way the neutral stance does, nor, by the same token, is it a good stance to assume throughout any public presentation. Sitting on a hip must be judiciously used at those times when your message is a more relaxed and friendly one. Use the neutral stance in all important moments.

Technique #17: What to Do with All Those Arms and Hands

Beginning trial lawyers often feel at a loss as to what to do with their arms and hands and so end up doing all sorts of strange things, without realizing the interpretations to which their arm and hand positions are subject. More experienced trial lawyers have learned how to work with their arms and hands to their advantage, knowing how much judge and jury will read into their every move. The placement of your arms and hands indeed affects how your body language is read.

Express openness and nondefensiveness with the neutral arm position; that's arms hanging loosely by your sides, hands relaxed, palms facing your legs (Illustration 2–15). This position conveys nondefen-

2-15

siveness, a relaxed openness and willingness to deal with whatever happens. As with the neutral stance, the neutral arm position is a "safe" position. When in doubt as to what to do with your arms, return to this position. Because it is so open and nondefensive, this position is highly uncomfortable for many people and must be practiced often to feel even somewhat comfortable. Don't be surprised by the discomfort; it's normal and will disappear as the neutral arm position becomes more familiar.

The open and nondefensive aspect of this position will be destroyed immediately, however, if you fist your hand (Illustration 2–16). Fists convey hostility and are to be avoided. Fists with the fingers curled around the thumb convey angry powerlessness and are equally to be avoided (Illustration 2–17). Arms crossed in front of the body at chest

2-16

2-17

level project defensiveness, a closing off (Illustration 2–18). As with the other body expressions of anger, crossed arms need to be used with caution. Anger tends to alienate others unless you have a truly valid reason to be angry.

There are certain arm-holding positions trial lawyers quickly learn to avoid, those that convey fear and worry, the opposite of the self-confidence you are trying to project. For example, if you hold onto your arms with your hands in an across-the-chest position, you are literally "holding onto yourself," which conveys fear and worry (Illustration 2–19). Similarly, if you cross one arm chest height across your body and hold the other arm, you express insecurity or fear

2-18   **2-19**

(Illustration 2–20). Neither of these arm-holding positions are advisable, as they undermine your perceived confidence and self-assurance.

Another arm position that is to be used sparingly is the "arms akimbo" position. When you hold both arms akimbo, hands on hips, your position suggests readiness, interest and energy (Illustration 2–21). If, however, your body is pitched forward somewhat and your facial expression is very serious, you will be perceived as belligerent and confrontive. Women need to be especially careful of the arms akimbo position, as it will be interpreted as confrontational even without the body

2-20   **2-21**

pitched forward (Illustration 2–22). Women are better advised to use the one arm akimbo, hand on hip position, with erect posture, which will be understood as conveying determination, readiness, and some degree of confrontation (Illustration 2–23). Do bear in mind, however, that for women, arms akimbo (whether one or both arms), have a "fish-wife" connotation and should be used sparingly. For men, a one-arm akimbo, hand on hip, is interpreted as a milder version of both arms akimbo (Illustration 2–24).

The stereotypical understanding of other arm and hand positions are also gender-related. Arms in front of the body, hands clasped low, is more acceptable for women than for men (Illustration 2–25). In men, it is called the fig-leaf position and is highly protective, implying insecurity and fear of harm. In women, it does not have that connotation, although it is often perceived as indicative of submissiveness. Hands clasped at the waist for women express a spinsterish or teacher attitude and may be useful when you wish to instruct (Illustration 2–26). On men, however, the same position tends to be seen as "prissy."

For a man to hold his arms behind his back, hands clasped low, conveys an authoritative, quasi-military attitude, especially if the stance is wide (Illustration 2–27). On women, however, hands clasped behind the back tend to accentuate a "victim" or prisoner facet and as such is rarely effective in court (Illustration 2–28). If you choose to adopt such an arm position, be well aware of the connotations.

Hands hidden from view in any fashion—behind your back, in your pockets, and so forth—are often interpreted as secretive, as expressing a need to deceive or dissimulate, regardless of your gender, but such positions are more common with men. The exception to this is the conventional male stance with one hand in pants pocket (Illustration 2–29). Be aware, however, that this is a casual, relaxed position and should not be used in serious or formal moments. Also, if you favor this hand position, do not mess with your keys, change, or other contents of your pocket, as this is distracting. Many a juror has commented in jury debriefings that he/she was more intrigued by the lawyer's habitual investigation of the contents of his pants pockets than he/she was by what the lawyer had to say.

Technique #18: Head placement: Shifty, arrogant, or straightforward?

Most of us think of our heads as the location of eyes, ears, nose, and mouth. Trial lawyers are well aware that the head, in and of itself, is as potent a channel of information as those sense organs. Learn how to alter the position of your head to affect how you are perceived.

2-22

2-23

2-24

2-25

2-26

2-27

2-28

2-29

As with your stance, arms, and hands, there is a neutral "safe" position for your head: head held straight ahead, with the chin level, neither tilted up nor down (Illustration 2–30). The safe head position expresses self-confidence and forthrightness and will always stand you in good stead. A straight, level head position greatly enhances a perception of trustworthiness.

If you tilt your chin skyward, you project arrogance or aloofness; you are literally "looking down your nose" at other people (Illustration 2–31). If you tilt your chin a little in and down toward your neck ("tucking" the chin), the interpretations of your body language vary according to the angle of the tilt. A slight downward tilt is effective and conveys

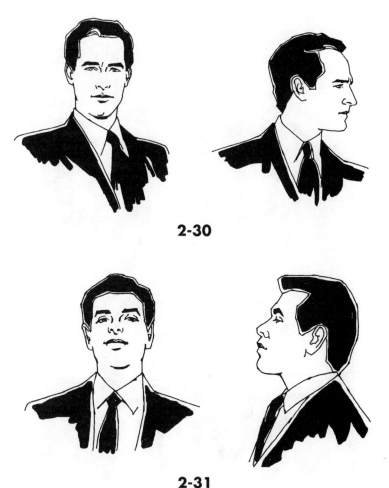

2-30

2-31

determination, strength, and a no-nonsense attitude (Illustration 2–32). A greater degree of tilt conveys stubbornness or belligerence and is to be used cautiously (Illustration 2–33).

If you tilt your head to either side ("cocking" the head), you convey interest, curiosity, or inquisitiveness. This is a good listening position to alternate with the neutral head position. Be careful, however, that you do not cock your head too much, which will make you seem insecure or weak (Illustration 2–34). Women, in particular, need to be careful not to overdo the degree to which the head is cocked.

If you turn your head to one side, but keep your eyes facing forward, you convey an impression of distrust, disbelief, or suspicion (Illustration 2–35).

2-32

2-33

2-34   **2-35**

Thought is greatly respected in our culture, and the ability to express thoughtfulness via your head position (the "dropped-head" position) has many rewards. For example, many trial lawyers using the dropped-head position have managed simultaneously to convey thoughtfulness and turn potential disaster into an advantage.

Case in Point

Jurors are unfavorably impressed by a lawyer's reaction of surprise: They feel a lawyer should know everything about the case if he/she is truly well prepared, and therefore jurors will evaluate surprise as unprofessional. Yet lawyers will tell you there are many instances during a trial when they are surprised, and consciously or otherwise, lawyers have to devise a way to mask that surprise. One of the ways to do that is to use the dropped-head position. When, for example, a witness has suddenly revealed something unexpected during cross-examination, rather than the lawyer letting his/her body give away his/her surprise and momentary panic, he/she simply drops his/her head down, as if consulting his/her notes or some deep inner wonderment. The truth of it is, the lawyer is covering his/her panic with a useful bit of body language, giving the jurors the credible impression of deep thought, rather than the internal panic the lawyer is in fact feeling.

Anytime you are in a situation where it would be to your disadvantage to let others know you are surprised by something, convey thoughtfulness by dropping your head down somewhat and letting your eyes go slightly to the side (Illustration 2–36). This position will give you the time to collect your thoughts and figure out what to do next without your body language betraying your discomfiture.

Whenever you want to buy time for any reason, drop your head down in thoughtfulness. People will wait the few moments you take to recover and will respect the serious consideration of the matter at hand that your body language conveys. Be careful not to drop your head too far down, however, as a bowed head is commonly interpreted as a sign of depression, grief, or despair (Illustration 2–37).

Technique #19: When "just sitting" becomes "power sitting"

A trial lawyer spends much of his/her time sitting, yet all eyes are still frequently on him/her and the lawyer cannot afford to ignore what his/her body language is conveying at that time.

The first and most important aspect of seated body language is the body shift. Whenever your body as a whole is leaning somewhat forward, you are expressing interest, energy, and involvement. This is an active

2-36   **2-37**

position that is favorably perceived (Illustration 2–38). As you shift your body back, you express a more passive and receptive orientation that can be interpreted as a gamut from simple listening to indifference to boredom to outright hostility (Illustration 2–39 and 2–40).

Because the leaning-back position can be so variously interpreted, the easiest way to know how to use body shifts is to lean your body forward anytime you wish to express interest in what is going on (Illustration

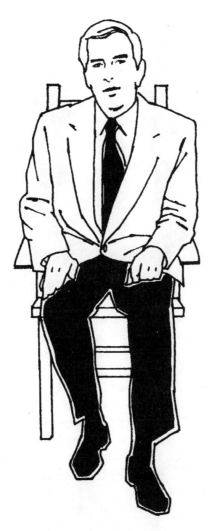

2-38

2-39   **2-40**

2–41) and lean back anytime you wish to express disinterest or disapproval of what is going on. Slumping forward on a table, or leaning way back in your chair are both to be avoided: slumping indicates depression, fatigue, and boredom, leaning way back expresses disdain and aloofness.

What you do with your legs and feet when seated depends entirely on how casual and relaxed you wish to appear. When in doubt, go to the "neutral seated leg position." For men, the neutral seated leg position is feet flat on the floor (Illustration 2–42). For women, the neutral seated leg position is feet flat on the floor, or legs slanted crossed at the ankles (Illustrations 2–43 and 2–44). The neutral seated leg position lends an air of readiness associated with energy and purpose. It ensures that your back will stay straight and your shoulders level. It makes it easier to keep your head level and straight without having to think about it. The neutral seated leg position is also an easy position from which to rise gracefully.

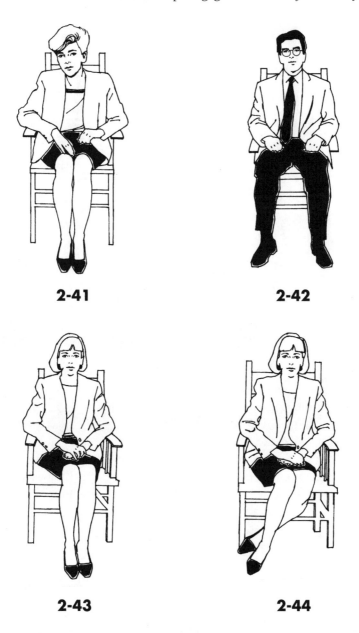

2-41   **2-42**

2-43   **2-44**

Other seated positions are to be used as dictated by the situation and how you wish to be perceived in the situation. The "four-square" position (Illustration 2–45) often adopted by men is relaxed and should not be used in formal situations, which is why you'll rarely see a lawyer

2-45   **2-46**

sitting that way in a courtroom. The crossed-legs position favored by
some men (Illustration 2–46) is easily interpreted as a sign of defensiveness and should be used with that consideration in mind.

Women are often very comfortable crossing their legs when seated.
If you enjoy sitting this way, however, be aware that when you are in a situation where you want to be able to rise easily and quickly (as lawyers do
during a trial, to make timely objections) it may take you too long to
uncross them to rise promptly. If you know you won't need to get up for
a long period of time, however, the crossed-legs position is perfectly
acceptable, as long as you resist any foot swaying, which projects insecurity or boredom (Illustration 2–47).

When you're seated, avoid arm positions that diminish your persuasiveness. If there is no table in front of you, allow your arms to simply
rest on the arms of the chair. If there are no arms to the chair you're sitting in, allow your hands to rest comfortably on your thighs, or clasp
them lightly in your lap.

As far as arm positions are concerned, you can keep both arms on
the table if desired, hands clasped or open (Illustration 2–48). Hands
clasped on the table is a mildly defensive posture and may convey some
protectiveness, but not nearly as much as arms crossed over chest. Resist
"steepling" your fingers as that is read as authoritative or "know it all,"
unless, of course, that's the impression you wish to convey.

2-47

2-48

The great temptations to be avoided when seated, with or without a table in front of you are:

- Running your hands over your face (Illustration 2–49).
- Putting your hands in front of your face, as both of these are very distracting (Illustration 2–50).

2-49 to 2-51

- Holding your head up with your arm, which causes you to slump and look fatigued and defeated (Illustration 2–51).
- Fidgeting and moving around unnecessarily in your chair, which makes you seem anxious.
- Shifting repeatedly from the left side of your chair to the right side of your chair, taking your whole body with you, which again makes you seem insecure.

Successful trial lawyers are winners, and as such, you won't catch one ever seating him/herself in anything less than a confident and self-assured manner. Learn to seat yourself in a way that conveys assurance. Under no circumstances allow yourself to seat yourself by plopping yourself down in your chair with an "ouf" of relief. You will seem like a tired old hound and will impress no one favorably. Regardless of how tired you may feel, seat yourself in your chair with energy and quiet self-determination.

How To Persuade with Your Body Language the Way Successful Lawyers Do

Technique #20: Suit your body language to your purpose

The elements of body language described in this chapter are by no means exhaustive: There are many more ways in which bodies "talk." Those described, however, are the most commonly used and interpreted in the art of persuasion. Once you know what these different elements mean, you can select which aspect of body language you wish to adopt depending on your current purpose.

You will not, however, be able to adopt any element of body language unless you know what your body is currently expressing. For example, you say to yourself, Well, I want to give the impression that I am listening attentively, so I'll cock my head slightly to one side. Great—that's a wise choice. What if your habitual head position is cocked to one side, however, and you are unaware of it? When you do what you think is "slightly cocking my head," you will be in fact leaning your head past the point of a stereotypically defined position of "listening" and your head cock will be read as "weakness," not at all the impact you were seeking. (Illustration 2–52). So, to effectively suit your body language to your purpose, start by figuring out what your body is presently "saying."

Step 1: How to Figure Out Your Current Body Language

1. Stand the way you usually stand and check yourself in a mirror. Be honest with yourself. How is your posture? What kind of foundation are you creating with your stance? How do you hold your head? Where are your arms? Use the worksheets provided at the end of the chapter to help you assess yourself.

2-52

2. Then ask yourself, what are the comments people have made over the years about the way you express yourself physically? Have people commented on your good posture, or have they asked you often if you're having a bad day when you're not (maybe you slump), or have they commented that you always seem to be going fifty places at once (maybe you fidget)? Use the worksheets provided at the end of the chapter to help you.

3. Look at pictures taken of yourself over the past few years, preferably candid. What do you see? What is your predominant expression? How do you stand, sit? Where are your arms? Again, use the worksheets provided.

4. For a week or so, observe your own body positions. Notice how you prefer to stand and sit naturally, what is the habitual position of your head? Don't try to change your body language in any way, just observe it. Use the worksheets provided.

Most of us take our bodies so much for granted, we never stop to attend to what our bodies might be expressing. We think, Well, that's just the way I am. No. That's the way you are given twenty or more years of habit formation; it is certainly not "just the way you are." Unless you are unfortunately heir to a body in some way damaged or deformed, your posture, stance, and expressiveness are in large part the result of your upbringing and environment, and as such, are highly changeable.

Step 2: How to Use Your Body Language Skillfully to Communicate Most Effectively with People

Once you know how you are currently expressing yourself with your body, you can choose those aspects you wish to keep, those you wish to change, and those you wish to practice so as to have available as desired, but not as a regular part of your body language repertoire. In this way, you will be using your body effectively as a communication channel; you can then make deliberate choices that will enhance and support your primary message to those you wish to convince.

CASE IN POINT

A trial lawyer I was working with determined from his personal observation of himself, his photographs, and what others said of him that he tended to slump, that he often folded his arms across his chest, and that he had a habit of cocking his head.

Given this information, he decided to make the following changes in how he communicated with jurors:

- He decided to correct his posture and make that a permanent change, to express self-confidence and energy to the jurors at all times.
- He decided to use the arm-across-the-chest position deliberately and only at certain moments to express to the jurors hostility or disagreement with what might be going on at a given time in the trial.
- The head cock appeared to be an effective listening position, and the lawyer decided to use it for that purpose, both in voir dire and with witnesses, working with himself to keep his head upright the rest of the time.

The lawyer's awareness of how different body language postures are interpreted and what his specific postures are allowed him now to use his body language skillfully to communicate, rather than letting it distract from or distort his message to the jurors.

Use the same process of first figuring out your habitual body language and then making appropriate choices, given your understanding of stereotypical ways body language is interpreted, to communicate your message powerfully to those you wish to convince.

How You Can Use Powerful Ways Lawyers Communicate with Facial Expressions

Technique #21: Express serious concern to win people's trust

A good trial lawyer masters, as his/her basic facial expression, an expression of serious involved concern. Anytime someone finds him/herself on trial, it is a serious matter, and any lawyer whose facial expressions do not reflect appropriate concern to the jurors will seriously undermine his/her credibility. Use Illustration 2–53 to guide you as to how to compose your face to express serious, involved concern. You will thus be conveying a professional and trustworthy attitude, which is critical to your ability to win people over to your point of view.

2-53

Technique #22: Convey your disapproval subtly

Case in Point

A trial lawyer hears opposing counsel say something she does not like, and the lawyer wants to make sure the jurors realize she doesn't like it. The lawyer does not look over at the jurors with a "see what the idiot is doing now" expression (no matter how much she'd like to do that), she simply frowns and holds the frown as she listens to opposing counsel (Illustration 2–54). The lawyer's nonverbal message of disapproval will be clear to the jurors, without her having to say a single word.

When you use this technique, it is important to hold your frown in place the entire time the person is saying that which you disapprove of. Instinctively, many people would frown upon hearing something they disapprove of; however, most of us will let go of the frown quickly. When

2-54

your objective is not just to express yourself, but also to persuade, it is important to maintain facial expressions throughout the duration of whatever it is you disapprove of, for maximum nonverbal impact.

Technique #23: Convey your approval subtly

CASE IN POINT

A witness during the course of cross-examination says something helpful to a lawyer's case. It is extremely poor form for the lawyer to break out into a smile, turn to the jurors and say "See, told you he/she was a liar!" Instead, the lawyer must find a subtle way to alert the jurors to his satisfaction with what the witness has just said. The lawyer could express his approval subtly by allowing his face to relax somewhat from its normal serious expression, which will let the jury know the lawyer likes what he is hearing, and might perhaps allow a slight smile to cross his face (Illustration 2–55).

2-55

Technique #24: Use your smile judiciously

In a courtroom, smiles are to be used with great care, as jurors do not feel court is a lighthearted experience. Smiles are stereotypically interpreted as invitations or signs of welcome, approval, and warmth. A smile used in a serious situation might be interpreted as disrespect or smugness. Smiles are stereotypically more expected from women; however, women need to guard against using smiles automatically. A facial expression becomes meaningless if used without conscious intent.

When you are in a serious situation, smile if it is appropriate, for example, if a person blurts out something obviously funny, and let the size of your smile vary according to the degree of humor expressed. All teeth out smiles (that is, a full-toothpaste-commercial-type smile) are generally to be avoided.

When you are in a more casual or relaxed setting, smiles are more appropriate; however, anytime you begin to talk about something serious, make sure your face returns to the serious, involved concern expression described earlier.

Some people smile when they are nervous. If you find yourself reflexively smiling when nervous, follow the guidelines given under "Technique #27" on page 79 to help you counter this tendency, so that your nervous smile is not misread as approval of what is going on.

Technique #25: Communicate interest or distrust with your brows

Brows are a wonderfully expressive yet often overlooked part of body language. If you observe good trial lawyers at work, you will see they are, whether they realize it or not, adept at using their brows to convey how they feel about various witnesses, issues, and testimony.

Raised brows are useful for indicating overt interest or curiosity (Illustration 2–56); they make your face look alert and alive. Both brows raised is a good listening position when you want it known that what you are listening to is relevant and worth hearing. Be careful, however, that your brows are not raised too high, which conveys great surprise or shock (Illustration 2–57), unless, of course, that is your intent.

One brow raised by itself conveys suspiciousness or distrust and can be used to great effect (Illustration 2–58). Practice different brow positions in the mirror until you are comfortable with them. Figure out, for example, just how much you need to raise your brows to express simple interest and how much is too much.

2-56

2-57

2-58

Technique #26: Give value with your eyes

In Chapter 1, we discussed how to use eye focus to establish credibility. We also mentioned that maintaining eye focus on an individual signifies that you value that person. As part of your use of facial expressions to persuade others, make and maintain good eye focus whenever you wish to indicate that you approve of someone or of what he/she is saying.

Let's say, however, that you're in a situation where you are listening to an individual talk, but you want to let the other people present, those you really want to persuade, know that you don't value what the individual is saying. Your objective is really to—on the contrary—discredit this individual. In this case, don't even attempt direct eye focus. Simply glance over at the person, letting your look hit wherever it wants, preferably not looking at the individual's eyes or face, just looking in a vague general way at him/her, and quickly at that. The rest of the time the individual is speaking, put yourself in a "thoughtful" mode (head slightly down, eyes to the side). The nonverbal statement you will have thus made is that this person barely exists for you; you disassociate yourself from him/her in any meaningful way. The implication is that this person's opinion is valueless and not to be taken into account.

A word of caution: Eye focus is powerful, and withholding it must be done only with good reason. To be trustworthy, you must be respectful, and not looking at someone does imply disrespect.

How to Profoundly Influence People with Your Facial Expressions

Technique #27: Let your intent guide your expressions

Just as you shape your body language in accordance with what you want to communicate and with a knowledge of how people stereotypically interpret body language, so too choose your facial expressions in function of what you want to communicate and how others interpret different facial expressions.

The four primary facial reactions used to persuade others are as follows:

1. Frown when worried, concerned, or upset.
2. Raise both brows when interested or curious.
3. Raise one brow when suspicious or distrustful.

4. Allow your face to relax when pleased, with the possible addition of different degrees of smile when appropriate.

Always be sure to allow your face to hold any given expression sufficiently long enough for others to clearly see and "read" it. People will form their opinion of how you feel about what is going on by following your facial expressions and body reactions to the proceedings.

There are two keys to how to use these facial expressions persuasively: Know what your face is currently expressing and be congruent. With the first key, start with a clean slate. If you don't know what your habitual facial expression is, you cannot change it to something more effective.

Figure out your habitual facial expressions as follows: Ask close friends or family how they perceive you: does your facial expression usually connote sadness, happiness, anger, worry? You'd be surprised how often people are not aware of the impression their faces convey. You may feel like a happy-go-lucky person, but others may perceive you as serious. Why? Is it because your forehead is permanently creased in a frown? Or do the corners of your mouth naturally turn down? What specific aspects of your face create this impression? Use the worksheets at the end of the chapter to help you.

Next, sit down in front of a mirror and deliberately set your face in the expression others say is your habitual expression. Often the lines in your face will give you a clue as to how you ordinarily express yourself. A deep line set vertically between the eyes, for example, is generally the result of a habitual frown (Illustration 2–59). Look in the mirror at what your

2-59

face expresses now and then figure out what you have to change to help your face express what you want it to express, not what it expresses as a matter of habit. Use the worksheet provided at the end of the chapter.

The second key is to be congruent. When you speak, make sure your facial expressions are congruent with what you are saying. If you're commenting on a sad state of affairs, don't smile. If you smile while commenting on a sad state of affairs, you convey sarcasm. You should convey sarcasm only if that is what you wish to convey. Know your intent and let it guide you.

CASE IN POINT

When a trial lawyer describes how nice things were for the plaintiff before that awful car crash, the lawyer will allow her face to soften and warm up at the niceness. This expression provides an excellent contrast for the lawyer when she later speaks with a heavy frown about the crash itself. Each part of the lawyer's speech will have been congruent, her nonverbal communication effectively supporting and enhancing her verbal message.

People are more believable when they are congruent. If you say you're sorry and you look sad, people are more likely to believe you than if you say you're sorry, but you smile fully. Trustworthiness is one of the fundamental traits you must express if you are to be successful in convincing anyone of anything. Keeping your facial expressions and body language congruent with your words contributes significantly to the perception of your trustworthiness.

A word of caution: In using your facial expressions to influence people, be subtle—very, very subtle. When you are attempting to convince people, they are scrutinizing your every expression for clues as to how sincere you are, how truthful you really are. If you grimace or you overdo a facial expression, it will be obvious at once, given the intense focus you're subject to, and people will promptly react to you as you do to a bad actor: You will not be believed, you will be perceived as manipulative and "phony." Your credibility will be out the door.

To learn more complex facial expressions in addition to the primary ones listed earlier, watch a good television program or movie with the sound turned off. Watch how good contemporary actors express themselves both in body and face, and practice the facial expressions and body language you think would be useful to you. Bear in mind that you are not trying to become an actor; you are simply learning a broader range of reactions than you have currently available to you.

Successful Lawyers Are "Body Smart": Develop Gestures that Clarify and Illustrate Your Important Points Convincingly

In addition to body language positions and facial expressions, successful trial lawyers also communicate nonverbally by the use of gestures. Gestures are hand, arm, shoulder, and head movements that are used to clarify or illustrate a point. Any good trial lawyer is facile in the use of gestures that emphasize and give power to his/her words.

THE SLAM THAT MADE JURORS JUMP

At a recent trial, I observed plaintiff's attorney slam his fist into his hand to emphasize the word "struck," as in "And then the metal bucket *struck* my client in the head." The sound of his fist hitting his hand had such impact that some of the jurors literally jumped in their seats. Upon debriefing, the jurors told me how that simple gesture brought the lawyer's point home more effectively than words could have.

If body language and facial expression can be said to enhance and support your message, gestures accent it; they provide the emphasis with which to add punch to any given point. Gestures, although highly personal in the sense that people will tend to express themselves repeatedly through certain gestures and not through others, are amenable to stereotypy, and each culture recognizes a stereotypical meaning to specific gestures.

THE HANDS THAT THREW IN THE TOWEL: HOW THE JURORS READ MARCIA CLARK'S BODY LANGUAGE

"Marcia [Clark] would just get too frustrated. I'm sitting right in front of her and I'm watching all her sighs and that to me was a sign of weakness. You're here to do a job and if something is bothering you, don't let them see you sweat. . . . A lot of times Marcia would sigh and make gestures with her hands as though she were throwing in the towel. That didn't help her."[4] It is difficult for jurors to follow the guidance of a lawyer who appears to be giving up on her case. Such gestures can be extremely detrimental to persuasiveness.

In our culture, shrugging the shoulders is interpreted as "I don't know" or "So what?"; pushing the hands down and away from your body means "Stop" or "Stay away"; bringing the hands up, palms up, connotes innocence (Illustration 2–60); nodding the head means "Yes," shaking it

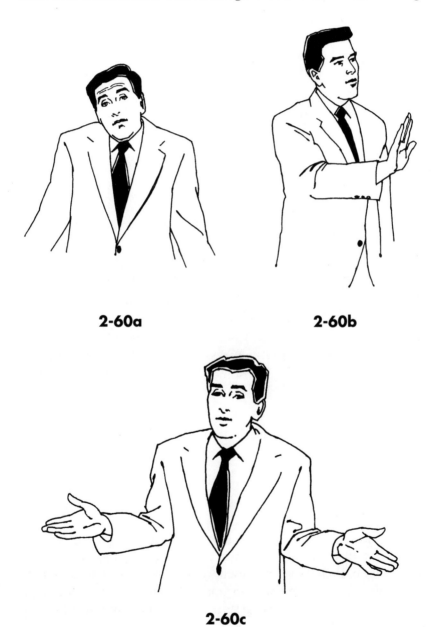

2-60a   **2-60b**

2-60c

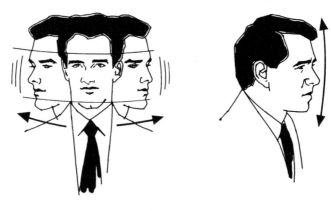

2-61

means "No" (Illustration 2–61). These are just a few examples of the many gestures commonly understood by people. You will notice that you tend to use certain gestures over and over, whereas others are not in your repertoire at all.

Technique #28: Weed out irrelevant habitual gestures

Anything you do out of habit rather than by choice becomes ineffective. Before you can select effective gestures to underline and give impact to your points, you must know what your habitual gestures are. How do you illustrate a point? Do you use few gestures, many gestures, and what are they? A practical way to observe your habitual gestures is to videotape yourself in two conditions:

- Having a conversation with a good friend, making sure to spend some of the time standing, and some sitting.
- Giving a "speech" directly to the camera, a presentation where you give your opinion, for example.

Use the worksheet at the end of the chapter to help with this exercise.

Persuasive trial lawyers use many illustrative gestures, for example, indicating with the hand that something is far away, shaking the head with dismay over an unfortunate event (Illustration 2–62). Nonpersuasive individuals use either too few or too many gestures, but most important, nonpersuasive individuals use gestures that do not illustrate anything.

2-62a   **2-62b**

Nonpersuasive individuals use gestures haphazardly and give the appearance of gesturing for the sake of gesturing, rather than gesturing in service of a point to be made.

Notice your use of gestures when you watch the replay of your conversations on the videotape. If you turned the sound off, would you know from your gestures what was happening? Would you be able to estimate, with considerable accuracy, not so much the content of the conversation, but how you felt about the different points, what your opinion was? If your gestures have no apparent relationship to the conversation, if they do not in some way *comment* on the content, then they are not illustrative.

Now that you are aware of what your gestures are, you are ready to increase the persuasive impact of your gestures. If you find that your gestures are not illustrative, or that they are, but your repertoire is restricted, then, once again, watch a good television program or movie with the sound turned off. Imitate and practice the gestures you see that feel comfortable to you and that seem to illustrate a point clearly. Then practice, practice, practice until those gestures are truly yours: comfortable, fluid, and second nature.

Most gestures are persuasive as long as they illustrate a point and are appropriate to the setting. Shaking your fist at someone may indeed illustrate your point, but is inappropriate to most settings. Be aware of the social significance of different gestures and use them in a way that is consistent with your purpose.

The single exception is pointing your finger. Pointing is highly useful as long as it is not done in someone's face. You can very effectively point in the direction of an object, a visual aid such as a chart or a slide, or to identify someone at a distance. It is not wise, however, to point your finger at someone directly in front of you, nor at a group you are addressing unless you are really aware of what you are doing. Pointing is experienced as intrusive and threatening; it carries too many memories of domineering third-grade teachers and makes people feel powerless and intimidated.

CASE IN POINT

Even when a trial lawyer wants a witness to feel powerless and intimidated on the stand, the lawyer will rarely point a finger directly at the witness while the witness is testifying; this is far too aggressive a gesture to use. The jurors will immediately identify with the person being pointed at and will feel compassion for the witness. This is hardly the lawyer's intent.

Equally problematic is shaking your finger in front of someone's face. This too is experienced as invasive and is best avoided.

Technique #29: Time a gesture to maximize its impact

Timing is very important in the effectiveness of a gesture. If you observe good trial lawyers, you'll see that their most persuasive gestures are made before or after a verbal point. Gesture before you speak if you wish to set up your point, after if you wish to provide a reaction to that point.

CASE IN POINT

A defense lawyer wanted to emphasize her client's innocence. She set her point up nonverbally by opening her arms, palms up, a gesture that conveys innocence, and then said very simply, "My client is innocent" (Illustration 2–63). Later, the lawyer wished to negate opposing counsel's point. She started by saying, "My learned colleague will have you believe the evidence incriminates my client"; then she shook her head, a gesture

2-63

that is stereotypically read as meaning "No." Nonverbally, she contradicted opposing counsel's statement. She then went on to say, "We will show this is not the case." The jurors, upon debriefing, commented on how the defense attorney's gestures illustrated and accented her points effectively.

This is the purpose of timing. If you use gestures right on top of your spoken message, you're likely to blur the message rather than illustrate it. It is far better to develop a few clear, direct, easily understood gestures and use them sparingly but well-timed than to develop a whole collection of gestures you simply throw out at random. This would defeat the purpose of gesturing.

Technique #30: Get rid of useless mannerisms

Gestures must be distinguished from mannerisms. Gestures are socially shared movements, movements that illustrate a point in a way that is similarly understood by members of a given culture. Mannerisms are quite different. Mannerisms are personalized gestures performed repetitively by a given individual. For example, you may rub your chin when thinking, or tug at your earlobe, or twist the ring on your finger (Illustration 2–64). Your mannerisms are uniquely yours; they convey messages that others figure out only over time, as they get to know you. Since mannerisms are not on the whole available to a stereotyped definition, they tend to distract from the more important part of your message, as people try to interpret the significance of your ring-twisting, earlobe-pulling, and so forth, and in the process, ignore some (often much) of what you are saying.

2-64

JINGLING KEYS AND JIGGLING LEGS: CHRIS DARDEN LOSES JUROR POINTS

"You know, I wouldn't know what was happening . . . but he [Chris Darden] would be doing his jingle thing with his keys and his legs jiggled when things got tense. It made me think, Well, if your case is so strong why are you so frustrated?[5] Not only are mannerisms distracting, they are often interpreted as indicators of how the case is going, whereas for the lawyer involved, mannerisms may be just a way of letting off steam.

Often, mannerisms are so distracting and annoying, they hardly seem worth trying to figure out at all.

CASE IN POINT

Jurors have been known to comment endlessly on attorney mannerisms, generally to the lawyer's detriment. Jurors have often told me how watching a lawyer constantly stroke his beard as he sits listening to opposing counsel, or watching a lawyer chew busily away at a hangnail, while another lawyer twirls her pencil obsessively between her fingers, can be so irritating that it makes it difficult for the jurors to attend to the matter at hand.

These are all examples of mannerisms that get in the way of people's effectiveness. Persuasive trial lawyers are persuasive because they are single-mindedly devoted to the task at hand, unself-conscious, self-assured, and calm. Such focus is reflected in their ability to use their bodies to express what they *want* their bodies to express, rather than allowing their bodies to dissipate their message with useless and irrelevant mannerisms. Learn to quiet your body so it does not detract from your essential message, but rather adds to the perception of your credibility.

How to Get Rid of Useless Mannerisms

Observe your habitual mannerisms

Become aware of your mannerisms. Most of us have no idea what are our personal tics and twitches until they are pointed out to us, and then we are often quite distressed. I can't tell you how many times I have pointed out a distracting mannerism to a witness I was preparing only to hear a vivid disclaimer, for example: "What, I gnaw my lower lip to death? Never!" Then I play back the videotaped session to the witness, and there he/she is, vigorously chewing away on his/her lip.

Ask your friends and family what your mannerisms are, or ask a friend to mimic you. He/she will undoubtedly exaggerate your mannerisms (much to your horror), which will make it much easier for you to see them and realize the effect they have. Use the worksheets provided at the end of the chapter.

Observe your mannerisms under stress

Many of the trial lawyers I have worked with have some mannerisms that show up only in intensely stressful conditions, such as during cross-examination. Again, appeal to friends and family for help. Ask them what are your mannerisms when you are under stress, or, if possible, have someone videotape you when you are in a stressful situation.

Some people unconsciously lose all sense of social decorum when under stress and find themselves indulging in mannerisms (pulling at nose hairs, paring fingernails, scratching near the groin) they are appalled to discover they've been doing in public. Still others have very mild, almost unobtrusive mannerisms until they are nervous, at which point they turn into churning windmills. An occasional licking, of dry lips, in itself quite acceptable, becomes a constant and obtrusive licking; an occasional rubbing together of the hands becomes, under stress, a hand-wringing marathon.

Awareness: a simple solution

Once you are aware of what your mannerisms are, quieting them becomes a matter of reminding yourself that they will only detract from the effectiveness of your message and then not doing them. Awareness is the key. Practicing *not* doing those mannerisms whenever you catch yourself doing them is what will facilitate their eventual disappearance.

Learn Ways Lawyers Use Movement to Persuade

Movement serves many functions. A good trial lawyer uses movement to keep jurors awake and interested, to emphasize a point, to break up the often deadening monotony of a trial. To be persuasive, however, movement, like gestures, must be deliberate, purposeful, well timed and well executed.

Technique #31: Use movement to establish control of a place or a situation

One of the most obvious uses of movement is how it helps you establish control of a place or a situation. A seasoned trial lawyer moves through the courtroom with ease and grace. He/she knows exactly where to place him/herself during opening and closing statements, where to move to, what position in the courtroom best catches the jury's attention, where to stand when showing exhibits for maximum juror impact. For some attorneys, such knowledge comes from trial and error over years of working courtrooms; for others, it comes from knowing the skills of how to make a courtroom theirs.

CASE IN POINT

When I work with a lawyer who either is just beginning his/her trial practice or is on the eve of an important case, I suggest that he/she visit the courtroom when no one is there prior to the actual trial date. I have the lawyer walk all through the courtroom, stand in various places, sit at the appropriate table, in the jury box, in the audience, and walk the room in all directions thoroughly, until the lawyer really feels as if he/she knows it.

In so doing, the lawyer has made the courtroom *his/hers*. The courtroom is now so familiar to the lawyer that he/she can move within it as easily and as confidently as he/she does in his/her own home. This gives the lawyer an aura of belonging there, which in turn makes the lawyer seem in charge and in control. The lawyer will exude the confidence that comes naturally with a feeling of belongingness, in addition to which the lawyer will actually feel more confident and secure from having made friends with what up to then was alien territory.

Making a space your own ahead of time, before the actual event occurs, during which you want to be at your persuasive best, not only gives you confidence and a sense of control over the situation, but also shows you how you will look through other people's eyes. As you sit, for example, where your audience will later sit, as you place yourself at the position at the head of the table where your boss will later be as you present your report, you give yourself the opportunity to sense how your actual physical placement of yourself will impact others. You will be much more sensitive to how you are coming across to those watching and listening to you, having, in a sense "been in their shoes." You can make adjustments to where you sit and stand knowing now how those positions influence your presentation. If at all possible, visit the space prior to the actual event, when no one is there. Walk the space thoroughly, remembering to place yourself wherever others will be to gain the advantage of their perspective, until you really feel like you know the space well. Then sit quietly a moment, with eyes closed, and recreate the room in your mind. Open your eyes and see if you were accurate in your mental reconstruction, make any necessary adjustments. Now you will be able to actually see yourself in the space as you prepare various parts of your presentation; this will help you prepare more effectively.

Anytime you are preparing yourself to persuade someone, walk the space ahead of time. Even if the meeting is set for your own office, walk the space so as to refamiliarize yourself with it.

If you cannot visit the space prior to the event, imagine the space as best you can in the privacy of your own home or office. It doesn't matter if you don't really know what the space will look like; using your common sense, you can imagine something close to the real space. For example, if you're giving a speech, you'll either be on an elevated platform or you'll be level with your audience, but either way you'll be in front of the audience, which will be seated most probably in rows. If you're giving a presentation, the setup will be similar, only smaller. If you're going to someone's office or living room for a meeting, imagine how a typical office or living room might be set up. Close your eyes and mentally explore the area, mentally trying to feel what it is like to stand or sit in the various places, what it's like from the point of view of those who will be there with you. Once you get to the actual space, simply make the adjustments you need to in order to fit your imaginings to the real thing.

Mental rehearsal is one of the key ways to ready yourself for any event so that you come in to the situation confidently, in charge and in control. Olympic athletes and successful trial lawyers have been using this technique for years. You can join the ranks of the winners by using mental rehearsal in this as well as in many other situations.

During the event itself, use the space given you freely and fully. Expansive use of space connotes comfort and well-being. Confident people are not afraid to stride from one place to another. A good trial lawyer will use the courtroom to the extent the judge allows. Even if you are restricted to a podium, having explored the space will make you more comfortable and relaxed, and you will not tiptoe between podium and table, but rather will stride comfortably, having walked this same passage many times before, even if only in your mind.

Technique #32: Use movement to keep people interested and attentive

Movement has a special function in the courtroom: It wakes people up (including the lawyers). This may seem like a strange consideration, until you take into account that the average adult attention span is only eighteen minutes. A trial lasts a good deal longer than that. Breaking up the constant flow of verbal communication with movement is one of the ways trial lawyers keep the jurors' interest and attention.

Movement keeps people alert by appealing to our basic survival mechanism. If something moves, you may be in danger, so whenever something moves, you will pay attention. Do not misunderstand, however: Movement is not a cue for danger. Movement simply signals us to be alert; in case there is danger, movement cues alertness. Movement, however, does not equate with nervousness. Fidgeting and shuffling make people aware of your nervousness, not of your points. Erratic moving around does not constitute persuasive movement.

HOW CHRIS DARDEN'S SHIFTING BODY DAMAGED HIS CAUSE

"[T]here was the body language conveying a lack of confidence. Darden constantly shifted his body from side to side in front of the jury, rarely establishing eye contact with the jurors. In fact, *The New York Times* claims, I believe erroneously, that Darden 'never did look at the jury.' "[6] You cannot let your nervousness or anxiety dictate how your body moves if you expect to be persuasive. Your body language, at rest or in movement, will always be "believed" over your words.

Movement, in order to be persuasive, is motivated, purposeful, and appropriate. A hyperactive child running erratically around the house is not moving persuasively; the child is just driving everyone nuts. Motivated and purposeful movement, such as a flawlessly executed dance movement or a ski slalom is marvelous to behold. Well-timed and well-executed movement in the courtroom has the same effect.

Case in Point

Even when movement is motivated and purposeful, it must still be appropriate to the situation in order to be persuasive. Pacing, for example, may be motivated and purposeful, but it is not appropriate in a courtroom. Why? Pacing is motivated by worry, and a trial lawyer is supposed to know what to do. Jurors expect a lawyer to be serious and concerned about things, but not be overtly worrying about them in the courtroom. A worried individual makes a poor guide for others to look up to for direction and authority.

If worry is inappropriate to the situation, you can endanger your credibility by pacing. The bottom line is, movement should never be accidental. Movement makes such a powerful nonverbal statement that you must move only when you have good reason to do so.

Technique #33: Use movement to make an effective transition between points

The most common motivator of movement is the need for a transition. Movement is a way of nonverbally stating, I have finished with thought number 1, I am now going to move on to thought number 2.

CASE IN POINT

A lawyer is cross-examining a witness. The lawyer starts by facing the witness and stating, "What you are saying, then, is that you did not see your wife before you left the house that night. . ." Then the lawyer turns and takes a few steps away from the witness, stops, and turns back toward the witness and says: "Would you say that your marriage was a happy one, Mr. Jones?"

The brief walk the lawyer took allowed the jury to digest the first bit of information, let them know nonverbally the lawyer was on to something new, and woke them up to be ready to hear the next bit.

Taking a few steps breaks up what might otherwise be the soporific rhythm of the spoken word and helps people know when you have finished with one subject and are on to a new subject. Your listeners are less apt to get confused or blur one point with the next.

Movement must be well timed to be effective. If you move all the time, people will react to you just as they do to a hyperactive child: negatively. If, however, you move only when you have a reason for doing so, your movement will be persuasive.

Technique #34: Use movement to drive a point home

Aside from moving to change the subject, what are some other reasons for moving? Movement can be used as a signal to indicate you are thinking something over; when you come to your conclusion, the point you want to drive home, you stop.

CASE IN POINT

In the previous Case in Point, let's say that the lawyer wanted to drive home the point that, in fact, the witness had not seen his wife before leaving the house on the night in question. Here's how the judicious use of movement would have helped the lawyer give the point maximum impact:

Lawyer: Did you see your wife when you came home from work?
Witness: No
Lawyer: Did you see your wife when your brother-in-law came over?
Witness: No
Lawyer: Did you see your wife during the time your brother-in-law was visiting?
Witness: No

Then lawyer would walk a few steps, as if thinking this over, then stop and say:

Lawyer: What you are saying, then, is that you did not see your wife before you left the house that night.

By walking a few steps and then stopping before the lawyer made the last, most significant point, the lawyer drew the jury's attention to the last sentence, which was, in fact, the one sentence the lawyer really wanted the jurors to notice. The walk alerted their attention, the jurors knew something was coming, the stop before the lawyer spoke was an application of the principle of holding still when you have something important to say, discussed in Chapter 1. Movement followed by stillness is an absolutely dynamite way of driving an important point home.

Technique #35: Use movement to create special relationships with people or things

The science called "proxemics" studies the use of space. There are well-established rules that govern the normative use of space in our culture. Simply put, the farther away you stand from someone, the less intimate your interaction. Mother and child are closely intertwined, friends stand side by side easily and comfortably, strangers respect a certain distance.

CASE IN POINT

Good trial lawyers are well versed in the persuasive use of space. When a trial lawyer first interacts with the jurors, the lawyer will generally stand a certain distance away, anywhere from around four to seven feet away. Slowly, as the lawyer gets acquainted with the jury, he/she will begin to move a little closer to the jurors, eventually standing very close to the jury rail, sometimes even touching the rail for a time.

Standing too close to someone too fast will scare them away. This is true whether you are an individual getting to know another individual or a trial lawyer seeking to influence an entire jury. Never moving toward people as you spend time with them and become familiar to them is, however, off-putting. You seem aloof and cold.

As you interact with those you are trying to convince, start by respecting their personal space, then allow yourself to move a little closer to them. If people back away from you, you've mistimed your movement; back off a little and wait a while before attempting to step in a little closer. Proxemics apply also to how a jury perceives the relationship between a lawyer and his/her client.

CASE IN POINT

When a lawyer sits fairly close to his/her client, the jurors will assume a friendly relationship between the lawyer and the client. If the lawyer is credible, his/her willingness to sit near the client implies that the client and/or his/her cause is also credible. Similarly, if the lawyer occasionally touches his/her client on the arm (on the back of the forearm so as to be nonsexually threatening), a certain friendliness will be assumed.

If you want to create the impression of a special relationship of warmth or favor toward either a person or an object, get close to it. Observe the laws of proxemics by not getting too close too soon, but get close.

Technique #36: Use movement to distract from or discredit a person

Movement can also be used to distract or discredit.

CASE IN POINT

A lawyer doesn't want the jury to focus on something the witness is going to say. While the witness is talking, the lawyer walks away, taking just a few steps to the side. Movement always takes precedence over words, and the jury, by watching the lawyer's movement, will be distracted from hearing what the witness is saying.

This technique is to be used with great care. Walking away when someone is speaking to you is considered rude; doing such discredits the person you move away from by taking respect away from the person. It connotes that the person, or what the person is saying, is not worthy of ordinary consideration. There's a fine line between discrediting what someone is saying so that you retain your credibility and coming across like a rude individual. You can minimize the rudeness of your movement so as not to alienate people by doing it quite slowly, or by not going too far, for example, moving only a few steps away.

Technique #37: Coordinate movement with your gestures, facial expressions, and eye focus to maximize your persuasiveness

Movement is used in conjunction with gestures, facial expressions, and everything we have covered so far to create the desired effect. Watching one of the great trial lawyers in action is like watching an impeccably choreographed dance, one in which everything works together seamlessly and effortlessly. It takes practice to achieve such mastery, but with time and patience you will succeed.

Learning how to make it all come together is a little like learning how to juggle: First you learn how to toss one ball in the air and catch it, then you add another ball and learn how to toss and catch two balls, then you add another and learn how to toss three balls, and so on until finally you can juggle many balls. So, too, with body language—first you learn to use eye focus, then you learn body positions, then you learn how to use eye focus and body positions together, then you add gestures, and so on until you can work all the techniques together.

The easiest way to master these skills is to practice each of the techniques separately and get comfortable with each on its own before you try to put them together. It's also in your best interest to work on these techniques *outside* the situations in which you really need to be persuasive, so that you feel totally comfortable *before* using the techniques in an "on-the-spot" situation. You have enough to worry about during an important presentation, for example, without giving yourself the extra stress of the first-time tryout of a whole new set of nonverbal communication techniques.

How to Make an Overhead Projector, Flip Chart, Lectern, and Podium Work for You Rather than Against You

A lectern or a podium reduces your ability to express by limiting your movement, so if at all possible, follow the example of good trial lawyers and work to one side of the podium or ignore it and work mostly in front of it. If, however, you find yourself in a situation in which you are constrained to a fixed position behind the podium, follow the guidelines I give to lawyers who frequently find themselves in a similar situation, for example, in the federal courts.

Rest your hands lightly on the podium, stand straight and true, and basically follow all the guidelines for effective body language as given previously. Remember the only difference between being behind a podium and standing free without one is that we don't see your body from about midchest on down. We still see all the rest, so head positions, gestures, and posture are as important as ever.

This is how to make a podium work *for* you. A podium will work *against* you as soon as you treat it as a prop or a crutch. You then cease to convey an impression of self-confidence and assurance and rather convey an impression of fear and insecurity. So do not under any conditions *grip* the podium, which makes you look terribly out of control ("drowning rat clings desperately to sinking ship") and do not lean heavily upon it. People's perception of your ability to stand on your own two feet is seriously impaired if they observe you hanging all over the podium for support.

Even though people can't see your bottom half when you're behind a podium, it's usually advisable to use a neutral stance nonetheless. A neutral stance gives firm support to your erect posture and helps avoid any involuntary compensatory head angles (Illustration 2–65). In addition, you can "root" your body firmly with the neutral stance, since swaying from side to side and shifting weight from one foot to the other are both to be avoided.

When using an overhead projector or flip chart, face your audience and point with your arm sideways to indicate the material, rather than facing the chart, which causes your back to be turned toward your audi-

2-65

ence. I find that many expert witnesses get so caught up in what they are trying to explain that they forget the importance of facing their audience and excitedly focus on the chart in front of them. Unfortunately, once the expert has turned his/her back to the jurors, the impact of much of his/her valuable testimony is lost.

Think in terms of referring to your chart or projected material occasionally, but keep your eye focus primarily on the people you are addressing. Know your charts well enough so you don't have to look at them too often. If you want to write something on a chart turn your back if need be to write it down, then step away from the chart, and refer to your written comment while facing the audience, arm pointing toward the chart. Expert witnesses who testify in this manner when referring to charts and diagrams are highly praised by jurors.

WORKSHEETS
BODY LANGUAGE: HOW TO FIGURE OUT
YOUR CURRENT BODY LANGUAGE

As you evaluate your body language according to this checklist, be honest in your assessment. The more accurate your observations, the more easily you can shape your body language so that you communicate effectively.

1. Your assessment of your habitual way of standing:

   (Looking at yourself standing in front of a mirror)

   Posture: erect ____ curved forward ____ arched ____

   Shoulders: square ____ slumped forward ____ tilted ____

   Stance: feet appropriate distance apart ____

     feet too close together ____

     feet too wide apart ____

   Knees: relaxed ____ stiff ____

   Hands: relaxed ____ fisted ____ fidgeting ____

   Head placement: level ____ tilted skywards ____

     tilted down ____ cocked ____

   Face placement: face straight ahead ____

                      face slightly turned to either side ____

2. Comments others have made about how you express yourself physically:

   _____

   _____

   _____

   _____

   _____

3. Assessment of recent candid photographs:

Note the number of times you adopt a certain way of standing, holding your shoulders, and so forth. For example, taking the category of "posture" from a total of twenty photographs, you stand erect in eighteen of them, curved forward in two. This gives a different assessment than if out of twenty, you are curved forward in eighteen of the photographs, and standing erect in two.

Posture: erect ____ curved forward ____ arched ____

Shoulders: square ____ slumped forward ____ tilted ____

Stance: feet appropriate distance apart ____

       feet too close together ____

       feet too wide apart ____

       sitting on a hip ____

       with feet close together ____

       with feet too far apart ____

Knees: relaxed ____   stiff ____

Arms: hanging relaxed at sides ____

       crossed in front of you ____

       crossed in back of you ____

       one arm holding the other ____

       both arms holding on ____

       one arm akimbo ____

       both arms akimbo ____

       other _____

_____

Hands: relaxed ____   hands fisted ____

hands fidgeting ____

one hand hidden from view ____

both hands hidden from view ____

other _____

_____

Head placement: level ____   tilted skywards ____

tilted down ____   cocked ____

Face placement: face straight ahead ____

face slightly turned to either side ____

4. Your overall assessment of your body language, taking into account the information from the above three categories. Note here the adjustments you need to make so that your body language expresses confidence and self-assurance.

Posture_____

_____

_____

_____

Shoulders _____

_____

_____

_____

Knees _____

_____

_____

_____

Arms _____

_____

_____

_____

Hands _____

_____

_____

_____

Head placement _____

_____

_____

_____

Face placement _____

_____

_____

_____

FACIAL EXPRESSIONS: HOW TO FIGURE OUT
YOUR HABITUAL FACIAL EXPRESSIONS

1. Comments friends and family have made about your facial expressions:

You usually look:

sad ____	cheerful ____
depressed ____	surprised ____
anxious ____	vexed ____
worried ____	irritated ____
suspicious ____	spaced out ____
wired ____	puzzled ____
guilty ____	curious ____
upset ____	bored ____
hostile ____	expressionless ____
intrigued ____	excited ____
other	_____

_____

_____

2. Your assessment of your facial expressions:

Look at recent candid photographs of yourself. Be as objective as possible in evaluating your facial expressions. Note how many times you look a certain way. For example, out of twenty photographs, note that you look anxious fifteen times, intrigued three times, and puzzled twice.

You usually look:

sad ____	cheerful ____
depressed ____	surprised ____

anxious ____   vexed ____

worried ____   irritated ____

suspicious ____   spaced out ____

wired ____   puzzled ____

guilty ____   curious ____

upset ____   bored ____

hostile ____   expressionless ____

intrigued ____   excited ____

other _____

_____

_____

3. Look at yourself in a mirror. Notice the lines in your face; they accent the habitual cast of your face. Think about what your lines say about you.

Do the crow's feet around your eyes

    go up ____   or go down ____?

What is the usual position of your mouth?

    lips curved up ____   lips curved down ____

    lips pursed ____lips relaxed ____

    mouth slightly open ____   mouth tightly shut ____

    mouth shut but relaxed ____

What is the usual position of your brows?

    held straight across ____

    held slightly up ____

    furrowed together ____

    one brow held up, the other level ____

How do the lines on your forehead go?

horizontal frown lines ____

One vertical line between your brows ____

Two vertical lines between your brows ____

4. Practice the four basic facial expressions so that you can use them deliberately and at will, according to your purpose:

    a. frown (brows furrowed)

       a little

       a little more

       brows furrowed together as tightly as possible

    b. raise both brows

       a little

       a little more

       as high as you can

    c. raise one brow leaving the other level

       (People differ as to which brow raises most easily; experiment until you figure out which one raises most easily for you)

       a little

       a little more

       as high as you can

    d. face relaxed

GESTURES: HOW TO FIGURE OUT YOUR GESTURES

Videotape yourself in two conditions:

1. Nonstressed condition: having a casual conversation with a friend

2. In a stressed condition: giving your speech, argument, sales pitch, or stating your position directly to the camera. Then observe your gestures in each condition and assess them according to the following guidelines:

1. Nonstressed condition:

Gestures: few ____   a moderate number ____ many ____

What are your habitual gestures?

_____

_____

_____

_____

_____

Are your gestures:

illustrative ____ nonillustrative ____

Do you point your finger and/or shake it?

point ____   shake ____

2. Stressed condition:

Gestures: few ____   a moderate number ____ many ____

What are your habitual gestures?

_____

_____

_____

_____

_____

Are your gestures:

illustrative _____ nonillustrative _____

Do you point your finger and/or shake it?

point _____ shake _____

3. Given the preceding observations, what adjustments would you like to make so that your gestures are persuasive?

_____

_____

_____

_____

_____

MANNERISMS: HOW TO FIGURE OUT YOUR MANNERISMS

Using the same videotape you made for the preceding gestures worksheet, assess your mannerisms, both in non-stressed and stressed conditions. Then ask your family and friends what they think are your mannerisms, both when you are under stress and when you are not.

1. Self-observation:

   Mannerisms in nonstressed condition:

   _____

   _____

   _____

   _____

   _____

   Mannerisms in stressed condition:

   _____

   _____

   _____

   _____

   _____

2. Observations of friends and family:

   Mannerisms in nonstressed condition:

   _____

   _____

   _____

   _____

Mannerisms in stressed condition:

_____

_____

_____

_____

_____

3. Given the preceding observations, what adjustments would you like to make so that you avoid any distracting mannerisms?

_____

_____

_____

_____

The Third Step:
Be Persuasive
With Your
Voice

"Imagine, for a moment, nine disembodied brains hovering over the chairs in the jury box. One brain is wondering if it's still snowing so he can run his plows that night; another brain is thinking of what the substitute teacher should be working on with her second graders. Another is confused over the matter of $56.64 void on the cash register that the defense lawyer keeps going over; two brains are fighting sleep, and another is trying to decide whether one of the lawyers wears a hairpiece. That leaves three minds following the proceedings, and they may not agree on the point being made. One day we each took eight-minute periods to pay attention so that at least one person was alert during the afternoon."[1]

The preceding paragraph does not describe the experience of uncaring jurists, resentful of their duty. On the contrary, it describes the experience of individuals honored by the opportunity to participate in the trial process, individuals who were deeply concerned that their determinations of guilt or innocence would be accurate. Yet even these highly motivated jurists found themselves fighting boredom and the intrusion of unwanted thoughts. Their boredom was not the result of boring substantive issues. The jurors' boredom was the inevitable outgrowth of how our judicial system operates—slowly. The problem is, no matter how exciting and stimulating your substantive issues, no matter how motivated the jurors, if the trial lawyer's delivery does not command the jurors' attention, that lawyer will not be persuasive.

BOREDOM: A FORMIDABLE OPPONENT

"The judicial process and the rules of evidence which govern it are not tailored to minds honed by the information explosion of our media-dominated society. The facts come in through the slow, orderly, drip, drip, drip of testimony from the witness stand. If it were a TV show on the same subject, what takes two hours of court time would be concentrated in a 30 second sound bite. The time spent/information received ratio of the courtroom is way out of whack with the pace of our lives in the outside world. Even though this was an interesting, exciting case which was tried efficiently before an experienced judge, I found myself fighting off boredom at times. But I kept reminding myself of the gravity of the charge, not to mention how bad it would look for the only lawyer on the jury to doze off."[2]

How Lawyers Use Their Voice to Transform Simple Presentation of Facts into Dynamic Persuasion of People

There is little a trial lawyer can do to speed up the "drip, drip, drip" of testimony. Even in the midst of one of the decade's most compelling courtroom dramas, the O. J. Simpson trial, jurors and public alike decried the weary tedium of the trial. There is much, however, that trial lawyers can do vocally to transform a trial into a far more interesting process, and the most successful among them are masters of vocal persuasion.

The human voice is a powerful instrument; your voice can profoundly move people or it can put them to sleep. Why do you think, for example, it is so difficult to drum up an audience for a lecture on theology, yet so easy to get thousands of people spellbound by TV preachers? The very word "lecture" conjures up yawns and sighs: You may love or hate TV preachers, but they are never boring. What is the difference? The content of the lecture is in all likelihood more intellectually stimulating, the message preached on television tends to be more simplistic and repetitious, so it's not a question of intellectual challenge. No, the main difference between a lecturer and a TV preacher is that the TV preacher is sincerely dedicated to persuading people to join his/her flock, the lecturer is presenting his/her point of view as the correct one.

There is a world of difference between *presenting* and *persuading*. Lawyers who get caught up in presenting the case when they need to be persuading jurors, lose. Successful trial lawyers whose main thrust is persuasion use the full range of their voices, vary the volume, pitch, and pace to keep that jury listening with both ears, ready and willing to hear more, and then use emotional techniques and skills to make sure the jury is truly convinced. And it works. The top trial lawyers' passionate commitment to getting their message across is absolute: It is that passionate commitment that leads them to use persuasive vocal techniques a less zealous lawyer might overlook.

If people are to be persuaded, first they must be awake. Good trial lawyers are ever mindful of the "snoozer" on the jury panel and realize how important it is to make their presentation interesting enough to keep all the jurors awake—at least most of the time. When I put together mock trials for lawyers, I am often kidded by the hiring attorney that I forgot to include a "snoozer" among the mock jurors; that's how common a problem the sleepy juror represents for trial lawyers. Keeping your listeners awake is your responsibility, and it is a basic rule of verbal persuasion. In addition, the voice must be easy and interesting to listen to and must reflect the speaker's credibility. Only if people are attentive and listening can you attempt to persuade them.

How to Use Lawyers' Vocal Techniques Guaranteed to Keep People Attentive and Listening

The voice is truly a magical instrument: It can enchant, delight, and captivate. Unfortunately, as with all magic, there's also a dark side: A voice can distract, annoy, and bore. As with body language, there are stereotypes for voices, and these will work for or against you. Trial lawyers are often instinctively aware of these stereotypes and modulate their voices accordingly. Conscious knowledge of the main vocal stereotypes will give you the benefit of knowing how to modulate your voice in function of your purpose.

Technique #38: Vary pace to keep people awake and interested

Pace refers to how quickly you speak. When trial lawyers speak too quickly, the jurors have trouble following them and eventually stop trying. If the lawyer speaks too slowly, jurors find themselves fighting sleep. What is desirable, then, is a basic pace that is easy for people to follow, but quick enough to remain interesting.

Use Pace to Reflect Good Energy

Good pace reflects good energy, which, as we have seen, is one of the components of competence and credibility.

A LISTLESS MARCIA CLARK SIGHS JUROR VOTES AWAY

According to *New York Times* reporter David Margolick, Marcia Clark, in delivering her closing argument was "largely listless . . . Ms. Clark sighed frequently, occasionally rubbed her eyes, forgot facts, reached for words and tripped over phrases."[3] Your energy is what rouses others, galvanizes them so they are ready to accept your point of view. Poor energy loses people's attention and focus.

Good energy in you induces good energy in others. Have you ever noticed that if you sit around with a group of people who are feeling blah and out of sorts, you end up feeling equally blah and out of sorts, whereas if you're with a group of people laughing and singing and dancing, how your own energy comes up to theirs? When a trial lawyer maintains good vocal energy, it's the vocal equivalent of walking at a brisk pace; it induces good energy in the jurors. When a trial lawyer allows his/her pace to drag, jurors' energy wears down, and suddenly the court day seems unending.

Use Pace to Express Confidence

Good energy also reflects confidence. A good expert witness, knowing his/her subject well, will speak more quickly, whereas an expert who is unsure about an issue will automatically speak at a slower pace, which reflects his/her internal search for ideas and words. Your basic pace, therefore, should be, as already mentioned, easy for people to follow but quick enough to be interesting. You then vary that pace according to your different purposes.

When to Slow Down or Speed Up Your Pace

Anything done the same way for long periods of time becomes monotonous. A lawyer who speaks at a good pace, but never varies that pace will eventually become boring. To counteract boredom, use your basic pace most of the time, and vary it in two ways from time to time.

Slow your pace down when you wish to appear *thoughtful* or when you want to give people the impression that you are working through a process of induction or deduction even as you are speaking. Slow your pace down when you have something particularly *important* or serious to say, slow your pace down when you wish to show great *respect*.

Speed up your basic pace (but *not* so much that you become impossible to follow or difficult to understand) when you are *reviewing* information you have given before or when you wish to make something seem *unimportant*. You can also speed up your pace somewhat when you're driving a point home, but be careful to go back to your basic pace when you get to the point itself.

How to Determine Your Natural Pace

To use the preceding techniques, you first need to determine your natural pace. What comments have people made over the years? Have you often been asked, "Could you slow down, please?" or do people say to you, "All right, so get to the point already"? These are clues to your pace.

Tape-record the voice of a television personality whose pace you think reflects good energy and self-confidence, then tape record your own voice during two or three informal conversations. Compare the two voices. If relative to the personality's voice you find that you are speaking much more rapidly than he/she is, that you seem to be going at ninety miles per hour all the time, slow yourself down. If, on the contrary, in comparing your voice to the personality's, you make John Wayne sound like a speed freak, you need to speak more quickly. Then, it's just a question of practice.

Establish your basic pace first, then learn to vary it by speeding up a little, or slowing down a little. Deliberately use speeding up or slowing down according to the guidelines given previously, so that your variation in pace is *motivated*. The change in pace must reflect a thought change; it should not be gratuitous. If you simply vary your pace for the sake of varying your pace, you are likely to sound slightly crazy, which is not consistent with the credible and competent image you need to present in order to persuade.

How to Cope with the Effects of Stress on Pace

Be aware that pace is significantly affected by nerves. Most people "rush" when nervous, that is to say, speed up their rate of speech. If you know this is what happens to you, compensate for it. When you're in an anxiety-provoking situation, deliberately speak more slowly than you usually would, and that will correct your "rushing." If the opposite is true for you, that under stressful conditions you suddenly develop a voice reminiscent of trudging through swamps, compensate by increasing your pace.

Technique #39: Use pitch to create an impression of authority and strength

In our culture, deeper voices are stereotypically interpreted as reflecting authority and strength, for both men and women. In addition, a deeper voice is stereotypically considered to be more believable, indicative of an individual's sincerity and trustworthiness. The "depth" of your voice is created by the pitch of your voice. The pitch is basically where your voice is placed on a musical scale. If you talk up where the high notes are, your voice is high-pitched; if your voice resonates to the frequency of the low notes, your voice is low-pitched. A high-pitched voice is stereotypically considered weak, somewhat irritating, and is often associated with flaky personalities or "airheads." A voice lower in pitch is considered knowledgeable, authoritative, indicative of self-assurance, and is often associated with people in power. This holds true for women as well as men.

To convey vocally the self-assurance and self-confidence that is the foundation of a trial lawyer's credibility in the courtroom, a lawyer will either have or will find him/herself developing a deep enough voice. There are very few (if any) high-pitched "Minnie Mouse" voices coming out of successful trial lawyers of either sex. In terms of your credibility as a persuasive individual, this does not mean you need to develop a basso profondo if you've been a soprano all your life. It does mean you need to broaden the *range* of your voice as it exists on the low end of the musical scale.

How to Determine Your Natural Pitch

Your first task, then is to determine whether your voice is high-pitched, low-pitched, or somewhere in the middle. An easy way to do this is, again, to tape a television personality who portrays a person of authority (for example, an anchorperson or famous mainline interviewer) with a voice that you find appealing and can identify as low-pitched, and then tape your own voice. Be sure to tape your own voice as it really is. You can accomplish this by simply leaving the tape recorder on during a breakfast conversation at home, or at other such candid moments. Then compare your voice with that of the television personality's. This should give you a good idea of your own pitch. If your pitch is already on the low end, great; if not, your pitch can be lowered.

How Your Pitch Gets Too High

Unless you have medical complications (for example, a problem with your palate or placement of your jaw), high pitch is usually a function of poor breathing, habit, and nerves. In general, when I work with trial lawyers, I find that correcting their breathing automatically lowers their pitch to a more assured and authoritative level.

Proper breathing is diaphragmatic breathing, as is taught in Lamaze for childbirth. The principle behind proper breathing is that you allow your belly to do the work. Improper breathing is breathing from the chest, where the chest heaves in order to allow the passage of air. When you make your chest do all the work, you don't fill your lungs fully with air, and so there is very little air to support your words. The tightness or constriction this creates makes your voice tight and constricted, and by extension, high-pitched.

A word of caution: You can learn to breathe properly on your own, as is demonstrated in the following exercise. However, DO NOT DO THIS EXERCISE IF IT IS THE LEAST BIT PAINFUL OR ANXIETY MAKING. There are excellent vocal coaches and singing teachers who are trained to teach proper breathing and who can supervise you as you learn if this process is even remotely stressful. Look in the telephone directory or ask friends in the entertainment business for a reference, and tell the instructor of your specific need to learn proper breathing.

How to Use Breath to Lower Your Pitch

I have taught the following exercise to many trial lawyers with good results. It is an exercise you can do easily on your own. Sit in a straight-backed chair with both feet flat on the floor. Place one hand on your belly and one hand on your chest (Illustration 3–1). Now breathe in through your nose, allowing your belly to swell out to a bit of a potbelly. You should feel this movement with the hand that is on your belly (Illustration 3–2). Then breathe out through your mouth, letting your tummy help by pushing the air out gently (Illustration 3–3). Your chest should not move at all during this, and the hand you placed on your chest should help you keep it still. This exercise should be accomplished without strain in your

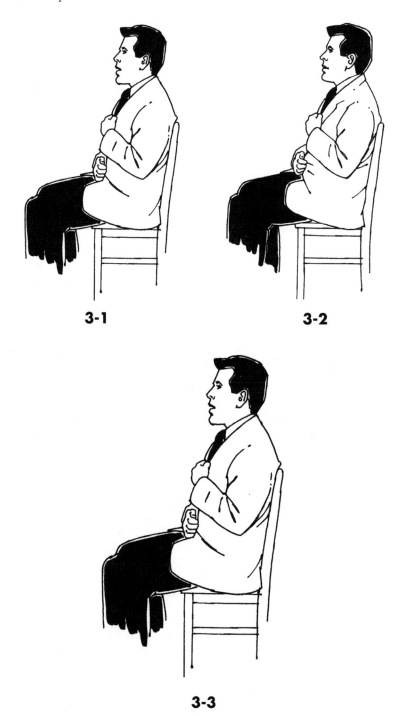

3-1

3-2

3-3

throat. If you find yourself straining with your throat, stop at once. Do the exercise slowly, taking about four counts to inhale, hold your breath two to four counts, then exhale in four counts. This will help you develop strength and flexibility in your diaphragm and belly. Do the inhale-hold-exhale sequence about six times, then stop and rest a moment. Then repeat the sequence. Do this for about ten minutes total, then before you get up from your chair, sit still a moment before you attempt to rise, as you may feel slightly dizzy if you're unaccustomed to getting all that oxygen.

Another exercise that has helped many an attorney broaden his/her range and deepen the voice is to sing along with the radio, *one octave down*. What I mean by this is sing along with the singer, but one octave down from where he/she is singing. This is going to sound peculiar and feel strange, but it will get you accustomed to working with a deeper voice. Lawyers tell me it's also more fun than practicing scales.

How Nervousness Affects Your Pitch

Many trial lawyers I've worked with have found that in general their voices are deep enough to convey authority and strength, but that when they get nervous or have to be "on," the voice suddenly flies up in pitch and they start sounding distinctly pre-pubertal. Nervousness and anxiety are major determinants of high pitch. Marcia Clark's voice, for example, during particularly anxious moments in the O. J. Simpson trial, sometimes raised surprisingly in pitch.

When you are nervous, you unconsciously contract your muscles, ready for fight or flight. But when your stomach and chest muscles are tight, you do not breathe in enough air to properly support your voice and you get the same tightness and constriction I spoke of earlier in reference to improper breathing, with the same results: a tight, constricted, and therefore high-pitched voice. In addition, when you are nervous, you tighten the throat muscles, which further constricts your voice.

How to Use Breath to Counteract the Effects of Nervousness

Proper breathing will help you relax and, consequently, will lower your pitch back down to its normal level. When you feel yourself getting nervous, take a few deep breaths, from the belly as described earlier, then say inside yourself the word "Now." If Now feels as if it's at your normal pitch, say a few more words to yourself to be sure your pitch is where you want it; then you can speak out loud with confidence that your voice will be where you want it and not high and squeaky. If Now isn't hitting the desired pitch, take a few more deep breaths and try again. Once your voice has internally settled down, it will be in the right place for all to hear.

Getting Past the Pitch Habit

Habit plays a large part in how we speak. You learned to speak from your parents, teachers, and peers, and once you learned a certain way of speaking, it became yours; you have spoken that way ever since. Your pitch is as much a part of you as how you walk. You probably have never questioned it until now. Don't be surprised, then, if you decided your pitch is too high and are working to change it, how uncomfortable it may be to do so. You will probably sound very strange to yourself. This is normal. You have been sounding one way for your entire adult life; any change is going to feel uncomfortable until it becomes the new habit. It should *not,* however, feel painful. If working to lower your pitch feels painful in any way, stop and consult a speech therapist.

A Special Note for Women Regarding Pitch

Women are caught in a bind regarding pitch. Culturally, women's voices are encouraged to be higher in pitch, in order to express greater vulnerability or delicacy. Many women learn therefore to speak in high, almost wispy voices and feel threatened in their femininity when it is suggested they allow their voices to drop down in pitch. The business of lawyering demands, however, that a woman appear confident, strong, and in control. A high, wispy voice does not stereotypically express these characteristics, so I often find myself working intensively with women trial lawyers who are sufficiently dedicated to their success and the success of their clients' cases to do the work necessary to deepen such a voice. In the process, however, these lawyers often fear becoming unfeminine, and so I have developed the following approach, which has eased these fears for many women lawyers.

If you are afraid that you will become unfeminine by lowering your pitch, I suggest that you allow your pitch to lower just a little. Speak like that a while and take the time to really get comfortable with the slightly lower pitch, then lower it again just a little, and so on, until you have achieved the voice you desire. Eventually, you will find a pitch that both conforms sufficiently to our cultural stereotypes to be considered worthy of serious attention, yet at the same time does not compromise your femininity.

Technique #40: Project confidence and competence by using good articulation

If pitch is the vocal tool that gives trial lawyers an impression of authority and strength, articulation is the primary vocal tool that allows a trial lawyer to be perceived as confident and competent. Stereotypically, poor articulation is associated with lack of education, mental retardation, laziness, and nervousness. None of these project confidence and competence. A successful lawyer, a credible and professional one, is expected to be well educated, endowed with a higher than average IQ, energetic, and sure of him/herself. Whether or not you are any of these (well-educated, high IQ, self-confident), good articulation will lend you an aura of confidence and competence and will contribute significantly to your ability to persuade others.

In addition, good articulation produces clear, crisp language that is easy to follow. If you make it easy for people to listen, they are more likely to pay attention. If you make it easy for people to understand you, they are more likely to get your point.

Poor articulation has no redeeming virtues. It is never effective as a communications device. Poor articulation just makes other people say "What?" a lot. As a matter of fact, one way to find out if you are a mumbler is to notice if people say "What?" a lot to you. Either your volume is way down, or you mumble. In a trial, jurors are at a distinct disadvantage in this respect. They cannot say "What?" The result is, anything the jurors cannot understand does not exist for them. A trial lawyer may make a vital statement, outline the very heart of his/her argument; if the jurors can't figure out what that lawyer is saying, it's as good as unsaid. So too, whenever you find yourself attempting to persuade an audience of any kind, it is imperative that you articulate clearly. If people can't understand you through your mumbles, that important point you just made may be completely lost.

Most people, as long as they are fairly easily understood by those around them, don't make efforts to produce clear speech. What you don't realize is that most people around you have become used to the way you speak, and in a sense "interpret" your mumbles. If you're speaking with a stranger, however, he/she may make efforts to understand what you are saying or may not care enough to do so and may simply let the not-understood parts stay that way. You have no way of assuring that the stranger will make those efforts. Certainly jurors don't, nor will most audiences, if that is a type of group you are attempting to persuade. Jurors cannot ask for clarification; good trial lawyers, being aware of this, take the responsibility for clear communication themselves and do whatever it takes to be fully and properly understood. Groups and audiences, if they are willing to make efforts to understand you in the beginning, will eventually tire and not be able to maintain that degree of constant attention. Audience members will not conclude, from their difficulty at attending to and understanding your speech, that their hearing is impaired; they will conclude that you are incompetent or insecure. Neither conclusion contributes to your ability to persuade.

How to Determine Your Articulation

You can figure out whether or not your articulation is good in the same way you figured out your pace and pitch: tape-record your voice and compare it to that of a television personality whose voice seems clear and easy to understand. Ask your friends and family if you speak clearly most of the time. If your articulation is poor, much can be done to improve it.

A word of caution: In some rare cases, poor articulation is due to a physical impairment (for example, misaligned teeth or a slight deformity of the palate or placement of the tongue). If you have such an impairment, consult a speech therapist; usually your speech can be significantly ameliorated.

How a Lazy Tongue Impedes Articulation

With the exception of certain physical impairments, poor articulation is caused by a lazy tongue. A lazy tongue is a tongue that doesn't work hard enough. The tongue is a muscle and needs to be treated as such. An underdeveloped muscle does not have the strength to permit control of movement. You can't play tennis well if you are completely out of shape: You won't be able to control the position of your tennis racket. Similarly, if your tongue isn't developed, you cannot control how you shape words, and it is difficult for you to speak clearly and vigorously.

Tongue Twisters: The Cure for a Lazy Tongue

I have found that the easiest way to improve trial lawyers' poor articulation is to have them do tongue twisters daily. Rather than going for speed in doing the tongue twisters, as you may have learned to do in school, however, I tell the lawyers to aim for muscular development. In other words, the tongue twisters need to be done as isometric exercises for the tongue and lips rather than as mental gymnastics. Granted, as your muscular development increases, you will be able to impress friends and family as you whip off the tongue twisters with amazing speed, but that is not your primary objective.

You will find a set of tongue twisters to practice at the end of this chapter. Read them aloud very slowly, pressing your lips tightly together for the *m, b, p* sounds, pushing your tongue hard against the roof of your mouth for the *n, ng* sounds, hard against the back of your front teeth for the *th* sounds, and really feel the sides of your tongue against your back teeth for the *k, y,* and *ch* sounds. Don't concern yourself with the vowel sounds; those are open sounds and do not build up the tongue. Concentrate on making the consonants firm. Really exaggerate. Remember you are pressing against yourself (that is, tongue against roof of mouth) to get the necessary resistance that creates muscular development. Focus on treating your tongue as a muscle, and don't worry about making the words sound right. They won't. This exercise, by the way, is an updated and less strenuous version of Demosthanes' projecting his voice across the ocean with a mouthful of marbles. The principle is the same: The marbles provided resistance the tongue had to work around. Tongue twisters are a lot easier and achieve the necessary effect.

Once you've done your tongue twisters slowly and laboriously for about ten minutes, read some of them naturally, without effort, and you'll notice that your speech is already clearer. This a momentary improvement, which will last only as you strengthen your tongue over time, but nonetheless, it's amazing how quickly articulation improves.

A word of caution: DO NOT STRAIN YOUR THROAT OR JAW WHILE DOING THIS EXERCISE. Doing tongue twisters should not cause any pain at all, simply some muscular effort from your tongue. IF YOU FEEL ANY STRAIN OR PAIN, *STOP AT ONCE* AND CONSULT YOUR DOCTOR OR A SPEECH THERAPIST. You're either doing the exercise incorrectly or you have a physical impairment of some kind.

You will find that some of the tongue twisters are more difficult for you to do than others—do those more; they are pointing up a problem area for you. Since tongue twisters require no thought, you can do them in the car and take advantage of time otherwise wasted in traffic jams, at red lights, and so forth. Do them in five-to-ten-minute sessions, for a total of twenty minutes daily, with rest periods in between. Articulation should be something you never think about, so good articulation must become second nature, as comfortable and automatic for you as walking.

Do not fall into the error of overarticulation. Although you should exaggerate in *practicing* your tongue twisters, you should not exaggerate in *speaking*. The tongue twisters will develop your muscles on their own; for the rest, just speak naturally, and as your muscles tone, your daily speech will automatically become clearer and more articulate, thereby reinforcing your image of a competent and confident individual.

Technique #41: Regulate your volume for maximum impact

Once you have worked with pitch to create an impression of authority and strength, reinforced people's impression of your confidence and competence with clear articulation, and learned to vary your pace to keep those listening interested in what you have to say, it's time to learn an important trial lawyer's technique: how to use volume to achieve *impact*.

To have impact, the trial lawyer's voice must first of all be easily and comfortably heard.

JUDGE ITO: SOFT VOICES ARE FOR BEDROOMS, NOT COURTROOMS

"In this case, in addition to their both [Marcia Clark and Christopher Darden] speaking softly and without force (at one point, Judge Ito had to tell Darden, 'Mr. Darden, if you would keep your voice up just a little bit so I can hear you') . . . far too casual in the delivery of their words to the jury."[4] A soft voice is appropriate in intimate situations, not in a courtroom. What people cannot hear, they will not be convinced of.

The opposite is equally true. When trial lawyers speak too loudly, jurors become annoyed and irritated. Overly loud voices literally give people headaches. You are not likely to convince someone who is suffering pain on your account. But when trial lawyers speak too softly, jurors will try to listen to the lawyer at first, but eventually the effort becomes too great and they just give up. So before we can discuss using volume for impact, we must consider appropriate volume.

How to Determine Your Natural Volume

Tape-record your voice in a number of different situations, through a variety of conversations, and compare your voice to the other speakers' voices. Is your voice significantly louder or softer than other peoples? Do you find that your volume gets much louder when you're intense about something, or perhaps much softer when you get nervous about something?

Changes in volume are dead giveaways to people's emotions. When people are angry, they raise their volume; when they're embarrassed or anxious, their volume dies down. Ask friends and family their opinion on the loudness or softness of your voice, then use those opinions in conjunction with the tape recordings you have made to figure out what your basic volume is and how that volume changes in function of different emotional states. Then all you need to do is practice raising or lowering your volume, so that you develop an appropriate, easily heard basic volume and practice compensating for any changes emotions create in your volume.

How to Regulate Your Volume for Emotional Effectiveness

To be successful, a trial lawyer must be in control of his/her vocal changes. A trial lawyer's voice must express what he/she wishes it to express, not what happens to be going on emotionally with the lawyer at the time. Do not misunderstand: Certainly your voice is an expression of yourself and generally should faithfully reflect your internal states; however, when you are in a situation in which your primary objective is to persuade others, as is true for trial lawyers, your voice should be at the service of that persuasion and therefore must be controlled to be effective. A trial lawyer must be in sufficient control of his/her voice so that it does not express emotions the lawyer doesn't want made known to the jurors.

CASE IN POINT

1. A beginning trial lawyer was nervous about what her star witness might unexpectedly divulge; she tipped off the jury to her nervousness by unconsciously lowering her voice. The jury attributed the lawyer's nervousness to a lack of faith in her own witness: The lawyer's credibility suffered considerably.

2. Voices were often raised in anger by counsel for both parties during the O. J. Simpson criminal trial. Jurors and commentators alike

spoke of such increased volume as "childlike" and "inappropriate," lending credence to a less than professional atmosphere.

Learn to use volume *deliberately* for impact, rather than letting your volume change unconsciously.

How to Lower Your Volume for Impact

Interestingly, raising volume for impact is rarely effective. It is the least subtle way of emphasizing a point and has been so overused that it has just about lost all its power. Once in a while, strategically placed, raised volume can be powerful, but it should be reserved for special cases, and more subtle alternatives should be carefully considered. What is effective, however, is *lowering* volume for emphasis: "Speak softly and carry a big stick." People who do not raise their voices in emotional moments are considered more steady and reliable, more competent and capable of dealing with crisis. A good trial lawyer will use lowered volume to capture the jury's attention, either to set up an important point or to bring one home. This is especially effective in an emotional moment.

Bear in mind, though, you must still be heard easily and comfortably, so when you lower your volume for impact, don't lower your voice too much. It is best to practice lowering volume for impact with the help of a tape recorder. Practice reading a paragraph out of a book, for example, using a basic comfortable volume for the most part; then lower your volume in specific places to get maximum impact. Listen to the recording, figure out when it was effective to lower your volume and when it wasn't, and do it again.

Learn Lawyers' Powerful Vocal Techniques Designed to Persuade People

In the first part of this chapter, we looked at vocal techniques trial lawyers use to keep jurors attentive and interested in what they are saying, as well as impressed with their credibility and professionalism. In this section, we will discuss lawyers' techniques of vocal persuasion. These techniques, however, will be effective only if you add them to the first set of techniques. Bear in mind that you cannot be persuasive if you have not created a background of competence and self-confidence, and even less so if you are putting those you are trying to persuade to sleep.

"The ability to handle language effectively is absolutely essential to success in court. It is the trial lawyer's ultimate tool."[5] Again and again, master advocates emphasize the role of language in the courtroom. The following techniques will help you handle language with the ease, grace, and power of successful trial lawyers.

Technique #42: Use phrasing to make sure people get your point

Because of the life-and-death nature of many of the matters lawyers bring to a courtroom, trial lawyers must weigh the value of the content of their words heavily and at the same time must *express* that content so that what the lawyer has to say will be readily understood and appreciated in the way the lawyer wants it to be. This is not as obvious as it may seem. Spoken language is not the same as written language. A juror cannot, if he/she has missed a point, "read that last paragraph over again." If a juror has missed a point, he/she will in all likelihood miss the next three points because he/she is busy worrying about the original point he/she missed while the next three fly by.

GARBLED SPEECH PRODUCES GARBLED THOUGHTS: MORE ON HOW THE PROSECUTION LOST THE O. J. SIMPSON TRIAL

"She [Marcia Clark] then proceeded to tell the jury in garbled language: 'now, although we don't know for a fact that he certainly did not receive that cut on some razor-sharp cell phone, it certainly does not make sense that when he went out to get the phone [Clark is actually embracing what Simpson told Baden as true] he opened the door to the Bronco and his knuckle grazed the wall of the door handle reopening the cut [he had received during the murder].' If you are a little confused at this point, you can imagine the jurors' confusion."[6] Clarity is key to persuasion. You cannot possibly hope to persuade anyone of anything if they can't even understand what you are talking about.

To have the necessary impact, spoken language must be organized differently from written language. In addition, anytime you are trying to persuade someone of something that person isn't familiar with, you must take this unfamiliarity with the subject into account. Points that may be obvious to you may not be at all obvious to the person you are addressing. You must design your delivery so that the points that *you* deem important are those perceived as important by those listening to you.

In the course of preparing for a trial, lawyers often become quasi-experts in the subject matter of the trial. A prominent medical malpractice lawyer, for example, pleading on behalf of his client in a dental matter, ended up knowing more about dentistry than the average practicing dentist. Yet for all his expertise and understanding of his client's problem, the lawyer lost the case. During jury debriefings, jurors complained that even though they sensed that there was malpractice here, they couldn't sort out what was important and relevant from what wasn't: The lawyer's overfamiliarity with dental matters had led him to forget how important it was for him to get the jurors up to speed. In the absence of being able to peg the important points, the jurors gave up and brought back a verdict in favor of defense.

How to Phrase to Get Your Meaning Across

Phrasing is a primary way trial lawyers use to assure that the jurors will hear what the lawyer wants them to hear. Phrasing is a way of grouping words together in logical fashion, with slight pauses on either side of the phrase, so that the thought can be easily grasped. Phrasing is how you make sense out of what you're saying.

When you are dealing with spoken language, think in terms of phrases, not sentences. Sentences are often too long to be easily understood; sentences can run whole paragraphs, whereas a phrase is usually only five to seven words long. Most important, a phrase represents a single thought. It is much easier to be persuasive if you are expressing one thought at a time. People can then follow your thinking with minimal effort and can better absorb your point.

A lawyer needed to make juror sense out of the following statement: "Shortly after he'd been examined by Doctor Searle in the emergency room Jack did regain consciousness although exhibiting many of the symptoms associated with brain concussion."

Said all together without a pause, this statement was difficult to digest, yet it is a relatively simple sentence. With the addition of pauses (indicated by /), it became easy to follow: "Shortly after he'd been examined / by

Dr. Searle / in the emergency room / Jack did regain consciousness/ although exhibiting many of the symptoms / associated with brain concussion."

How to Use the Pause to Appear in Charge and in Control

A word of warning: These are *pauses,* not stops. A pause is just what it sounds like, a momentary phenomenon; it is not to be confused with an ending (a stop). It's the difference between slightly letting your foot ease up on the accelerator (pausing), and putting it on the brakes (stopping). Pauses, then, are the tool that allows you to phrase, and you phrase according to thought.

Notice how each of the phrases in the preceding Case in Point contains only one thought. The *placement* of the pause is not absolute; there are other ways to phrase the above sentence. The important point is that you restructure written language so it is easily and effectively understood as spoken language. When you phrase, you appear to be in command of language: This is actually the vocal equivalent of "doing things one thing at a time" we discussed in the context of creating credibility. By expressing one thought at a time, you appear to be in charge and in control, the very basis of power.

At the end of this chapter is an exercise to help you learn to use phrasing effectively and naturally. When you do the phrasing exercise, be sure you do it out loud. This holds true for all the vocal exercises in this chapter. Your voice as you hear it inside your head is not the same as your voice when it is heard out loud. As with the techniques given throughout this book, practice is of the essence. With practice, these skills become second nature and powerful; without practice, they are useless. I encourage you to practice the skills in your daily life so that they become easy to manipulate and so that you become expert at them.

Technique #43: Use the pause to highlight important points

The pause is not only useful in making language intelligible, it also is a prime way of highlighting important points. As any good trial lawyer will tell you, the days of histrionic oratory are long gone; contemporary speech must use subtle means of emphasis and persuasion. The pause is a wonderfully subtle technique. Judicious use of the pause provides you with the ability to make a point crystal clear, to give it maximum significance with very little effort and no histrionics.

Case in Point

An example: in the following statement: "The car was going eighty miles per hour when it hit the child," a lawyer wanted to emphasize the *speed* of the car. Rather than using the pause simply to phrase her statement, I encouraged the lawyer to use the pause both to phrase the statement for clear meaning *and* to emphasize her point.

The result was as follows: "The car was going // eighty miles per hour / when it hit the child." The longer pause (//) was really unnecessary in terms of clarifying meaning, but it brought attention to the speed of the car effectively, without the lawyer's having to be overly obvious about it.

How to Use the Pause Subtly to Emphasize Important Points

The pause for emphasis is a setup: It is the nonverbal communication of "Are you ready, folks? Something important is coming." The pause has tremendous power. It is the vocal equivalent of stillness, and stillness pulls attention. It is important not to "punch" or emphasize with *volume* the "eighty miles per hour" in the preceding Case in Point that follows the pause: This is overkill and would sound melodramatic. It is critical that the words following the pause are not said in a louder voice or in a different voice from those preceding it, or you will lose the subtlety of your effect.

How to Change the Placement of the Pause to Emphasize an Important Point

By maneuvering the placement of the pause, you can change the point you wish to emphasize.

Case in Point

Taking the previous example, let's say, for instance, that the lawyer had wanted *the child* who was hit to be the focus of the jury's attention.

All she had to do was change the placement of the pause: "The car was going eighty miles per hour when it hit // the child." Try the sentence out loud with this new pause. Now the important point is the child.

If the lawyer had wanted to highlight the fact that the car *hit* the child, she could simply have moved the pause over: "The car was going eighty miles per hour when it // hit the child."

The guideline for effective use of the pause is to pause *in front of* the point you wish to emphasize. Don't pause three words away from your point; pause right in front of *the* critical word.

How to Use Pitch Skillfully in Conjunction with the Pause for Effective Emphasis of a Point

Be careful that your voice does not pitch down right before the pause. Pitching your voice down undermines the value of the pause. Bear in mind that the pause used to highlight a point is essentially setting up that point: If your voice pitches down, you won't set up your point, you will shoot it down. Your pitch should remain level or even go up a little to set up a point, but never down. The pause is a powerful tool and should be used only for important points. Don't pause for every point; your speech will become choppy. Reserve it for your main point.

How to Use the Pause to Minimize the Importance of a Point

If pausing highlights a point, then taking out the pause will diminish its importance. For example, a lawyer who wants to diminish the importance of something opposing counsel said can do so just by restating opposing counsel's statement without taking any pauses; opposing counsel's point will seem less important.

CASE IN POINT

For example, in a recent murder trial, prosecution announced:

"The // bloodstains / on the carpet were of // human origin." The emphasis was on "bloodstains" and "human origin." Defense attorney reduced the impact the prosecution achieved with the pauses by simply removing them. Defense reiterated the statement during cross-examination, saying:

"The bloodstains on the carpet were of human origin."

No one word was pointed up more than any other; the overall statement was rendered monotonous and thus lost its impact.

Defense could have also changed the emphasis prosecution had made by changing the *placement* of the pause.

CASE IN POINT

Using the same example, prosecution had stated: "The // bloodstains / on the carpet were of // human origin." The emphasis was on "bloodstains" and "human origin."

Defense could have reinterpreted the significance of prosecution's statement with: "The bloodstains on the // carpet were of human origin."

Defense would have nonverbally lessened the importance of "bloodstains" and "human origin" and would have shifted attention to "carpet," a relatively innocuous word.

The pause is an excellent example of how it really isn't just what you say, but *how you say it* that makes all the difference in persuasive speech.

The exercise on pauses at the end of the chapter will help you develop the ability to use the pause naturally and convincingly. The pause is a powerful tool. The more you work with it, the more you will come to appreciate just how powerful it is. Be sure to practice out loud.

Technique #44: Make dull material come to life using "Color," "Peaks," and "Valleys"

Phrasing and pausing are techniques trial lawyers use to help them make their words make sense and to call the jurors' attention to certain points; "color," "peaks," and "valleys" are used to help make their words interesting. If trial lawyers' language is not interesting, they will not be persuasive. Trial lawyers have the challenging task of talking for long periods of time in front of the jurors, who, try as they might, may not find the substantive issues as compelling as the lawyer does. Trial lawyers must engage the jurors' interest regardless of the sometimes dull and uninteresting nature of the issues (oh, the D.N.A. material at the O. J. Simpson trial!) and over longer periods of time than most of us listen to anything. Color, peaks, and valleys are ways of making what the lawyer says exciting, so that the jurors want to continue listening to that lawyer's point of view, not to opposing counsel's.

How to Create a Compelling, Vicarious Experience for Your Listeners By Using Color

In addition to making otherwise uninspiring testimony inspiring, color brings an event right into the courtroom, through the power of the voice. When the jurors are in the jury box, they cannot see the event the lawyer is describing, they cannot experience that awful/triumphant/heartbreaking moment, unless the lawyer makes that moment happen for them.

CASE IN POINT

In talking about how to describe a man with a broken leg, top trial lawyer Gerry Spence says: "Don't say he suffered pain. Tell me what it felt like to have a broken leg with the bone sticking out through his flesh. Tell me how it was! Make me see it! Make me feel it! Make me understand! Make me care!"[7]

Successful trial lawyers are masters at making that moment real for the jurors; it is a primary secret of their persuasiveness. Color is how to bring a moment to life, vocally. Color is, literally, painting pictures with your voice.

How to Manipulate Words in Order to Create Color

How is this accomplished? You give life to a word by making it sound like what it *means*. As Oliver Wendell Holmes so beautifully put it: "A word is the skin of a living thought and may vary greatly in color and content according to the circumstances and time in which it is used." Attending to the meaning, the thought, that the word represents is how you give a word *power*.

Technically, color is achieved by either stretching the word (lengthening it), or shortening the word. Words such as "hit" or "kick" are shortened to give a vocal rendition of a blow. Words such as "lonely" or "painful" are stretched, lengthened to give them an aspect of suffering. The word must not simply be lengthened or shortened however; you must try to put into the word what its value is. How boring can you make the word "boring" sound? How hurt can you make the word "hurt" sound? If you really *think* about what you are saying, you'll find you do this quite naturally. It is only when we speak without truly attending to our choice of words that we lose the dimension of color.

Case in Point

A lawyer wanted to add color to the following sentence: "John's headaches have been going on a long, long time." See if you can accomplish that by doing as the lawyer did: Try stretching the word "long" by stretching the "ng" sound. Make the word "long" sound long. Now say "long" in the context of the sentence, taking care to stretch only the first "long," leaving the second one alone. Do this out loud.

If you absolutely do not raise your volume when you color the word "long," you will effectively have brought the sentence to life *without* resorting to melodramatic effect, which is exactly what the lawyer did. He was thus able to help the jury feel just what was going on with John in a sincere and believable way.

A word of caution: Do not stretch the vowel sounds (a,e,i,o,u) when lengthening a word. Stretching vowel sounds is what you do when you sing, not what you do when you speak. Work the *consonants,* consonants are the meat of the word, consonants are what give a word texture and definition.

How to Use Color to Get People to React Emotionally to a Point

Color is a useful alternative to the pause in emphasizing a point, especially when you have several important elements in one sentence. You can use the pause to emphasize some points and color to emphasize others. The rule of thumb as to when to choose color rather than the pause to emphasize is as follows:

Use *color* when the emphasis is a more *emotional* one, when you want people to react emotionally to a point; use the *pause* when you are looking for a more cerebral or *logical* reaction to your point.

Case in Point

Let's go back to our earlier example: "The car was going eighty miles per hour when it hit the child."

The lawyer could make the word "hit" sound like a blow, by shortening the word, and giving the final "t" emphasis. She then could phrase the statement, and use color on the word "hit": "The car was going eighty miles per hour / when it *hit* the child."

You can almost feel the impact.

As you plan out whatever it is you have to say, as you think about how you want to present your point of view to others, think as trial lawyers do, in terms of coloring words, of giving words their true value so as to make your speech more alive, more exciting.

How to Practice Using Color

In addition to the color worksheet included at the end of the chapter, an easy way to practice coloring is to work with a romance or adventure novel. Romance and adventure novels are loaded with color words, since their goal is to bring an adventure to life with words. Deliberately, and with exaggeration, make as many of the words from the novel sound like what they mean as you possibly can. Do this out loud, one word at a time. Then, once you've practiced in exaggerated fashion for about ten to fifteen minutes, forget about it.

As you do this exercise on a daily basis, you'll find your everyday speech becoming more interesting, richer, more varied, without your making any special effort. You are training yourself in a general fashion to attend to the value of words, to color, and this will naturally find its way into your daily speech. So although you practice in exaggerated fashion, you end up coloring subtly.

How to Keep People Interested and Attentive by Using Peaks and Valleys

There is nothing worse than trying to listen to someone speaking in a monotone. Jurors are vocal in their complaints against trial lawyers who, brilliant as they might be, persist in speaking in a monotonous drone. Even if the content of the lawyer's speech is riveting, it is difficult to stay tuned into and attentive to a monotonous voice. Trial lawyers have no choice: To be successful, they must keep the jurors interested and attentive. You must keep your audience interested and attentive if you are to be persuasive. Simply put, a monotonous voice is death to your argument. In addition, trial lawyers are faced with an inescapable reality: the shortness of adult attention. You may be fascinated and wide awake for hours on end as you speak, but that's no guarantee the people who will be listening to you are. Vocal variety is a constant challenge.

How to Create Peaks and Valleys that Work

Peaks and valleys are important ways of keeping people listening to you. Peaks and valleys are slight changes in your basic pitch. In other words, you have a basic pitch level with which you are comfortable, but within that level, you need variety. In order to accomplish this, you raise some words up a bit ("peaks"), and drop others down a bit ("valleys"). A "bit" here means about a one-note value on a musical scale (Illustration 3–4).

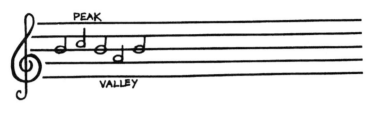

3-4

The peak has a dual function: It both keeps people attentive by the simple fact of pitch variety, and it brings attention to a word in the same way a pause or color does. It is the vocal equivalent of underlining a word in red.

CASE IN POINT

Go back to an earlier example: "The car was going eighty miles per hour when it hit the child." The speed of the car had already been established through expert testimony; now the lawyer wanted to remind the jurors of that fact in her closing argument. See if you can do what the lawyer did to accomplish this. Simply raise the "eighty miles per hour" in this case: "The car was going "eighty miles per hour" when it hit the child." You have brought attention to the relevant point, but in subtle fashion (Illustration 3–5). Be careful to drop back down to your basic pitch; don't allow the peak to seduce you into a higher than normal pitch once the word has been said.

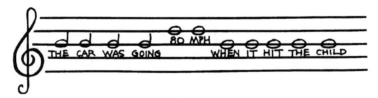

3-5

Valleys are roughly one-note *drops* of a word or a phrase. Valleys are often used to indicate personal comments or information deemed important but not crucial.

A lawyer wanted to make a comment without appearing heavy-handed: "This photograph, as a matter of fact, was added to the evidence just today."

The phrase "as a matter of fact" represented a personal comment, and as such, was dropped slightly in pitch, to set it off from the rest of the sentence without appearing too obvious.

Taking a different example: "This photograph, already entered in evidence, shows John on April 2, 1979."

Since the entire phrase "already entered in evidence" represented information already noted and was not crucial at the moment, it was dropped slightly in pitch (Illustration 3–6).

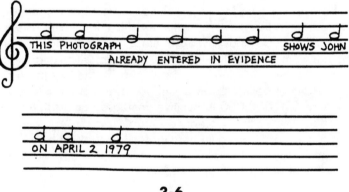

3-6

Peaks and valleys, to become a natural part of your speech, must be practiced. The worksheets at the end of the chapter provide you with sentences that are best practiced out loud. Use a tape recorder to help you determine when you are truly raising a word or lowering your pitch. Although it takes patience and practice, vocal variety is well worth the effort. There's nothing quite as reassuring as an awake, alert audience, be that an audience of one or an audience of 1,000, attentive to your every word.

*Technique #45: Use the five senses to portray a scene
or situation vividly and persuasively*

Bringing a scene to life relies not only on the use of color, as described earlier, but also on the trial lawyer's choice of words. For the jurors to be persuaded, they must be moved, as we shall see in detail in Chapter 7, and in order to be moved by a scene, they must experience it. The trial lawyer must, to be persuasive, be able to describe the situation in such a way that the jurors experience the event as if they were there and feel, for example, the client's suffering as if it were their own and the client's outrage as if it were theirs.

How do we experience an event? Through our five senses. Experiencing an event is actually the synthesis of how we see, hear, touch, taste, and smell that event. Depending on the event, some of the senses are more prominent than others: sight, hearing, and touch are almost always included.

THE $10,000,000 PIGPEN:
SILKWOOD VS. KERR-MCGEE

A worker at the Kerr-McGee uranium plant, Jim Smith, testified on behalf of the Silkwood family (*Silkwood* vs. *Kerr-McGee*) in the following vivid terms: "I never saw anything so filthy in my life [as the uranium plant]. . . . If you ever walked into it, you could hardly breathe when you went beyond the door. The ammonia fumes and the uranium around there was just one big pigpen."[8] The jury came back with a verdict of $500,000 in actual damages (for the Silkwood family) and $10,000,000 in punitive damages against Kerr-McGee. Notice how Mr. Smith's description engages the senses: how compelling it is to say "you could hardly breathe" in describing the fumes, how easy it is to visualize a "pigpen," and how descriptive "pigpen" is of dirt as well as disorder.

When you describe an event, deliberately choose words and phrases that engage the senses.

How to Choose Words and Phrases That Powerfully Engage the Senses

CASE IN POINT

A lawyer wants to convey the following information about his client: "John lies in his hospital bed, paralyzed from the neck down."

It may be intellectually sufficient to give the jurors the information in such a straightforward unembellished statement, but the lawyer knows such a rendition will not allow the jurors to experience the truth of John's life as he lives it.

The lawyer will therefore choose words and phrases to engage the senses, such as: "John lies in his hospital bed very still; a fly buzzes in front of his face, but he cannot shoo it away, despite the annoying sound. The sun pours brightly onto his bed; he can see it and the sight warms his heart, but it does not warm his body, because he cannot feel it. The phone rings beside his bed; John looks longingly at the phone, but he cannot pick up the receiver. John can't do a lot of things we all take for granted. John is paralyzed from the neck down."

Certainly, engaging the senses takes a good deal more work and effort than simple sharing of information. However, information in and of itself rarely won a case or convinced anyone of anything.

Learn to engage the senses by practicing describing events to friends and family using all five senses. You will undoubtedly find that you use some of the senses to the exclusion of others. Try to work with *all* the senses, so that you can make an experience as rich as possible for the listener. Bear in mind that by engaging the senses, you not only make it easier for yourself to persuade, you also are more interesting to listen to, and if people are attentive and interested, they are much more likely to get your point.

Technique #46: Use emotions appropriately in order to sway people

Emotions, properly used, are a primary tool of persuasion; improperly used, they are a primary tool of dissuasion. When a trial lawyer fails to convey feeling in his/her arguments, jurors state that such a lawyer appears robotlike, unconnected to the rest of the human race and, more important, unconnected to the world as the jurors know it. Yet if a lawyer uses emotions melodramatically, jurors comment that the lawyer came across as insincere and phony and had lost all credibility.

Emotions, therefore, must be used with care, but must be used. Emotion, as we will see in Chapter 7, is critical to people's decision-making process and is therefore critical to your ability to persuade.

How to Choose Specific Emotions to Convince People of Your Point

The first step in using emotion is to determine which emotion it is that you want the listener to feel. If you want the listener to feel outrage, then *you* must sound outraged; if you want the listener to feel pleased, then *you* must sound pleased.

CASE IN POINT

Let's look at which emotions would be appropriate for the lawyer to use in the previously used example: "John lies in his hospital bed very still; a fly buzzes in front of his face, but he cannot shoo it away, despite the annoying sound. The sun pours brightly onto his bed; he can see it and the sight warms his heart, but it does not warm his body, because he cannot feel it. The phone rings beside his bed; John looks longingly at the phone, but he cannot pick up the receiver. John can't do a lot of things we all take for granted. John is paralyzed from the neck down."

There are several emotions here for the lawyer to choose. For example, the lawyer could express *annoyance* through the phrase "a fly buzzes in front of his face," feelings of contented pleasure through the phrase "he can see it and the sight warms his heart," and longing through the phrase "John looks longingly at the phone." These emotions will help the jurors connect to John's experience.

Notice that the lawyer did not choose to convey emotion through the whole statement. A little emotion goes a long way. Specifically, avoid putting emotions on phrases that are already highly emotional just by virtue of their content. For example, there is no need to express emotion through the phrases "but he cannot shoo it away," "because he cannot feel it," "but he cannot pick up the receiver," because these phrases already have plenty of emotional impact purely on an informational level.

How to Use Your Voice to Convey Emotion Persuasively

A trial lawyer must not only choose emotion properly, he/she must also carry that emotion successfully through his/her voice. In other words, the jurors must perceive the emotion the lawyer *wants* them to perceive, and not something else.

To find out if you are able to convey the emotion you wish to convey, practice saying phrases with different choices of emotion into a tape recorder and then play back the tape. Were you successful? Can you recognize in your voice the emotions you chose? This is a skill that takes some time to develop, but that is wonderfully effective.

Keep talking into the tape recorder and listening to the feedback until you are easily able to express the emotion of your choice. A list of different emotions is given at the end of the chapter. This is by no means a list of all emotions, but has been included to give you an idea of the diversity of emotions available to you that you may want to consider using. Some emotions will be more difficult for you to convey than others; these require more practice.

How to Avoid Emotional "Overkill" (Melodrama)

Emotion becomes melodrama only when it is inappropriately used. Unfortunately, emotion is inappropriately used a great deal. For example, a broken leg is cause for annoyance, irritation, certainly frustration, but it is not cause for heartrending grief. So if in speaking of a client's broken leg, a trial lawyer adopts a tone of profound grief, the jurors are sure to comment on such misuse of emotion during jury debriefings. The lawyer's succumbing to excesses of melodrama can easily lose him/her all jury sympathy. On the other hand, if a trial lawyer rattles off a child's death caused by a drunken driver as if he/she were measuring out oatmeal for breakfast, he/she is also guilty of misusing emotion in the worst way: by not using it.

The use of emotion is governed by *appropriateness*. All you need do to avoid melodrama is choose the emotion that fits your subject matter; if anything, underplay a little and choose an emotion slightly less powerful if you are afraid of becoming melodramatic. Do, however, use emotion. Just because it must be used cautiously does not mean you should avoid it. On the contrary, the fact that emotion must be used cautiously reflects its enormous power, and you should avail yourself of that power.

Technique #47: The "Build-Drop": A master technique for creating dramatic effect to emphasize a major point without appearing theatrical

There is no place in today's courtroom for rhetorical flights of fancy. A trial lawyer must somehow be able to create dramatic effect subtly. Any effect that smacks of theatricality will also smack of being phony and must be avoided. The build-drop is an effective technique that, without seeming dramatic, has a dramatic effect.

How to Create a Build-Drop

The build-drop consists of a setup and the point you want to get across. The setup is whatever information leads up to your important point and is delivered with consistently rising pitch. The point you want to get across is delivered with a drop in pitch.

Case in Point

The lawyer wants to drive an important point home. She decides to do a build-drop using the statement: "John can't do a lot of things we all take for granted. John is paralyzed from the neck down."

Her *setup* would be "John can't do a lot of things we all take for granted"; her *important point,* the one she wants to drive home, is: "John is paralyzed from the neck down."

The lawyer then delivers her build-drop as follows (Illustration 3–7): The setup is *built up* in pitch, then there is a *pause,* then the important point is *dropped down* in pitch.

Let's take another example, this time within a single sentence "John is paralyzed from the neck down."

Here the *setup* is "John is paralyzed," then comes the pause, then the *important point* "from the neck down" (Illustration 3–8).

In delivering a build-drop, *do not* alter your volume when you say the important point or you will lose all subtlety.

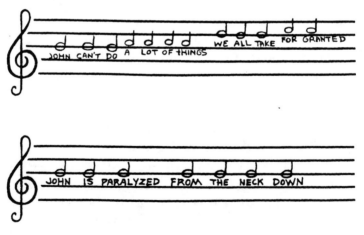

3-7

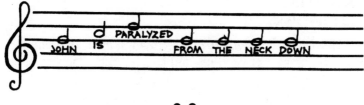

3-8

How to Use the Build-Drop in a Question/Answer Format

Trial lawyers often use the build-drop effectively in a question-answer format, for example: "Did Mary run from the scene of the crime? No." The setup is the entire question, then comes the pause, then the word "no" (Illustration 3–9). If you use the build-drop in this manner, you will have created dramatic effect with great subtlety and persuasiveness, *as long as you don't alter your volume.* Bear in mind that because the build-drop is dramatic, it must not be overused. Reserve it for statements that really need to be delivered with maximum impact.

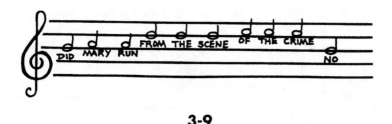

3-9

SUMMARY

There is nothing worse than having to strain to understand or to hear someone. Curing your mumbles will guarantee that you will be easily and effectively heard. Correcting your speech for pitch, pace, volume, and articulation is a necessary first step. Using pauses, phrasing, color, peaks, and valleys will further the effectiveness of your speech. Using emotion will then make your words truly persuasive.

WORKSHEETS
TONGUE TWISTERS

Do the following tongue twisters as described in the text, going for the muscular development of your lips and tongue, rather than for speed.

- Bim comes, Ben comes, Bim brings Ben's broom, Ben brings Bim's broom, Ben bends Bim's broom, Bim bends Ben's broom, Bim and Ben's broom bends, Ben's bent broom breaks, Bim's bent broom breaks, Ben's broom is broke, Bim's broom is broke, both brooms are broke.

- When beetles fight these battles with their paddles in a bottle and the bottle's on a poodle and the poodle's eating noodles they call this muddlepuddle tweedle poodle beatle noodle battle paddle bottle.

- A maid in Grathum mum once played the national anthem mum and broke a crysanthemum mum.

- Which is the witch that wished the wicked wish?

- If a doctor doctored another doctor would the doctor doing the doctoring doctor the other doctor in the way the doctored doctor wanted to be doctored?

- A tooter who tooted a flute tried to tutor two tooters to toot. Said the two to the tooter is it harder to toot or to tutor two tooters to toot?

- Leith listlessly lisps and lips lots of lengthy lectures.

- Never need nine of nothing not new nor old.

- If Roland Reynolds rolled a round roll round a round room, where is the round roll which Roland Reynolds rolled round the room?

- Whether the weather be fine or whether the weather be not, whether the weather be cold or whether the weather be hot, well we'll go whatever the weather, whether we like it or not.

- Freshly fried flesh of fresh fried fishes is fine for fat folk.

- Gailey gathered the gleaners the glossy golden grain and garned it gladly in granny's great grainery in Godfrey's green grassy glen.

- The monk's monkey got in the ink, the monk's monkey drank it. The monk woke up his uncle. He thought it was a prank, ink the monkey drank.

- One violet winkle veering west was Worthington went working around Vermont.

- Triangular tangle gangs that wangle anger Tommy Prangle, they're from a jungle Prangle says, but not to be outfangled.

- Who sews crows clothes, Sue sews crows clothes, Slow Joe crow sews who's clothes, Sue's clothes, Sue sews socks of fox-in-socks, now Slow Joe crow sews socks of fox-in-socks, now Sue sews roses on Slow Joe Crow's clothes.

PAUSES

Try pausing at different places in the following sentences and see how you vary the importance of what you are saying according to where you have placed your pause. Remember, a pause brings attention to what *follows* it.

1. Was the speed of the vehicle excessive?
2. Mr. Smith was traveling at 95 mph.
3. This is a dangerous stretch of road.
4. Mr. Smith hit the child at that speed.
5. Mrs. Jones visited her only doctor twice.
6. The impact could not have caused that much damage.
7. Was Mrs. Jones in danger?
8. Whose handwriting is that, Doctor?
9. Mr. Smith was driving 75 mph at the time, but he was not drunk.
10. There was kind of a bump in the road.

PHRASING

Try phrasing the following sentences so that you make sense of what you are saying. Experiment with different choices of phrasing until you are satisfied.

1. How could Mrs. Smith forget to get her brakes fixed?

2. According to Dr. Jones, Mr. Smith's injuries are minimal.

3. Mr. Jones attempted a right-hand turn from the left-hand lane.

4. We do not know just when Mrs. Smith arrived on the scene.

5. So whatever information the doctor gets is from the patient himself if he is able to talk.

6. Was Mr. Smith driving erratically at the time, or did he swerve to avoid the child?

7. Mr. Smith did not have time to come to an appropriate stop, or he wasn't paying attention.

8. Was he speeding when he hit the side of the barn?

9. You stated in your deposition that you had brought the documents to Mr. Jones before the meeting June 8th; is that correct?

10. You stated previously that you were in the vicinity of the plant at approximately 9:15 A.M., which was the time of the explosion, did you not?

COLOR

Make the words you want to emphasize in the following sentences sound like what they mean. For example; make the word "pain" sound *painful.* Be careful not to use volume to do this.

1. At this particular area, there are no curves in the road—it is relatively flat—is that correct?

2. Then you weren't speeding at the time, you were paying attention to your driving.

3. And were there any complications on this repair job?

4. There were treatments given in an effort to strengthen the leg and restore proper motion.

5. The headaches occur daily, the duration being as long as an hour or two.

6. Mrs. Jones has noticed that her husband, previously a happy, thoughtful man, is now nervous and preoccupied.

7. The photographs will show the severity of the impact.

8. It was a clear, bright day; driving conditions were excellent.

9. There was never any discussion as to the implications of the new will.

10. The head trauma was severe, no doubt; however, I am not convinced that Mr. Jones's distress is solely a consequence of that injury.

PEAKS AND VALLEYS

Find as many *peaks* (raising a given word) and *valleys* (dropping a word or phrase down in pitch) as you can in the following sentences. Have fun with this exercise; exaggerate to get the feel of peaks and valleys.

1. Ladies and gentlemen, the evidence shows that my client did not embezzle the funds.

2. Mr. Smith will never walk properly again.

3. Dr. Beck is a highly reputable physician, whose standing in the medical community is well known.

4. Mrs. Jones sustained severe injuries and is still under medical supervision.

5. Is it your opinion that Mr. Jones was traveling in a reasonable manner?

6. You wouldn't know whether Mrs. Smith stopped at the stop sign, would you?

7. I am confident that the evidence will show Mr. Jones did sustain a bump on the head and was rendered unconscious because of it.

8. There is nothing in the evidence to substantiate Mrs. Herbert's claim.

9. Late in the afternoon of May 30, Mr. Jones was seen talking with Mr. Ames, which needless to say put him in a very embarrassing position with his own department.

10. There is no excuse, ladies and gentlemen of the jury, for the shabby treatment my client has endured in the course of this trial.

EMOTIONS

The following is a list of emotions for you to work with in the Emotions Worksheet and when practicing with romance and/or adventure novels. It is not a complete list of all emotions, simply a list to give you an idea of the emotional range available to you in order to be persuasive.

happy	serene	at peace
wonderful	indifferent	bored
depressed	disappointed	anxious
nervous	uneasy	scared
angry	hostile	embarrassed
heartbroken	distressed	pessimistic
confused	troubled	helpless
hopeless	ridiculed	criticized
belittled	devastated	trapped
jittery	awkward	outraged
concerned	worried	desperate
annoyed	irritated	puzzled

EMOTIONS

Select an emotion from the Emotions List and say one of the sentences below, deliberately making your voice carry the emotion you chose. Tape-record yourself and listen carefully when you play back the recording; does your voice indeed convey the emotion you chose? If not, try again. Then pick a different emotion from the Emotions List and say the same sentence as before, but with your voice carrying the new emotion. Tape-record yourself again and listen. Do you hear a distinct difference? Were you able to clearly convey the second emotion you picked? If so, great. If not, try again. Then pick a third emotion and repeat the exercise. When you have run as many emotions as you want through a sentence, go on to another sentence and follow the same procedure.

Patience and persistence are the key to learning how to persuade with your voice. So, practice! You'll be impressed with the results.

1. The impact was very minor.
2. To put it another way, four-year-old children are simply not responsible.
3. Doctor, would you describe the results of your operation as a failure?
4. Now do you remember these questions being asked of you and the answers given?
5. The facts of the case are relatively uncomplicated.
6. Maybe Mr. Smith was drunk at the time.
7. He impacted the car because he was traveling 45 mph in a 15 mph zone.
8. Mr. Smith was drunk at the time, and he was speeding.
9. Mrs. Smith did hit the side of the barn, but she was not speeding.
10. Perhaps Mr. Jones was careless in forgetting to turn his lights on.

The Fourth Step:
Develop Trust By Developing Relationship

Twelve blank faces stare out at the trial lawyer, waiting to hear what the lawyer has to say, waiting to see how the lawyer measures up, to see if he/she is any better than the attorney representing the other side. Twelve strangers, whom the trial lawyer must convince to adopt his/her point of view rather than opposing counsel's. But how? How is this lawyer going to persuade these twelve unknowns that he/she is right and opposing counsel is wrong? The truth of the matter is, if they remain strangers, the lawyer will not succeed. Persuasion is based on trust, and people trust those who are familiar to them. Successful trial lawyers start, not by trying to convince the jury of their version of the facts of the case, but by becoming familiar to the jurors, by winning the jury's *trust*.

This is no easy task, yet good trial lawyers do it, day in and day out. Almost magically, they transform a cold group of twelve complete strangers into an audience of familiars who are willing at least to consider the lawyer's interpretation seriously, open to being convinced.

How Lawyers Win Jurors' Trust by Developing Relationship

Whom do we trust? We trust people we know and feel comfortable with, those with whom we have "rapport." Rapport means relationship: The creation of rapport means entering into a "sympathetic relationship"[1] with an individual. When we say so-and-so has good rapport with a person, we mean he/she relates easily with that person, seems to understand the person, gets along well with the person. When you create rapport, what you are doing in essence is establishing trust. Without trust, there can be no persuasion.

All those bad jokes about the stereotypical used-car salesman are really reflections of the used-car salesman's failure to create rapport. The salesman is trying to get you to trust him/her regarding the worth of a car (and therefore persuade you of the purchase) before any rapport has been developed. That's virtually impossible. There is no relationship, how can there possibly be any trust?

Usually, the tighter the relationship, the greater the degree of trust. The closer you are to someone, the more likely you are to trust him/her. And in turn, the more you trust someone, the more likely you are to allow yourself to be persuaded by that person. Your best friend, for example, has a great deal more influence on you than the checker at the grocery store. A trial lawyer's first task, then, is not to persuade the jury of anything, but to enter into a sympathetic relationship with the jurors that will, in turn, engender their trust.

A trial lawyer does not, however, have unlimited time or situations in which to do this—far from it. Trials frequently take place over a period of just a few weeks, if that. Recent high-profile cases such as the Menendez brothers, O. J. Simpson, or Heidi Fleiss, which take months to play out, are the exception rather than the rule. The trial lawyer has little time in which to generate rapport with the jurors.

The friendship you have with your best friend probably took years to develop and grew naturally out of the many experiences you shared together; a trial lawyer doesn't have the benefit of pretrial years with the jurors and sees them only within the limited setting of the courtroom. A trial lawyer, therefore, does not expect rapport to manifest itself spontaneously with the jurors in the way it does with a good friend. Successful trial lawyers rely on other ways of developing a close and trusting relationship. This chapter is devoted to showing you how trial lawyers create a relationship with the jurors similar in persuasive power to that you have with a very good friend, given the structural and time limitations of the courtroom. You can then apply these same principles to creating such a relationship with those you wish to persuade.

Learn How to Develop Relationship as Lawyers Do by Establishing Common Ground with Others

Aligning your initial position with that of those you wish to influence is known as "establishing common ground." It puts you on their side, you become one of them, thus more acceptable. Once you've established common ground, you can lead people to your point of view with far greater ease and effectiveness.

HOW A HOT, SWEATY DAY WON A NEW YORK JURY'S HEART

Norman H. Sheresky relates: "Once, during the course of a trial in New York City during early summer, Bruno Schachner, an old and respected trial warrior, arose and suggested to the court that the jury would be more comfortable if they were permitted to remove their jackets. The trial judge became infuriated and told the jury that the suggestion was improper, that Mr. Schachner could not care less if the jurors fried in hell, and that he was only trying to solicit their favor.

"The tirade was so stern," recounts Sheresky, "that I, as associate counsel, felt the perspiration pouring down my sleeves. Schachner replied, 'Your Honor, I had no idea that my suggestion would be considered improper, but if it was, I most respectfully apologize to you and particularly to the jury." Upon which he sat down and whispered in my ear, 'Screw him, look at the jury; they love me.' "[2]

And they did! The jury loved Schachner because he had definitively sided with them. He had established common ground: "It's hot, I'm hot, you must be hot," and by doing so made himself one of them.

People relate best and most easily to that which is familiar to them.

CASE IN POINT

The secretary you've employed for five years is familiar to you, you know how she works, you can depend on her to do certain things consistently very well, and you can equally depend on her to do certain things not so well. You may or may not like her, but you know her. Ever noticed how your life changes when your secretary is on vacation and you hire temporary help? The temp may be a terrific person, but he's an unfamiliar entity, and you don't know whether he will file things in the right places and get reports done on time, much less with what degree of accuracy. Anything the temp does differently from your regular secretary will make you uncomfortable. You feel as if there's a guest in the office, not a teammate.

Novelty causes uncertainty and conflict, which may be stimulating in certain situations, but not in the already anxiety-producing situation of a trial. There, the unfamiliar will cause only discomfort.

If people relate comfortably to that which is familiar to them, what does that imply? That people relate best to that which is *similar* to themselves, because they know themselves better than anything or anyone else.

CASE IN POINT

If you like baseball and you find yourself among a group of people all enthusiastically talking baseball, you'll feel right at home and decide that these are terrific people you could easily become friends with; after all, you have a lot in common. If, on the other hand, you find yourself with a group of people raving about gymnastics, who don't say anything against baseball, but are completely indifferent to your baseball enthusiasm, you probably won't stick around; you'll find it difficult to relate to them, you have nothing in common.

This ties in with an interesting result from communications research: When people don't know you, if in the beginning you clearly indicate that your own position is in accord with theirs, people are more likely to accept your message, even if your message actually ends up being quite different from that original position.

Persuasion, then, can be thought of as a process that starts from the establishment of common ground (similarities), that creates familiarity, that facilitates rapport (relationship), that engenders trust, that is the precursor to persuasion. Bear in mind, however, that this is an additive process. The psychological aspects of persuasion will be effective only if you've established your credibility and expertness as described in the previous chapters, but if those *have* been established, then the psychological dimension will greatly enhance your persuasive power.

Common ground also implies common footing. Good trial lawyers address the jurors as equals, not as lesser beings. Rapport implies mutuality. A sympathetic relationship is one that goes both ways. Research in the area of social power has demonstrated that your ability to persuade someone is far more effective when the acceptance is reciprocal, in other words, when you accept people as much as they accept you. When a good trial lawyer or expert witness is at work in the courtroom, the jurors feel that the lawyer or witness is *with* them, working side by side with them, guiding them through his/her version of the facts.

ON EQUAL FOOTING:
A KEY WITNESS IMPRESSES THE O. J. SIMPSON JURORS

"I thought Gary Sims, from the California Department of Justice, was an outstanding witness, too. He's professional. He knows his job. Matter of fact, it was through him that I started to learn a little bit more about the DNA processing because he spoke to us at our level."[3]

Sims facilitated juror learning because of his willingness to treat the jurors as competent human beings who simply needed guidance to understand a scientific matter. He never talked down or "at" the jurors. To persuade people, treat them as equals and treat them with respect.

If you respect the people you are seeking to convince, they will respect you; it's that simple. If you talk down to people, as many not-so-successful trial lawyers and expert witnesses have been known to do, people will rebel by not attending to you.

WHEN AN EXPERT TALKS DOWN, JURORS' EARS SHUT DOWN

"What happened is, she [Robin Cotton, who testified as a DNA expert in the O. J. Simpson trial] lost us, and I say us because I believe that everybody felt the same way. She talked down and when you talk down to people, you tend to lose them."[4] Robin Cotton had some fine points to make and was considered very knowledgeable by the jurors. Had she simply addressed the jurors as equals, she would have been not only knowledgeable, but convincing.

Jurors interviewed in jury studies often complain of being treated as if they were stupid or retarded. When a lawyer treats the jurors like idiots, the jurors promptly turn toward someone who treats them better. Validate people's self-worth by treating them as equals and they will reward you with trust and acceptance.

Beyond common footing, successful trial lawyers establish rapport with the jurors by accentuating the similarities between themselves and/or their clients and the jurors. Rapport is not a generic concept; rapport must be created differently for every case, because every jury is different. Successful trial lawyers are careful to emphasize their similarities with the jurors both verbally and nonverbally.

CORRUPTION FALLS BEFORE CALICO AND OVERALLS: THE VERDICT AGAINST THE SPEAKER OF THE TEXAS HOUSE OF REPRESENTATIVES

William P. Allison of Lynch, Zimmerman, White & Allison in Austin, Texas, on what happens when trial lawyers ignore this precept: "The out-of-town defense lawyers walked into the modest West Texas courtroom dressed in their finest, most expensive apparel. The jurors came from the community, and they wore calico and overalls. The case was the corruption trial of the speaker of the Texas House of Representatives, but because of the environment of the trial, it became the case of the Brooks Brothers lawyers versus the Sears, Roebuck jurors. The well-dressed defense lawyers lost, and so did the speaker of the House."[5]

The point is not that the defense attorneys should have come in wearing overalls and affecting a West Texas dialect; that would have been imitation, not the establishment of common ground. Rather the defense attorneys should have recognized the less formal, down-to-earth character of the jury as a whole and emphasized their own less formal, down-to-earth side. By choosing to ignore the issue of rapport and failing to make the jurors comfortable by emphasizing the similarities between the jurors and themselves, the defense lawyers lost.

Mirroring: A Dynamic Technique Lawyers Use to Set the Stage to Persuade People

How could these defense lawyers have emphasized the similarities between themselves and the jurors? By a process called "mirroring." Mirroring is a technique whereby you reflect physically and vocally another individual's physical attitudes and vocal characteristics.

How Mirroring Establishes Common Ground by Emphasizing Similarities

We all have different aspects to our personalities. There are times when you are more formal than others, times when you are willing to unwind and act silly, times when you're quiet and reflective. To emphasize the similarities between him/herself and the jurors, a good trial lawyer will bring forward that facet of his/her personality that is most similar to the dominant personality of the jury as a whole. The trial lawyer is not attempting to be someone he/she is not, adopting a phony persona for the benefit of the trial; that would be virtually impossible, and quite frankly, ineffective unless the trial lawyer is an actor on a par with Dustin Hoffman or Meryl Streep. The lawyer is simply choosing to express that part of him/herself that most closely resembles the character of the jury, to make the jury feel more comfortable with the lawyer and thus more trusting and more open to the lawyer's interpretation of the facts.

The four main areas where mirroring is used are dress, body language, voice, and vocabulary.

Technique #48: How to mirror dress and body language

Because Mr. Allison focused on dress in his comments, let's first take a look at how mirroring would apply to the defense attorneys' dress. The jury panel was down to earth, wearing overalls and calico. Reflecting the simple, homespun quality of this style, the defense attorneys (who were male) could have worn a suit without the vest, leaving the jacket unbuttoned, and could have chosen to wear a suit appropriate to the local weather both in cloth and color. This attire would have reflected or "mirrored" the jurors' values.

The operative word here is reflect, not imitate. People are highly offended by imitation of themselves; too often imitation feels like mockery, and it is invariably phony. When, however, you reflect the predominant tone of body language, dress, and voice, you point out in nonverbal fashion the likenesses between you and those you are seeking to influence, making yourself easier for them to identify with, without denying your own personality.

The steps to successful mirroring of dress are as follows:

1. Research your audience's background: Do your research; figure out how your audience is likely to dress. For the trial lawyer, this means finding out how the jury is likely to dress given the community, time of year, and socioeconomic background of the jurors.

2. Select your wardrobe appropriately for mirroring: Select from your wardrobe clothes that express the side of you that is more like those you wish to influence, still remaining true to your basic persona. For the trial lawyer, this means selecting an outfit that reflects the jury's attire, although still staying appropriately dressed for the courtroom. The question the trial lawyer asks is, "How can I dress to make this jury feel I am one of them, while retaining my professionalism?" The question you need to ask yourself is, "How can I dress to make this person/group of people feel I am one of them, while retaining my identity and being appropriate to the occasion?"

3. Adjust your wardrobe to your specific audience: If you thought, based on your research, that your audience would be conservatively dressed but in their Sunday best, and when you walked in, dressed in your best going-to-meeting outfit, they were in jeans, plaid shirts, and cowboy boots—adjust. Unbutton your jacket or take it off, roll up your sleeves, do whatever you can do that will subtly let your audience know you are one of them. Be flexible and use your common sense.

Mirror with Body Language to Create a Relationship of Acceptance and Trust with Your Audience

Dress is the easiest way to mirror and certainly contributes in an important way to people's first impression of you. Mirroring body language allows you to go beyond creating a sympathetic first impression to helping people feel accepted and trusting of you.

Mirroring body language is based on the same principle as mirroring dress: reflection, not imitation. When a trial lawyer wants to facilitate a witness's cooperation, that lawyer might start by mirroring the witness's body language. Illustrations 4–1 to 4–3 demonstrate how to accomplish a successful mirror, with a female attorney mirroring a male witness.

First, the lawyer would notice if the witness's body is shifted forward or back. The lawyer reflects that position. The lawyer would then notice the placement of the witness's head, arms, and legs, and the lawyer would allow her body position to suggest similar placement. The lawyer would not copy the witness's exact body position. That would look stupid and be resented.

When you begin to mirror someone you want to convince, take your time in fitting your body language to his/hers. Start with the overall body shift, then, for example, let the head be placed, then the arms. Don't

4-1

4-2

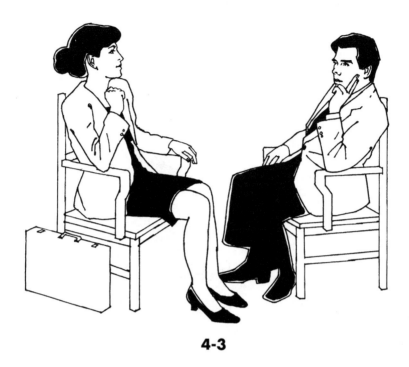

4-3

try to mirror a whole body posture all at once; it doesn't work. Mirrors are highly effective nonverbal tools, but they must be created with subtlety in order to be successful.

Mirrors do more than emphasize the similarities between yourself and the person you are mirroring. Mirrors are a tremendously powerful way of establishing your acceptance of an individual. In Chapter 2, it was pointed out that body language is believed over words: Whenever there is a discrepancy between your stated message and your body language, your body language will be believed, not your statement. By adopting an individual's body language, you have nonverbally stated, "Mr. Jones, whoever you are is fine by me. I accept you exactly as you are and show my acceptance of your present being by conforming to your physical attitudes and postures." Because the communication is nonverbal, it will be believed.

There's nothing quite like acceptance to make people feel worthy. Total acceptance is the essence of unconditional love. Think what power unconditional love has: using the same principle uses the same power, albeit to a different degree. When you mirror someone you want to influence, you nonverbally validate that individual as he/she is, and this acceptance encourages him/her to be open to you, to give you what you want.

If, as you go along talking with this individual, his/her body language changes, you can continue mirroring the changes if you wish to solidify rapport. Mirroring is most important, however, at the beginning of the interaction, to establish acceptance and rapport initially and can then be used sporadically throughout the interaction.

A word of caution: Be careful to mirror changes slowly and with somewhat of a lag. If the person puts his hand on his chest and you instantly let your hand fly to your chest, that person is going to know something fishy is going on and will not trust you. You are communicating acceptance, not playing "monkey-see, monkey-do." The distinction is important. Anytime you wish to establish rapport, you can do so with mirroring body language.

Use Body Language Mirroring to Obtain Cooperation From Someone Who is Being Uncooperative

What do you do, however, when faced with an uncooperative individual, someone you need to convince of something but who basically doesn't want to hear about it? Proceed no differently: mirror. This may sound strange, but it works. If the person sits there, shifted somewhat back in his/her chair, holding onto the chair arms defensively, a dour expression on his/her face, a typical nonverbal posturing of "I don't want to be here, and I don't want to hear this," do *not* attempt to warm the person up by smiling and opening up your arms; he/she will trust you even less. No, rather adopt the person's body language, shift your body back, maybe cross your arms to suggest the defensiveness of his/her chair-arm grip, and allow your face to assume a serious concerned look. At least you're now playing in the same ball park. You're not rejecting the person's reticence, you're accepting it and continuing nonetheless.

Case in Point

Think how awful it feels when someone comes up to you when you're depressed and claps you on the back, saying with a great big smile "Cheer up, things can't be that bad!" Oh, yes they can. And the last thing you will feel like doing is opening up to this person who obviously doesn't understand anything. If, on the other hand, someone comes up to you quietly, standing a little stooped, just as you are, and says, with a serious and concerned look on his/her face and in a gentle way, "Cheer up, things can't be that bad," you'll probably open right up and say "Oh, yes they can." The verbal message is the same, but the *body language* of the second person gave you permission to be you, and so you are willing to open up.

Try this on friends and family before taking it out into a situation in which you need to be persuasive; you'll be surprised at how effective this technique is.

Use Reverse Body-Language Mirroring to Make a Person Anxious and Uneasy

If mirroring an individual's body language implies acceptance, then not mirroring an individual's body language implies rejection and can be used as such.

CASE IN POINT

A lawyer wants to make a witness anxious and uneasy. All the lawyer has to do is fail to mirror the witness's body language. Reverse it, as it were. If the witness is sitting comfortably shifted back, relaxed, arms resting on the chair arms, the lawyer can shift his/her body forward, cross the arms, and tense the body overall somewhat. The witness won't know what is going on, but the witness won't feel accepted and will sense that something is off; the witness will get uneasy.

So too, if you are in a situation in which you want to make someone uncomfortable without being offensive or obvious about it, you can apply a reverse mirror. You can let someone know, for example, that you do not agree with his/her position on an issue by countering the other person's body language. People do this all the time, quite instinctively. You can use the same instinctive techniques consciously, by choice, in the pursuit of your objectives. Anytime you need to close someone off, or reject him/her, remember the power of body language. Countering someone's body language is a far more subtle and effective rejection technique than raising your voice or resorting to rudeness.

Use Mirroring to Set a Whole Group of People at Ease

A lawyer who wishes to create rapport with the jury as a whole will adopt a physical posture that reflects the predominant physical attitudes of the jurors. A group of jurors as a whole will be, for example, more relaxed and casual, or uptight and somewhat rigid, and so forth. Similarly, you can shape your body language to suggest the same overall physical attitude as that of the group you are addressing, so as to create a nonverbal bond between yourself and that group.

When listening to a third party, if you want to create the feeling that you and the person(s) you wish to convince are listening together, that you are in harmony, conform your body language to the predominant posture of the people you want to convince. *Anytime* you wish to create, reinforce, or express the bond between yourself and others, reflect their overall physical attitudes.

Technique #49: How to mirror vocabulary and vocal style

Mirroring is done with the voice just as it is done with the body. A trial lawyer seeking to create rapport with the jury as a whole will find out what the vocal pace of the community is, for example, and mirror it to the degree that is comfortable for him/her. Failure to create vocal rapport can seriously damage a lawyer's persuasiveness with jurors.

AN ARISTOCRAT SUCCUMBS: HOW HOUSE COUNSEL JOHN W. NIELDS LOST TO LT. COL. OLIVER NORTH

House counsel John W. Nields did not succeed in creating rapport during the investigation of Lt. Col. Oliver North. Nields's tone of voice, in particular, was mentioned as a factor unsympathetic to average Americans. "Nields's tone of voice was frequently sharp. . . . Nields projected the image of the aristocrat, and tended to be condescending towards North . . . it does not work when a witness has established a rapport with 'the jury' (here, the American people). North came across to the average American as 'one of us,' a working man just following his leaders and also as someone the average person would like to have living next door. By contrast, Nields's haughtiness turned him into 'one of them.' "[6]

A good trial lawyer, however, would *never* affect an accent or dialect that is not his/her own, nor should you. You are likely to sound fake and thus untrustworthy. With an individual, use vocal mirroring as a trial lawyer would with a witness or juror; use mirroring to establish rapport and use reverse vocal mirroring to prevent it.

CASE IN POINT

A lawyer wants to create rapport with his witness, an anxious middle-aged woman who speaks in a quiet voice with many pauses because of her anxiety. He mirrors his witness vocally by taking extra pauses when he speaks and asks his questions in a somewhat softer voice to make the witness feel at ease and accepted.

The lawyer wants to discomfit another witness, who has much the same vocal patterns as the middle-aged woman. He reverses the mirror. He rattles his anxious witness by asking his questions at a good clip, with hardly any pauses, in a normal-volume firm voice. The lawyer's reverse mirror is subtle enough not to be experienced as abrasive by the jurors, but rejecting enough to produce further anxiety in the witness.

Emphasize Similarities With Those You Want to Convince by Using a Common Vocabulary

A lawyer's training is literate. A lawyer has spent a good number of years in school and is proficient in the use of words. A lawyer reads and writes more than almost any other professional. He/she deals in complex concepts all day long and discusses cases primarily with colleagues who are familiar with the same concepts. Lawyers tend, therefore, to forget that the majority of Americans are not as well educated as they are and do not have the benefit of constant communion with higher level concepts and vocabulary.

This poses a problem. When I review opening statements for trial lawyers, I am appalled at how off-putting and lacking in juror-friendly language those statements are. I am not referring only to the use of "legalese." Good trial lawyers are well aware of how little jurors appreciate having unexplained legal terms thrown at them. I am more specifically referring to lawyers' overall use of language, which tends to be overly sophisticated and often so grammatically complex that only an English teacher could make sense out of it. A good trial lawyer doesn't try to speak the same way he/she writes a brief; a good trial lawyer speaks so that jurors will easily understand him/her. A good trial lawyer will speak in words and expressions already familiar to the jurors, making them feel comfortable, more trusting of the lawyer, and thus more available to the lawyer's point of view.

Follow the successful trial lawyer's lead: Avoid the use of professional or technical jargon, unless it is appropriate to the situation and understood by those you wish to convince. Otherwise, professional and technical jargon seriously puts people off. It makes you seem aloof and "better than"; people don't warm up to the condescending attitude implied by the use of special terms. Different communities use different expressions. A good trial lawyer will listen, during voir dire, to the actual words and expressions used by the prospective jurors. The lawyer will tune into the jurors' level of understanding and get used to thinking at that level. Your usual mode of speech may include phrases and/or slang that are not easily understood outside your community. Mirror the vocabulary of those you seek to convince rather than expressing yourself with your habitual vocabulary, and monitor your expressions so they fit the people and the situation you're working with.

Technique #50: How to mirror a person's energy

Consciously or otherwise, good trial lawyers tune easily into a jury's energy state and use it to their advantage. Juries, for example, are known to be perky and awake in the morning, sleepier and less alert in the afternoon. Individual juries have characteristic energy states: some juries are active note takers and even as they sit seem to exude alertness; others are more passive, seeming to require "spoon-feeding." A good trial lawyer will pick up on the jury's energy state and both mirror it and play to it, to gain the greatest advantage.

In convincing a group of people, you can similarly pick up on and work with the group's energy state. You can also mirror energy states effectively with individual people. Each of us has a familiar and habitual energy state. Some of us are usually relaxed or "mellow," others of us are somewhat "wired" most of the time. Observe yourself, know what your energy state is, generally speaking. Then, when you are attempting to convince someone of something, observe and pay attention to where the person's energy level is relative to your own. Gently adjust your energy level to mirror the person's energy level, being careful on the one hand not to mimic the person's energy or on the other, to push your personal energy beyond what is comfortable for you.

A word of caution: Mirroring is a powerful communication technique and should not be dealt with lightly. Mirroring with dress can be planned ahead and simply presented; body language, vocal/vocabulary, and energy mirroring must be performed in the heat of the moment. If your mirroring is clumsy, it will not enhance your persuasiveness. It is critical, then, that you practice mirroring before attempting to apply it to a "real" situation. Worksheets are provided at the end of this chapter to help you. Practice mirroring with your family, friends, and as many other people as possible before you start using it as a persuasion technique in a situation in which it really counts. With practice, however, mirroring becomes second nature and then is wonderfully effective. Practice is the key.

Perceptual Modes: A Powerful Technique Lawyers Use to Predispose People to Be Convinced by Them

The stronger the "kinship" a trial lawyer creates between the lawyer and the jurors, the more easily the jurors will allow themselves to be persuaded by the lawyer. It is no accident that in the O. J. Simpson trial, both prosecution and defense teams prominently included black lawyers.

MATCHMAKING: LAWYERS AND JURORS IN THE O. J. SIMPSON TRIAL

"When the district attorney's office first sent Chris Darden down, I remember thinking he was there as a token because the jury was predominantly black. . . . Another thing I wasn't quite sure of was what happened to that attorney, Bill Hodgman. Was he sick or something? I sort of felt, *Well, why did they throw Chris up in here?* Was it because they looked around and saw the jury was predominantly black and they threw him up thinking we can get a balance up here? Like, well, Chris, maybe you can communicate with them things that we are not able to communicate to them."[7]

Even though the jurors knew perfectly well that such a choice was deliberately made in order to make them feel more comfortable and trusting, the impact was still felt. We feel more trusting of those who are "like us."

It is therefore in your best interest to use every possible means of helping those you want to persuade feel comfortable and "like you." Remember that people relate best and most easily to that which is familiar to them. Well, communications research has recently demonstrated the power of the familiar in a most surprising context: "perceptual modes."

Perceptual modes are how we perceive the world through our five senses; the perceptual mode you favor in picking up information from the world around you determines the specific way in which you understand the world.

CASE IN POINT

What does this imply in the courtroom? When, for example, a trial lawyer addresses a prospective juror using the perceptual mode the lawyer has figured out is particular to this juror, the juror will get the impression that the lawyer really understands him/her; after all, the lawyer views the world in the same way the juror does. The lawyer will be experienced by the prospective juror as comfortable and familiar because, in a profound sense, the lawyer is truly speaking the language the prospective juror speaks. This automatically makes the juror more trusting and accepting of the lawyer, more willing to cooperate.

Facilitate Winning People Over by Perceiving the World the Same Way They Do

Attending to people's perceptual mode is an effective tool in the service of persuasion, yet few people are aware of perceptual modes and therefore do not have this powerful tool at their disposal. Paying attention to someone's perceptual mode is much like relating to a person in his/her native language. If you went to Greece, for example, and wanted to persuade a Greek of something, you would attempt to speak in Greek. Trying to get the Greek to change over to English so that you could persuade him/her of whatever it is you had on your mind would be three times more work and in all likelihood unsuccessful. The idea seems foolish, yet we usually ignore one another's perceptual modes, mostly because we don't know they exist, thus blithely disregarding one another's internal language.

Technique #51: How to recognize people's perception of the world

Although people have five physical senses through which they perceive the world, three of those are dominant (sight, hearing, and touch) and constitute the basis for the three perceptual modes. Of the three basic ways in which to perceive the world, people tend to favor one: We either *see* the world, *hear* it, or *feel* it. This is not to say that people who favor a visual mode, for example, experience the world only through their eyes, just that they first and predominantly experience the world in visual terms. Visually oriented persons certainly make use of the auditory and feeling modes, but only secondarily.

To effectively use perceptual modes to persuade, you must first be able to recognize them. You can learn to do this quite easily, by listening to the words an individual chooses to express him/herself.

Recognizing Visually Oriented People

Visually oriented people perceive the world mainly through their eyes. They understand the world by how it *looks* to them. Visually oriented people use phrases such as

> I *see* what you mean.
> I'm *clear* on that.
> How does that *look* to you?
> I can't *picture* it.
> I need to get a better *perspective*.

And so on. Visually oriented people tend to notice color and shape and mention these when asked to describe something.

Recognizing Auditory People

Auditory people perceive the world mainly through their ears. They understand the world in terms of how it *sounds* and what its rhythms are. Auditory people use phrases such as

> I *hear* you (for I understand you).
> That *sounds* good to me.
> Let's *talk* about it.
> That *struck a chord* for me.
> It doesn't *ring a bell*.
> I didn't miss a *beat*.

And so on. An auditory person comments on whether a person has a loud or soft voice, if a room is quiet or noisy, and is sensitive to such small auditory disturbances as noisy air conditioning units or street noises.

Recognizing Kinesthetic People

Kinesthetically oriented people perceive the world mainly through their *feelings*, through both the actual physical sense of touch and their internal feelings or emotions. A kinesthetic person speaks primarily in terms of how things feel to him/her, both on a tactile level and at an internal emotional level. Kinesthetic people will say

That *feels* right to me.
I understand how you *feel*.
That's a *heavy* problem.
That's a *hot* idea.
I'll be in *touch* with you.
I want to *get a handle* on it.
I'm not *comfortable* with the idea.

And so on. Kinesthetic people mention texture often and usually comment on how they feel about something when describing it.

An awareness of perceptual modes allows you to avoid the kinds of communication difficulties that prevent the development of rapport.

CASE IN POINT

Think of what happens, for example, when a visually oriented attorney is valiantly trying to explain to a kinesthetically oriented juror how something looks, while the kinesthetically oriented juror is trying to figure out from how it looks, how it feels.

Now that you know which perceptual mode is which, here's how to figure out the perceptual mode of the person you want to persuade. Ask a couple of questions of the person and listen carefully to how he/she responds. If at all possible, ask a question that does not imply any particular perceptual mode, for example, "So how are things with you today?" and pay attention to how the person answers. Then ask another question or two using what you think is the person's perceptual mode. If the person appears to be visual, ask how a given position "looks" to him/her; if auditory, how it "sounds" to him/her; if kinesthetic, how it "feels" to him/her. Listen attentively to how the person answers you. If you find, over the course of the next few questions, that you were off base, change to what now appears to be the correct choice of modes and go from there.

A word of caution: A perceptual mode cannot necessarily be determined by the first few sentences out of someone's mouth. Listen for a while before you decide which is the predominant mode. Be careful not to ask questions that slant the person's answer in a predetermined perceptual mode. If you ask, for example, "Did you see the girl sitting in the car, Bob?" regardless of his orientation, Bob will reply in visual terms. Notice rather how Bob expresses himself in more open-ended questions that do not imply any particular perceptual mode and notice his word preference over a period of time.

Technique #52: How you can use people's perceptual mode to ready them to be convinced by you

Once you've figured out a person's primary perceptual mode, incorporate as many words from that mode *as is comfortable for you* in speaking with that person. Don't become someone you are not in the interest of persuasion. Simply adjust how you present your points so that you rely more heavily on that person's perceptual mode in working with him/her. You will be infinitely more persuasive in speaking that person's "internal language" than you could ever be otherwise.

To benefit fully from the rapport-building power of perceptual modes, you must be able to speak in all three of the modes easily and at will. A little practice will enable you to do so. Use the worksheets at the end of this chapter to help you. As you become facile with recognizing people's perceptual modes, practice conversing with them in those modes. Practice especially those modes that are not your own.

CASE IN POINT

If, for example, your primary mode is visual, pretend you can no longer use sight, but must relate to something purely through the sounds and rhythms of it. This may seem difficult at first, but will get easier as you enlarge your perceptual vocabulary to include auditory-type words. Then, pretend you can relate to things and people only through feelings and the sense of touch. Figure out how to communicate via a kinesthetic mode to the exclusion of the others. Now you can incorporate feeling-type words to your habitual way of expressing yourself.

In Chapter 3, we discussed the different ways trial lawyers use their voices persuasively in the courtroom. Learning how to speak in a visual mode uses the skill described in that chapter as "coloring"; painting pictures with your voice. You use words to create a *vivid visual rendition* of the event you are describing. When you color, you also make words *sound like* what they mean. This automatically accesses the auditory mode. Learning to color, then, not only has a useful function in alleviating vocal monotony, but also allows you to access both the visual and auditory modes simultaneously. In addition, learning to use emotion as described in Chapter 3 will help you to access the kinesthetic mode. The different skills and techniques set forth in this book all work together to help you become truly persuasive.

How to Use Perceptual Modes when Addressing a Group

A jury or any other type of group will inevitably be composed of people of all three perceptual modes. Bearing this in mind, use words and phrases from all three modes in addressing a group, as a trial lawyer would in addressing the jury. This will give people of each perceptual type an opportunity to feel comfortable and at ease with you. As you make an effort to express yourself in all three modes, you ensure that you are heard by everyone in the group, in a perceptual language each can understand. This is where a knowledge of your own mode comes in particularly handy. If you are primarily visual, for example, then be sure you include auditory and kinesthetic words as you speak. If you are auditory, you must not ignore the visual and kinesthetic modes. If you are kinesthetic, learn to incorporate visual and auditory words.

Men tend to be primarily visual, and women tend to be primarily kinesthetic. There are fewer auditory types, and these tend to be fairly evenly divided by gender. Do not misunderstand; there are certainly men who are kinesthetic and women who are visual. If you are addressing a group that is primarily composed of women, however, you might want to stress the kinesthetic expression; if the group you're attempting to convince is primarily composed of men, pay more attention to the visual.

Use Perceptual Modes to Facilitate a Person's Cooperation

An awareness of perceptual modes can help you facilitate cooperation or obtain information from a person who isn't particularly inclined to be working with you.

CASE IN POINT

When a lawyer is having trouble eliciting what she wants from a witness, I suggest that the lawyer notice her witness's perceptual mode and then start speaking in that mode. For example, if the witness says, "I don't *see* how I can answer that," the lawyer might come back with, "Well, let me see if I can *clarify* it for you," and respond to the witness in visual terms. Or if the witness says "I don't remember exactly what happened, it just didn't *feel right* to me," the lawyer might well be able to jog the witness's memory by prompting with a question composed in the same perceptual mode (kinesthetic): "I can understand that. I mean it must have been a pretty *rough* moment; just how did it feel to you?"

Try this approach; you may be surprised at just how much more cooperative a person can become as you speak in his/her perceptual mode.

"Pace and Lead": A Rapport-Based Technique Lawyers Use to Successfully Handle Difficult People

There is more to being a trial lawyer than what you see in a courtroom: There is an enormous amount of pretrial and trial preparation. A trial lawyer, for example, must help people become good witnesses, must somehow get them to be patient with the unending details and repetitive nature of much of trial work, and must get them to be understanding of and work with the delays, last-minute changes, and other problems inherent to the operation of our system of justice. This is not always easy. Witnesses are often uncooperative, irritating, and full of complaints and criticisms, sometimes because they are just unpleasant people, sometimes because they are fed up with the situation. Regardless, the trial lawyer must find a way to work successfully with difficult witnesses and nice witnesses through difficult times.

By using a psychological technique called "pace and lead," you can learn to handle difficult people as trial lawyers do—with grace and ease and, most important, successfully.

How Acknowledging the Other Person's Point of View Opens the Door to Convincing Him/Her

If people are, for example, angry or hysterical or suspicious, denying their emotional condition will usually prove ineffective. The way they feel at the moment is the way they feel. Telling them they shouldn't be upset not only won't work, but will serve only to make the person more emotionally distraught. Now you've not only made the problem worse, you made it even less likely that the person will be receptive to anything you have to say; after all, if you can't even accept the person the way he/she is, why should he/she listen to you?

To "pace" someone is to acknowledge the emotional or mental state an individual is currently experiencing by mirroring his/her body language and reflecting his/her words. Pacing is an integral part of persuasion. As Gerry Spence states: *"Winning is getting what we want,* which often includes assisting others in getting what they want. . . . The winning argument may . . . take the form of . . . providing help, of understanding, of cooperating with the *Other."*[8] Understanding, cooperating with those you are attempting to persuade is very effectively done by "pacing."

Once a person feels acknowledged at that basic level, he/she is more willing to listen to you, and he/she is more willing to trust you. Your acceptance of the other's emotional reality has effectively created rapport in the same way that your acceptance of a person's perceptual mode creates rapport.

Technique #53: How to use "Pace and Lead"

Pacing, however, is not enough. A trial lawyer wants not only to create rapport with an individual, but also wants to use that rapport as a springboard to persuasion. Thus, once the trial lawyer has paced the individual, the lawyer will begin gradually to "lead" the person by shaping his/her body language and words to bring the witness to the understanding or behavior the trial lawyer needs from that person.

CASE IN POINT

The lawyer has just announced the cancellation of yet another deposition by opposing counsel. The witness exclaims in an angry tone of voice: "I can't believe I have to go through this again. I keep getting ready, and it's canceled. I get ready again, and it's off—this is driving me nuts! I want out—I'm sick of this!" The lawyer (who can't afford to lose the witness and needs his testimony and cooperation) answers by pacing (speaking in an angry voice, reflecting his witness's tone of voice): "Tell me about it! I hate this as much as you do—cancellations are hell!" At this point, the lawyer then begins to lead by dropping some of the anger out of his voice and saying: "Having this thing go on and on is very frustrating. And right now, what we're doing is . . ." as he begins to lead the witness to what the lawyer needs from the witness, by discussing the next steps to be taken.

The lawyer, although acknowledging the witness's anger, does not reflect the entire contents of the anger—that would be cloning, which, as we have seen in every instance of mirroring, is not a good idea. The lawyer simply reflected the witness's *emotion* and agreed with what the witness said to the extent that was truthful and accurate for the lawyer. Generally speaking, this is sufficient to defuse a tense situation. The witness feels he/she has been heard and therefore is now willing to hear what the lawyer has to say.

Along with the vocal and emotional mirroring a lawyer does as he paces a witness, the lawyer also mirrors his/her witness's body language. If the witness is all tensed up, for example, his/her body in an alert and ready-to-fight position, the lawyer will mirror the witness's body language by holding him/herself somewhat stiffly and in an energized way. The lawyer thus reflects the witness's emotional state through his/her voice, stance, and posture.

When you use pace and lead, you remove yourself from a position of having to defend yourself or somehow "fix" the person's emotional state before you can attempt to convince him/her. Instead, your acknowledgment of the person's emotional reality puts you in an empathic position, from which you can accept the person's reality (without necessarily agreeing with it or buying into it), and from that place of acceptance, you can establish the rapport that will facilitate persuasion. (See page 177.)

It may take several pace and leads before you can sufficiently acknowledge a person so he/she genuinely gets past his/her current emotional ground. Each time you lead the person, pay close attention to how he/she responds to your lead. If an angry person is still angry, he/she will go back to the anger and not allow you to lead. Be patient, pace once again by acknowledging the anger, and then try leading again. It usually takes no more than three rounds of pace and lead to help a person feel sufficiently acknowledged so that he/she can now move on.

As with all the other skills in this book, practice pacing and leading until you can do it comfortably and easily. Once in your arsenal of skills, pace and lead is an astonishingly valuable tool of persuasion.

Summary

Science continues to provide us with clearer and clearer understandings of how humans communicate. A skilled use of mirroring, perceptual modes, and pacing develops the necessary foundation of trust and acceptance that will most effectively support your persuasiveness.

A VICTIM TAKES THE STAND: SUCCESSFULLY COUNTERING THE "PRODIGIOUS POWER OF HELPLESSNESS"

Gerry Spence cross-examines a woman, Maria, who has been shot and horribly injured by his client, Leyland: "At the time of the preliminary hearing . . . Maria was still clinging to life. At the rehabilitation center . . . she [Maria] had learned to operate a mechanical wheelchair by blowing into a tube, and the therapists had attached a device to her that permitted her to form audible words. . . . I looked at this small, huddled remainder of a woman, and all I wanted to do was to get the hell out of there. She was, of course, the state's star witness. How does a lawyer take on one so horribly wounded? She demonstrated the prodigious power of helplessness."

" 'Maria, I wish neither one of us were here,'" I began in a very subdued voice.

" 'I do . . . too,'" she gasped through her talking machine.

" 'I know my job isn't nearly as hard as yours. It's easier for me to ask the questions than for you to answer them, and I wish I didn't have to ask them. Do you hear me?'"

" 'Yes, sir.'"

" 'You don't need to call me "sir." We are just two human beings struggling through this thing together.'"

" 'All right,'" she said through her raspy machine."[9] Mr. Spence's use of pacing is admirable. He began by using a subdued voice, thereby vocally pacing Maria's. He then acknowledged her obvious pain and physical difficulty at having to talk at all: "It's easier for me to ask the questions than for you to answer them, and I wish I didn't have to ask them." Finally, Mr. Spence acknowledged Maria's emotional reality: "We are just two human beings struggling through this thing together." Needless to say, once Mr. Spence had so brilliantly paced Maria, he proceeded to lead her to the questions he needed her to answer. Because he had so effectively acknowledged Maria, she was willing to answer him openly and directly.

WORKSHEETS
BODY LANGUAGE MIRRORING

1. Videotape yourself in a brief (five minute) conversation with a friend, with both of you seated.

2. During the conversation, practice mirroring your friend's body language to the best of your ability.

3. Watch the replay of the videotape and assess your mirroring skills using the following guidelines. Rank how well you are mirroring in terms of percentages, for example, you are able to pick up on body shifts well 70 percent of the time, fair 20 percent of the time, poorly 10 percent of the time.

	Good	Fair	Poor
Ability to pick up on friend's body shifts:	___	___	___
Ability to mirror specific movements: arms	___	___	___
head	___	___	___
legs	___	___	___
Ability to mirror subtly:	___	___	___
Appropriate timing in accomplishing mirrors:	___	___	___

Main problem in timing:

    Moving too quickly: ___

    Moving too slowly: ___

4. Given the foregoing assessment, indicate the corrections you feel are needed to improve your mirroring skills:

_____

_____

_____

_____

_____

_____

_____

5. Work on the corrections you have noted, then do another video-tape session, and observe your progress.

6. Now videotape yourself in conversation with a friend, only this time ask your friend to vary his/her position, so that some of the time he/she is seated and some of the time he/she is standing. Repeat the assessment process as described earlier, using the following guidelines:

	Good	Fair	Poor
Ability to pick up on friend's body shifts:	____	____	____
Ability to mirror specific movements: arms	____	____	____
head	____	____	____
legs	____	____	____
Ability to mirror subtly:	____	____	____

Appropriate timing in
accomplishing mirrors:

____   ____   ____

Main problem in timing:

Moving too quickly: ____

Moving too slowly: ____

7. Given the foregoing assessment, indicate the corrections you feel
are needed to improve your mirroring skills:

_____

_____

_____

_____

_____

_____

_____

8. Work on the corrections you have noted, then do another videotape session, and observe your progress.

VOCAL AND VOCABULARY MIRRORING

1. Audiotape or videotape yourself in a fifteen-minute conversation with a friend.

2. Mirror your friend's pitch, volume, and pace.

3. Listen to the replay of the audiotape or videotape and assess your mirroring skills using the following guidelines. Rank how well you are mirroring in terms of percentages, for example, you are able to mirror pitch well 70 percent of the time, fair 20 percent of the time, poorly 10 percent of the time.

	Good	Fair	Poor
Ability to mirror pitch:	___	___	___
Ability to mirror volume:	___	___	___
Ability to mirror pace:	___	___	___
Ability to mirror subtly:	___	___	___
Appropriate timing in accomplishing mirrors:	___	___	___
Main problem in timing:			
Mirroring too quickly:	___		
Mirroring too slowly:	___		

4. Given the foregoing assessment, indicate the corrections you feel are needed to improve your mirroring skills:

_____

_____

_____

_____

_____

5. Work on the corrections you have noted, then do another audiotape or videotape session, and observe your progress.

6. Audiotape or videotape another fifteen-minute conversation with your friend, only this time attend only to his/her vocabulary.

7. Mirror the level of vocabulary and type of words used by your friend and then assess your mirroring skills as described earlier, based on the following guidelines:

	Good	Fair	Poor
Ability to mirror local vocabulary:	____	____	____
Ability to mirror types of words	____	____	____
	____	____	____
	____	____	____
Ability to mirror subtly:	____	____	____
Appropriate timing in accomplishing mirrors:	____	____	____

Main problem in timing:

Mirroring too quickly:____

Mirroring too slowly: ____

8. Given the foregoing assessment, indicate the corrections you feel are needed to improve your mirroring skills:

_____

_____

_____

_____

_____

9. Work on the corrections you have noted, then do another audio-tape or videotape session, and observe your progress.

COMPLETE MIRRORING:
BODY LANGUAGE AND VOCAL MIRRORING COMBINED

1. Once you feel you can comfortably and easily mirror body language and voice separately, work on mirroring them both at the same time.

2. Videotape yourself in a fifteen-minute conversation with a friend and mirror both his/her body language and vocal qualities.

3. Watch the replay of the videotape and assess your mirroring skills using the following guidelines. Rank how well you are mirroring in terms of percentages, for example, you are able to pick up on head positions well 70 percent of the time, fair 20 percent of the time, poorly 10 percent of the time.

Body language assessment:

	Good	Fair	Poor
Ability to pick up on friend's body shifts:	___	___	___
Ability to mirror specific movements: stance	___	___	___
arms	___	___	___
shoulders	___	___	___
head	___	___	___
legs	___	___	___
Ability to mirror subtly:	___	___	___
Appropriate timing in accomplishing mirrors:	___	___	___
Main problem in timing:			
Moving too quickly:	___		
Moving too slowly:	___		

Vocal assessment:

	Good	Fair	Poor
Ability to mirror pitch:	___	___	___
Ability to mirror volume:	___	___	___
Ability to mirror pace:	___	___	___
Ability to mirror level of vocabulary:	___	___	___
Ability to mirror types of words:	___	___	___
Ability to mirror subtly:	___	___	___
Appropriate timing in accomplishing mirrors:	___	___	___
Main problem in timing:			
Mirroring too quickly:	___		
Mirroring too slowly:	___		

7. Given the foregoing assessment, indicate the corrections you feel are needed to improve your mirroring skills:

_____

_____

_____

_____

_____

_____

_____

8. Work on the corrections you have noted, then do another video-tape session, and observe your progress.

PERCEPTUAL MODES

1. Listen carefully to yourself. What types of words do you use to convey your experience of life? Do you primarily see things, hear them, or feel them? Determine your own perceptual mode, then determine that of different friends and co-workers.

	Visual	Auditory	Kinesthetic
Your perceptual mode:	____	____	____
Friend #1:	____	____	____
Friend #2:	____	____	____
Friend #3:	____	____	____
Friend #4:	____	____	____
Friend #5:	____	____	____
Friend #6:	____	____	____
Friend #7:	____	____	____
Friend #8:	____	____	____
Friend #9:	____	____	____
Friend #10:	____	____	____

2. Now that you can easily recognize another's perceptual mode, practice communicating in that mode. Audiotape or videotape yourself in conversation with a friend. Then listen to the replay of the conversation and observe whether or not you are accurately using your friend's perceptual mode. Rank your skills in terms of good, fair, or poor.

Accurate use of friend's perceptual mode:

	good	fair	poor
Conversation #1:	____	____	____
Conversation #2:	____	____	____
Conversation #3:	____	____	____
Conversation #4:	____	____	____
Conversation #5:	____	____	____
Conversation #6:	____	____	____

3. Note which perceptual mode is most difficult for you to use easily and practice it until you express yourself comfortably and with equal facility in all three modes.

five

The Fifth Step:
Gain The Advantage With Creative Listening

"What is it then which sets the winners apart? Why is it, since we all work in the same forum and under the same rules, that some are consistently successful while others are less so? . . . Consistently successful trial lawyers, in addition to properly preparing their cases, make maximum use of physical traits possessed by all of us in order to gain the edge. These traits are the senses of sight and hearing. The exceptional trial lawyers seem to possess that rare ability to press an advantage at the proper time; to find, through persistent and knowledgeable probing, the weakness in the armour of key witnesses; and to exploit those weaknesses with the explosiveness and decisiveness of Patton on the attack."[1] And the ability to press that advantage comes from the ability to *listen*.

HOW LAWYERS USE CREATIVE LISTENING TO GET THE ADVANTAGE TO WIN THEIR CASE

Persuasion is not a one-way street. Most of us think of exceptional trial lawyers as convincing speakers, "silver-tongued" advocates, individuals with the gift of influencing others with their oratory, and this is true. No matter how verbally gifted, however, a trial lawyer will succeed only if he/she is an equally astute and well-practiced listener

"I have seen very competent people," says noted trial attorney Richard "Racehorse" Haynes, "have an idea of the questions they want to ask, then mechanically go through asking those questions without really listening carefully to what is being said. If you only listen partially, you do not catch the nuances that suggest to a seasoned practitioner that this witness is not telling the truth. . . ."[2]

Persuading in the courtroom relies on the interplay of what the lawyer is expressing and how others react to that message. Good listening is what distinguishes an ordinary trial lawyer from a great trial lawyer. The successful trial lawyer is always listening to how others receive what he/she is saying and adjusting his/her approach, argument, and strategy in function of that feedback. No less a master than Gerry Spence has said: "If I were required to choose the single essential skill from the many that make up the art of argument, it would be the ability to listen."[3]

Learn How Good Listening Makes It Easier for You to Get Your Way by Increasing Your Ability to Discern Weaknesses and Spot Inconsistencies

Most people think of listening as something you do with your ears. A trial lawyer thinks of listening as something that is done with ears *and eyes*. As the Honorable Earl Strayhorn so accurately states in the earlier quotation, sight is every bit as important as hearing. Why is that? Because much of the feedback a trial lawyer uses in order to win is nonverbal. The "weaknesses" Judge Strayhorn speaks of are those inconsistencies of content, vocal tone, and *body language* that point up an area of vulnerability. You use your ears to determine inconsistencies of content and vocal tone and your eyes to read inconsistencies of body language. "Body language," explains Mr. Spence, "is words heard with the eyes. Bodies reflect fear, boredom, interest, repulsion, openness, attraction, caring, hatred. Bodies will speak to us, if we will carefully listen with our eyes."[4]

This is where solid, thorough preparation pays off. If a lawyer is still formulating arguments, racking his/her memory for some important point, or searching files for a misplaced document, the lawyer is not free to really listen. Even if the lawyer hears the main information being given, he/she will not hear and see the nuances that will give the lawyer the winning edge.

Be prepared. Let the excellent preparation you do before you walk into a situation where you want to persuade free you to truly listen. The better prepared you are, the more you can filter what you hear through your prior knowledge of the situation, so that you can quickly catch and make best use of when something doesn't sound quite right, doesn't ring true. The better prepared you are, the more energy you have available to

THE PROSECUTION IS CAUGHT OFF GUARD BY ITS OWN WITNESSES: THE PEOPLE VS. O. J. SIMPSON

"For instance, the prosecutors in the Simpson case did not prepare some of their witnesses for cross-examination nearly as well as they should have. Take Dennis Fung. Fung admitted to me there was no such preparation of him by the prosecution. 'We were just caught off-guard,' " he said.

Indeed, it was clear that the prosecutors didn't even put in enough time preparing themselves and their own witnesses for *direct* examination. Just one example: Clark, trying to establish that Officer Robert Riske, the first officer at the Bundy murder scene, had preserved the integrity of the crime scene . . . asked Riske rhetorically about his training in securing crime scenes at the police academy. Riske's answer, which stunned Clark: "They kind of glossed over it. They don't really train you."[5] Failure to properly prepare their witnesses led to too many surprises. Left with no choice at that point but to deal with the obvious, the prosecutors lost all the advantage creative listening could have given them.

watch the individual(s) you seek to persuade and be attuned to slight changes in body posture or expression that give you the necessary feedback to win.

What are you listening for, specifically? Lack of congruence. This is the true definition of an inconsistency. In Chapter 2, when we discussed body language, we defined congruence as a harmonious interaction of body language and content; for example, if, as you speak angry words, your fists are clenched and you are frowning, you are displaying congruence. All parts of your communication are going in the same direction, expressing the same idea: Your communication is therefore believable. When trial lawyers observe a witness or juror for possible weaknesses, they watch and listen for lack of congruence, for moments where one part of the individual's communication conflicts with another part.

THREE KEY VERBAL INCONSISTENCIES LAWYERS LOOK FOR AND HOW YOU CAN USE THEM TO YOUR ADVANTAGE

There are three ways verbal content may be incongruent: content clashing with content, content conflicting with emotional tone, and content conflicting with body language.

Technique #54: Look for content that clashes with content

This is the first and most obvious way trial lawyers listen for inconsistencies. The witness will answer one way to a question on day one, for example, and differently to the same or a similar question on day two. Although such an inconsistency may happen in obvious fashion, more often it is not so obvious and may make all the difference to a case. If a lawyer is not alert and listening, he/she might miss a vital point.

THE CASE OF THE "CONVENIENT" CANCER: A LYING DOCTOR SNARED

David M. Harney, the preeminent medical malpractice trial lawyer on the West Coast, representing plaintiff, was cross-examining an expert witness for the defense. The case involved a boy's cancerous condition. The cancer specialist, Ian Macdonald, ". . . offered as a basis for his expertise his observations of a man with a similar cancer in his arm at the New York Sloan-Kettering Hospital in the 1930s. This man's cancer, said Macdonald, was extremely slow-growing; he observed its slow growth because the patient refused surgery. But later in his testimony Macdonald—to support his opinion that the growth rates of this cancer are "variable"—said he had seen one "fast-growing" cancer, and he described the patient as a man in New York in 1936 with a cancer in his arm. When Harney cross-examined Macdonald and asked him to describe more fully the "slow-growing" cancer he had mentioned earlier, the doctor referred to the very same man in New York. Through his sharp listening skills, Harney had caught the redundancy in the examples and pointed out the doctor's mistake. Thus Harney completely discredited Macdonald as an expert witness."[6]

Once a discrepancy is pointed out, it becomes very noticeable. If, however, you are too focused on what you have to say, if you're already formulating your next point even as someone is speaking (a bad listening habit many people share), your failure to listen attentively can easily lead you to miss a valuable point—such as the one brilliantly exploited by Mr. Harney—altogether. If you find that you have a bad habit of interrupting, or formulating your next point while someone is still talking, you can readily improve your listening skills by learning to clear your mind and focus on what you are hearing. A worksheet is provided at the end of the chapter to help you improve these skills. Practice good listening in your daily life. It may take a while before you are able to stay focused on what you're listening to, but it is a skill critical to your ability to persuade and therefore well worth developing.

Technique #55: Look for content that conflicts with emotional tone

A good trial lawyer will carefully listen for incongruence between the content of the communication and the underlying emotional tone. If a witness, for example, says how upset he was, but his tone is calm, or even somewhat pleasant, something is wrong. If a prospective juror, for example, tells the lawyer she is in favor of the death penalty, but she sounds nervous and uneasy, something is wrong.

An incongruity between what a person says and the emotional tone underlying what the person says will not tell you *what* specifically is wrong; it operates rather like a red flag, warning you to pay attention. Such incongruence indicates an area to investigate: Something's going on here; things are not what they seem to be.

Technique #56: Look for content that conflicts with body language

Inconsistencies between an individual's body language and what that individual says are a veritable gold mine for attentive trial lawyers. This is where listening is done primarily with the eyes. There is incongruence when an expert witness states she is sure of a fact, but she is picking at her fingers or nervously adjusting her clothing. There is incongruence when a white prospective juror states he would consider a black defendant's testimony no differently from that of a white defendant's, but his arms are crossed tightly over his chest. As with content conflicting with emotional tone, the discrepancy between body language and verbal content will not necessarily tell the lawyer specifically what is amiss, but it does serve as a clear warning signal, that here is fertile ground for probing.

THREE KEY NONVERBAL INCONSISTENCIES LAWYERS LOOK FOR AND HOW YOU CAN USE THEM TO YOUR ADVANTAGE

Content provides a specific way to look for inconsistencies. You screen for direct contradictions to the content in emotion or body language. Other ways of spotting inconsistencies are not as direct, but are equally fruitful.

Technique #57: Look for variations in vocal tone

Vocal inconsistencies, for example, can tell an attentive lawyer a great deal about the "truth" of a statement. For example, let's say that during a witness's testimony, his voice rises somewhat in pitch, or that his pace increases. A rise in pitch or increase in pace is indicative of nervousness, so the lawyer would immediately begin to wonder: Why would this witness be nervous right now? Is he lying? Was there something about how I phrased the question that struck a sensitive spot? Is he worried about my present line of questioning? The lawyer would then probe accordingly.

Technique #58: Look for overly frequent pauses, "uh" sounds, and "I think"

A witness's vocal tone may remain even; however, the witness's speech may be full of "uh" sounds and pauses in between every word or two. Such hesitation is a typical sign of anxiety. The lawyer would then ask him/herself: What is causing this witness such anxiety? Does she reply like this to every question? Is it just courtroom anxiety? Or is it *this question*? What about my question might make her anxious?"

Similarly, a witness may preface his/her statements with "I think" or "I believe." or "I guess," all of which may imply insecurity of some kind.

TOO MANY HESITATIONS LOSE THE CASE: MARCIA CLARK'S COSTLY USE OF "I THINK" AND "I GUESS"

Marcia Clark's closing argument to the jurors was unfortunately riddled with such expressions of insecurity:

"Vannatter and Lange came out to Bundy, and *I guess* they showed up around 4:00, 4:30, *I think it was.*" "They still didn't run out to Rockingham, okay? *I can't remember, I think* he said it was around the time . . ." "Even then they didn't go immediately. It wasn't—*I think* about 5 o'clock when they finally went to Rockingham."[7] Even if only on an unconscious level, jurors would pick up on such signs of insecurity. The question then becomes: "Why should I believe someone who is this insecure about what they are saying? How can I be convinced of what they are saying if they aren't?"

Such prefaces ("I think" "I guess" "I believe") merit the same type of exploration as the "uh-uhs" aforementioned.

Technique #59: Look for inconsistencies in vocabulary

A lawyer's ears will also prick up if he/she hears a difference in the witness's vocabulary. If all of a sudden a witness uses words and phrases that seem too formal or too educated (given his/her prior responses) in response to a question, he/she may well have been coached in that response (and badly at that). Here is a weak spot to probe.

A prospective juror in voir dire who suddenly uses vocabulary that is inconsistent with the rest of his/her speech may be unconsciously signaling an area of greater interest, such as a well-developed knowledge of aviation or history or something that the lawyer would not have expected. The lawyer, noticing the change in vocabulary, can probe to see if this area of interest is a clue to biases and/or "special knowledge" that might influence the case.

THE BOILER MAKER AND WORLD WAR II: REVEALING A SUBTLE CASE OF PREJUDICE

A boiler maker with an eighth-grade education, during voir dire, mentioned "model airplanes" as a hobby. Defense attorney asked a question about the prospective juror's interest in model airplanes purely as a matter of rapport building. The juror used some highly specialized terms in briefly describing his hobby, which showed unusual knowledge about World War II aircraft. Defense counsel, who was doing an excellent job of listening, picked up on the change between the juror's habitual vocabulary, which was very basic, and his use of these specialized terms. Defense counsel asked a couple of questions regarding the man's interest in World War II planes and found out that the man's parents had been killed during the Holocaust and that the man was still profoundly affected by everything connected with the war.

Bottom line: the man was very prejudiced against Germans, and defense, whose client was of German ancestry and who had a distinctive German name, might not have weeded out this juror as biased against the client had defense counsel not been paying close attention to the inconsistency in the man's vocabulary.

HOW LAWYERS "LISTEN" TO BODY-LANGUAGE CUES TO GET THE ADVANTAGE

Body language is there for everyone to "read." A good trial lawyer is aware that just as jurors and witnesses can read the lawyer's body language, so can the lawyer read that of the jurors and witnesses. For a trial lawyer, the ability to read juror body-language cues during the course of the trial is critical, since the lawyer has no other source of juror feedback. How else can the lawyer know how the jury is responding to his/her presentation of the case? To just present the case without attending to how jurors are taking it in would be sheer folly.

You can use the trial lawyer's well-developed ability to read juror body language to your advantage any time you are similarly faced with people you want to persuade who will not be giving you much verbal feedback, for example, an audience to whom you're giving a speech.

Trial lawyers must also weigh and evaluate the impact of their questioning and opposing counsel's questioning on various witnesses. An individual's body language will tell you a great deal about how that individual is accepting or rejecting a point you are making. All through the trial, lawyers will be carefully watching and taking note of how witnesses and jurors alike are responding with body language to what's going on, using that constant feedback to help them develop the case successfully.

Three Lawyer Techniques You Can Use to "Listen" to Body Language Cues to *Your* Advantage

Technique #60: How to interpret body language cues accurately

The good news is, body language is always more "truthful" than words. The bad news is, in order for it to be genuinely useful to you, you have to know how to read body language accurately. A trial lawyer cannot read juror body language purely on the basis of stereotypy, as do the jurors. The lawyer needs more accuracy than stereotypy could give; the trial lawyer therefore learns to read body language in a context.

CASE IN POINT

Just because a juror is sitting straight in his chair, gripping the arms of the chair for dear life, does not necessarily mean he's a hostile, angry person who would be death on the jury panel. He may be, but he may also simply be intimidated by the trial process. A good trial lawyer will observe this prospective juror for a period of time, notice whether his position shifts in response to various questions and how he sits when he's *not* the object of questioning. The lawyer will also pay attention to whether the man adopts other postures expressive of a hostile attitude, or if he adopts postures that seem more indicative of anxiety.

Only once the lawyer has read the juror's basic position in the context of his overall body language will the lawyer make a determination as to what the juror's body language means to the present case.

When you start reading a person's body language, establish a base line for yourself. Watch the person for a while and notice what that person's usual body responses are. Once you have observed an individual for a little while, you will be in a better position to give an accurate interpretation to any one specific body response the person might give.

Technique #61: How to use body language cues to evaluate your impact on a person

Body language is particularly useful in helping a trial lawyer determine the impact of his/her cross-examination of a witness. A trial lawyer will watch for shifts in body position and changes in body language in response to a given question: These tell the lawyer what is really going on with the witness. Does a witness, for example, begin to fidget or shift in his seat, which would indicate nervousness? Does a witness suddenly sit up much straighter, which might indicate defensiveness, as would crossing her arms over her chest? Does a witness's foot begin to tap or move repetitively, which indicates annoyance or anxiety? Does a witness's body shift into a more relaxed slumped mood? If so, perhaps the lawyer just let him off the hook. Do a witness's eyes narrow or her lips tighten, which may indicate suspiciousness or defensiveness? Do a witness's hands fist, or curl tightly around the arms of the chair? If so, he's probably angry.

An individual's body language serves as a constant guide to whether or not you are being convincing. As you learn to read it, you will be able to figure out readily whether you're on the right track and being heard as you wish to be, or whether you're barking up the wrong tree.

Technique #62: How to use body language cues to guide you in the successful development of your point

A good trial lawyer will watch just as attentively when the witness is responding to opposing counsel, or when a prospective juror is being questioned by opposing counsel: There are valuable cues to be had from these interactions. If you are in a situation in which others are also seeking to influence the people you want to persuade, don't make the mistake of paying attention only to body language when you're the one talking. On the contrary, how individuals respond via body language to others will tell you a great deal about how you should adjust your presentation so as to be more effective.

A trial lawyer will notice in particular the shifts in juror facial expressions, for example, as well as major body shifts. The lawyer will look for signs of approval and disapproval, belief or disbelief as opposing counsel presents his/her case. Remember that, as with jurors, an audience is generally mute during your presentation; since the only avenue of expression available to audience members is their body language, they are likely to use it. Make adjustments to how you present your thoughts in function of audience reactions. A good trial lawyer always keeps in mind the idea of interplay; he/she will not make the mistake of falling in love with his/her own arguments. The lawyer will at all times take into account how the jurors are affected by the questioning and arguments of both sides and make changes accordingly.

Use Eye Contact the Way Lawyers Do

Although the ears are the sensory receptors for sound, if the eyes are not also "listening," we do not *feel* heard. Good trial lawyers are well aware of how important it is to maintain strong and direct eye focus to encourage witnesses to talk and support their testimony. Try the following experiment to show yourself just how valuable eye focus is to others' feeling "heard."

You'll need a friend's cooperation for this; be sure to warn him/her first of the experimental nature of the experience. Ask the friend to talk to you, about anything—the content is irrelevant. As your friend is speaking, look away from him/her: Without moving your head or body, just look over to the side. Keep listening attentively, however. Do this for a minute or so. Then stop your friend and ask him/her how it felt when you looked away. You'll find that although you could probably repeat the short conversation verbatim, your friend did not *feel* listened to at all when your eyes were off him/her. If anything, your friend may very well report feeling disrespected when your eyes were off him/her.

Then, ask your friend once again to talk to you. This time, keep your eyes on your friend steadily throughout his/her "speech" and nod your head occasionally. Do not, however, listen to him/her at all. Think about anything at all: an upcoming event, for example, or last night's party. Do your grocery list in your head, but do not listen. Just keep looking at him and nod from time to time. After about a minute of this, stop your friend, and ask him/her how he/she felt. You'll find that this time, your friend *felt* listened to, even though you weren't listening at all. Surprisingly enough, your eyes are far more critical to someone's *perception* of being heard than are your ears.

Technique #63: Use eye contact to make a person feel listened to and credible

A good trial lawyer knows the value of good eye focus and uses this knowledge assiduously in the courtroom. The easiest way, for example, to make a prospective juror feel listened to, feel that his/her words are credible and valued, is simply to look at the prospective juror the whole time he/she is speaking. The lawyer will wait until the prospective juror is finished with his/her entire answer before looking down at his/her notes. Similarly, to make a witness feel secure and comfortable on the stand, the lawyer will look at the witness clearly and directly the whole time the witness is talking. If a witness is giving a particularly long piece of testimony, the lawyer will start by looking at the witness to ensure his/her security and comfort, then may indeed look down or slightly to the side, as if thinking, but will look right back up at the witness whenever the lawyer wants to underline the importance of something the witness is saying or to reassure the witness of his/her value.

The power of eye focus cannot be overstated. When you want to let someone know that what he/she is saying is valuable, keep your eyes glued to that individual. Clearly, the "fishhook" technique will help you greatly here, especially when you find that you need to look at a person through a fairly long discussion.

Use Your Body Purposefully As Lawyers Do

In addition to your eyes, your body can be used to signal whether or not you value what someone is saying. When a trial lawyer wants to assure that the jurors will listen fully to a witness in order to absorb a given point, the lawyer will guide the jurors by listening fully to that witness. The lawyer will use his/her body language to project to the jurors that what the witness is saying is important.

Technique #64: Use your body to bring a person's attention to a point

How does the lawyer accomplish this? By adopting a body position that expresses "attentive listening." Face the person you are listening to square on, keep your face and body still, do not take notes, do not gesture. Lean your body in slightly if standing, a bit more if seated. Watch the person as he/she speaks, keeping your eye focus steady.

In court, this body posture accomplishes two things: it signals to the jurors to pay close attention to the witness, and it makes the witness feel valued and important.

Anytime you want to bring attention to a point, that you nonverbally want to say "Listen up!" use this position of attentive listening.

Technique #65: Use your body to distract a person's attention away from a point

On many occasions, however, lawyers seek exactly the opposite effect. They want to signal to the jurors "Hey, what this person is saying is hardly worth listening to; as a matter of fact, I don't even know what he/she is doing on the stand."

Some of the body language ploys trial lawyers use to distract from a witness, for example, thereby devaluing the witness's testimony are as follows:

- The lawyer does not face the witness when the witness is talking.
- The lawyer moves around or does something physical (take notes, clean his/her glasses, pour a glass of water).
- The lawyer leans back or away from the witness and does not maintain good steady eye focus.

Such lack of stillness and eye focus will accomplish two things: since movement pulls attention to itself, the jurors' focus will be split between the lawyer and the witness; and the lawyer's lack of stillness will project the message that what this witness has to say is not important, certainly not worth being still for.

Please bear in mind that this type of distracting maneuver is not something to try when you are face to face with one person, attempting to convince that one person. The person opposite you will think you are rude and probably stomp out the door. This is a technique that is effective only when you are trying to influence a third party (be that one individual or many) in his/her evaluation of the person speaking. For example, if you are in a group, seeking to influence the other members, and one person starts saying things you don't think have any merit, you can use a distracting technique. Be very careful, however, in using distraction; there is a fine line between distracting and failing to sufficiently respect someone. Lack of respect will always backfire against you. Be subtle in your use of distraction so you don't find yourself alienating the people you are trying to convince.

Use Acknowledgment as Lawyers Do

Good listening consists of more than simply staring at people; in order to be effective, you must acknowledge what you hear as well. Acknowledging is accomplished in two basic ways: by head nodding and by saying "uh-huh." Nodding your head every so often lets a person know that you are following what he/she is saying. It is a nonverbal signal indicating I'm with you, I understand, keep going. Saying "uh-huh" or any equivalent thereof, even as a murmur, serves the same function. Doing neither of these will generally lead an individual to believe that he/she is not understood, perhaps not even heard, and can be distressing.

An experiment similar to the one described earlier will demonstrate this point forcefully. Ask a friend to talk to you, and as your friend speaks, look at him/her with good eye focus, holding still, but do not nod, change your facial expression, or give your friend any verbal acknowledgments. Chances are your friend will complain that you were being very cold and may even perceive you as critical.

Ask your friend to talk to you once more, but this time, although you maintain good eye focus and a still body, nod every so often; allow your facial expressions to vary in function of your reaction to what you hear, and/or make acknowledgment noises, such as "uh-huh." This time your friend will perceive you as warm and will feel listened to and understood.

It is important, then, to add acknowledgments to your listening skills and to use them in conjunction with the other techniques described here whenever you want to project that a person or statement is significant.

Technique #66: Use acknowledgment to gain a person's cooperation

Making acknowledgment nods and sounds is important throughout a trial, and a good trial lawyer will use it right from voir dire in order to facilitate the development of rapport. The lawyer will certainly then use acknowledgment with witnesses whenever the lawyer wants to encourage the witness to continue. Acknowledgment makes the witness feel valued and worthy and thereby more willing to cooperate with the lawyer. A good trial lawyer will always remember to acknowledge anything the judge says, and the more skillful among them will even use acknowledgment with the jurors, insofar as is appropriate. For example, if something said during testimony strikes the jurors as funny and they laugh, the lawyer may, in addition to laughing, also nod toward the jurors, nonverbally saying, Yeah, I agree, I thought that was funny too.

Technique #67: Withhold acknowledgment to make a person uncomfortable

The converse is equally true. Attentively listening to a witness with eyes and body language but withholding all acknowledgment has a disconcerting effect. When a lawyer chooses to do this, the witness will feel riveted, impaled on the lawyer's look, and will react by either physically or mentally "squirming." Meanwhile, the jury will have no idea what the lawyer is up to, because the lawyer's body position and eye focus are signaling, Look here, something important is happening. And indeed it is; the unhappy witness is projecting nervousness all over the place. Creating such distress can rapidly lead a witness to discredit him/herself.

Be judicious and cautious in your withholding of acknowledgment. This technique is less likely to backfire on you because it is so much less obvious than, for example, lack of stillness or lack of eye focus, but it is extremely powerful, so be advised. People don't like being made to squirm; be sure you know what you're objective is if you choose to withhold acknowledgment.

How Lawyers Use Reactions to Influence the Jurors' Thought Process

Reacting is a more complex process than simple acknowledgment. Reacting consists of listening to and acknowledging the speaker, ingesting what you have just heard, connecting it to your own thought, and then nonverbally communicating a response in such a fashion that it can be easily and accurately interpreted by an observer. Although this sounds complicated, it is a process we perform unconsciously continually throughout our day. For example, someone says something that makes you happy: you smile. Someone says something that saddens you: you sigh. The difference with reacting naturally and reacting in the context of a trial is that trial lawyers often design their reactions so that they have a specific and predetermined effect. What is usually an automatic and unconscious process must therefore become conscious. Reactions are skillfully used in the courtroom to let the jurors know how the lawyer feels about what is going on.

CASE IN POINT

A lawyer was cross-examining a witness. After her question, the lawyer listened attentively, nodding her head, and then went on to ask another question. Doubting what she was hearing as the witness responded, the lawyer reacted, deliberately, by cocking her head to one side, giving a quizzical look. The jury, observing the lawyer's reaction, sensed there was something about the witness's answer that bothered the lawyer. In jury debriefings, the jurors stated that although they did not know at the time why the lawyer was troubled by the witness's response, they figured something was wrong and were then attentive to what might be suspicious about that particular witness. The lawyer, without saying a word and by the subtlest of reactions, had successfully led the jurors to considering her point of view.

When you let those observing you see how you feel about other people's comments, you guide your audience to think along the lines you want. You lead them to discover *with* you the conclusion you'll eventually reveal. By their participation in your thought process, people are more readily influenced by your conclusion. They see how you got there, and that's convincing.

Because reactions are expressed through body language, gestures, and facial expressions, they will always be believed more than your words. Knowing this, top trial lawyers use reactions to counter the impact of words when those words are not in their favor.

If you don't tip your hand, those listening to you will assume, by your positive and pleased reaction, that you made your point. Body language and your internal gut reaction are two different things. Develop

THE CASE OF THE ABSENT WITNESS WHO WAS NEVER ABSENT: A LAWYER'S PERSUASIVE SLEIGHT OF TONGUE

"Philadelphia attorney Charles A. Peruto, Sr. is well known for his ability to react quickly in bad situations. Peruto will handle a situation when a question seems to bury him like this:

Peruto: Then in fact you flew to Chicago the day before the killing and weren't even in Philadelphia the day you said you saw my client commit the murder?

The Witness: No, because it snowed the day before, and all flights were grounded. So I was in Philadelphia on that day.

Peruto, his case having gone down the drain, will then respond as follows:

Peruto: (Slamming his hand on the table and pointing his finger at the witness) Precisely! No further questions.

The jurors will say to themselves, I thought Peruto's case was badly hurt by that answer, but it seems to have been what he wanted. I must be missing something, or he wouldn't have reacted that way. I guess that answer isn't so important.[8] By his reaction, Peruto implied that he got the answer he wanted, even though the truth is the exact opposite! And the jurors believed that reaction.

the ability to separate the two, so as to use your body to convey what you want in your reactions, and not what just happens to be going on with you.

Reactions range from the subtle, expressed with a simple change of the brow, to the obvious, expressed through a major body shift with gesture. Use stereotypical definitions of the various body-language postures and facial expressions, as given in Chapter 2, to guide you in creating desired reactions. Bear in mind that reactions must be easily read; mannerisms are not a good choice as their meaning is too personal. Practice various reactions either in front of a mirror or with a videocamera until they become natural and easy.

A Powerful *Indirect* Way Lawyers Use to Influence People

Some years ago, social psychologists undertook interesting research that showed that when people think a person trying to influence them has an ulterior motive, they are more convinced by a conversation they overhear involving that person than by a direct communication from the person. In other words, when people suspect you are directly trying to win them over because you have something to gain by it, they are not open to you. When, however, people overhear you talking to someone from whom you have nothing to gain, they are far more likely to be convinced by you. Trial lawyers are well aware of the power of "overheard conversations" and use them to get their points across indirectly in a number of ways.

Technique #68: Use "overheard conversations" to get your point across

Good trial lawyers conduct their conversations in and around the courtroom with this knowledge in mind. A trial lawyer's "casual" conversations anywhere within earshot of the jurors are in no way casual. On the contrary, a good trial lawyer will see these as golden opportunities to convince the jurors of various points. Lawyers know that jurors are not only watching them all the time, the jurors are listening to them all the time as well. The discussions the lawyer has with co-counsel, the times when the lawyer explains to assistants how visual aids should be displayed and why, what the lawyer says to a colleague met in the hall who asks, "How's it going?"—all these are golden opportunities to give information that, overheard by a juror, will lead to a favorable assessment of the lawyer and the case.

The reverse is also true. If a juror overhears a lawyer being disrespectful of the judge in talking to a colleague, the juror will believe that statement more than he/she will believe the lawyer's appropriately respectful behavior when in the courtroom. If jurors overhear a lawyer denigrating the client in an aside to co-counsel, the lawyer's credibility will take a rapid downswing.

Anything overheard will be believed more than anything you say when you are in the active position of persuading. Knowing this gives you added power: Use the knowledge well and to your advantage.

SUMMARY

Listening constitutes half of all communicating. Listen with your ears, your eyes, your whole body. Listen actively, scanning for inconsistencies on many levels: content, vocal, body language, and emotional levels. Acknowledge, react, and be aware of the power of eye focus; these are valuable tools too often ignored. Use them, and you'll come out a winner.

WORKSHEET
ATTENTIVE LISTENING

1. Audiotape or videotape a fifteen-minute conversation with a friend.

2. Whenever your friend speaks, clear your mind of all other thoughts, including formulating your reply, and focus all your attention on listening.

3. Respond when appropriate.

4. Listen to the replay of the audiotape or videotape and assess your listening skills using the following guidelines:

	Seldom	Frequently	Occasionally
Do you have difficulty clearing your mind and focusing?	___	___	___
Do you interrupt your friend?	___	___	___
Do your responses incorporate what your friend just said?	___	___	___
Do you ignore what your friend says and just stay with your own thought?	___	___	___

5. If you find you have difficulty clearing your mind and focusing, learn the "back-pocket" technique. Create an imaginary back pocket, where you put all extraneous thoughts, to be pulled out and looked at later when it is appropriate. Then, when in conversation, try to focus on what your friend is saying. Whenever an extraneous thought goes through your mind, send it to your back pocket, where it belongs.

If you still have great difficulty clearing your mind and focusing, learn meditation techniques. These are helpful in quieting an overactive mind.

6. If you find that you often interrupt and ignore your friend's input, use clarification and reflection to improve your listening skills.

   These consist of carefully listening to your friend, and then asking him or her: "If I understand you correctly, what you mean is . . ." or "So what you mean is . . ." or "Then the way you see the situation is . . ."

   Reflect and clarify before you go on to your own response. This way you ensure that you do not interrupt and have indeed included your friend's input in your response.

VERBAL INCONSISTENCIES

1. Videotape a television program, preferably a dramatic show. Watch several short segments, from three to five minutes in length, one at a time and ask yourself the following of each segment:

	Yes	No

Segment #1

Does content conflict with content? ____ ____

If yes, how? _____

_____

_____

_____

Does content conflict with emotion? ____ ____

If yes, how? _____

_____

_____

_____

Does content conflict with body language? ____ ____

If yes, how? _____

_____

_____

_____

Segment #2

Does content conflict with content? ____ ____

If yes, how? _____

_____

_____

_____

Does content conflict with emotion?   ____   ____

If yes, how? _____

_____

_____

_____

Does content conflict with body language?___   ____

If yes, how? _____

_____

_____

_____

Segment #3

Does content conflict with content?   ____   ____

If yes, how? _____

_____

_____

_____

Does content conflict with emotion?   ____   ____

If yes, how? _____

_____

_____

_____

Does content conflict with body language?___   ____

If yes, how? _____

_____

_____

_____

Segment #4

Does content conflict with content? _____ _____

If yes, how? _____

_____

_____

_____

Does content conflict with emotion? _____ _____

If yes, how? _____

_____

_____

_____

Does content conflict with body language? _____ _____

If yes, how? _____

_____

_____

_____

Segment #5

Does content conflict with content? _____ _____

If yes, how? _____

_____

_____

_____

Does content conflict with emotion? _____ _____

If yes, how? _____

_____

_____

_____

Does content conflict with body language? ____   ____

If yes, how? _____

_____

_____

_____

2. Then replay each segment and observe how accurately or inaccurately you observed inconsistencies. Repeat the exercise until you can easily and comfortably spot verbal inconsistencies.

NONVERBAL INCONSISTENCIES

1. Television is a wondrous self-teaching tool. Teach yourself to notice nonverbal inconsistencies by watching characters on your favorite programs and observing the following:

   sudden or unexpected rises in pitch

   increases or decreases in pace

   increased frequency of "uh's"

   pausing between every word

   inconsistencies of vocabulary

2. Then ask yourself: What is motivating these nonverbal changes? Why, for example, would an otherwise strong and authoritative male character, start to say "uh" every three words?

3. Once you have a feel for inconsistencies via your television set, attune yourself to those inconsistencies as they occur in the people (including yourself) in your daily life.

BODY LANGUAGE CUES

1. Become more sensitive and receptive to body language cues using the following exercise:

   Observe the people around you, at work or at play. Note your first impression based on their body language, then note your impression after observing them for ten minutes, taking the context into account. The more you learn to take context into account, the more accurate your reading of body language cues.

Person's body language	First impression of what this body language means	Impression after ten minutes of what this body language means
#1 _____	_____	_____
_____	_____	_____
_____	_____	_____
_____	_____	_____
_____	_____	_____
#2 _____	_____	_____
_____	_____	_____
_____	_____	_____
_____	_____	_____
_____	_____	_____
#3 _____	_____	_____
_____	_____	_____
_____	_____	_____
_____	_____	_____
_____	_____	_____

#4 _____   _____   _____

_____   _____   _____

_____   _____   _____

_____   _____   _____

_____   _____   _____

#5 _____   _____   _____

_____   _____   _____

_____   _____   _____

_____   _____   _____

_____   _____   _____

#6 _____   _____   _____

_____   _____   _____

_____   _____   _____

_____   _____   _____

_____   _____   _____

2. Videotape a twenty-minute conversation with a friend. Watch the replay of the conversation and observe what body language cues your friend is giving you as to the *impact* of what you are saying. Notice in particular the following:

Your friend's   body shifts

eye positions

arm movements

leg changes

head movements

See if you can accurately pinpoint which comment of yours provoked which element of body language. Practice this exercise until you can comfortably and easily pinpoint body language reactions to your statements.

Statement   Body language elicited

#1 _____   _____

_____   _____

#2 _____   _____

_____   _____

#3 _____   _____

_____   _____

#4 _____   _____

_____   _____

#5 _____   _____

_____   _____

#6 _____   _____

_____   _____

#7 _____   _____

_____   _____

#8 _____   _____

_____   _____

#9 _____   _____

_____   _____

#10 _____   _____

_____   _____

EFFECTIVE LISTENING WITH THE BODY

1. Videotape yourself in conversation with a friend. Observe your body language as you listen. Note the following:

When listening:	Sometimes	Occasionally	Rarely
Is your body square?	____	____	____
Is your body still?	____	____	____
Is your head still?	____	____	____
Are you gesturing?	____	____	____
Is your body slightly leaning forward?	____	____	____
Is your eye focus steady?	____	____	____

2. Based on the preceding observations, note the corrections you need to make so that your body listens effectively:

_____

_____

_____

_____

_____

_____

ACKNOWLEDGMENTS

1. Videotape yourself in a twenty-minute conversation with a friend. Observe how you acknowledge him/her when he/she is speaking and note the following:

	Sometimes	Occasionally	Rarely
Do you maintain steady eye focus?	____	____	____
Do you nod your head?	____	____	____
Do your facial expressions vary in function of what you are hearing?	____	____	____
Do you make "uh-huh" or similiar acknow-ledgment sounds?	____	____	____

2. Based on the preceding observations, note the corrections you need to make so that you acknowledge effectively:

_____

_____

_____

_____

_____

_____

REACTIONS

1. Watch people as you go about your daily life and watch actors on television. Observe how people react to different situations. What do their faces and bodies do specifically to express different reactions? Use your understanding of stereotypes as outlined in Chapter 2 to help you figure this out.

   Observe people in various situations and note the following:

In reacting to a situation, people feel:	This is expressed in facial expressions and body language as:
disappointed	_____
	_____
	_____
	_____
disapproving	_____
	_____
	_____
	_____
disgusted	_____
	_____
	_____
	_____
sad	_____
	_____
	_____
	_____

interested

_____

_____

_____

intrigued

_____

_____

_____

curious

_____

_____

_____

suspicious

_____

_____

_____

annoyed

_____

_____

_____

righteously
indignant

_____

_____

_____

determined

_____

_____

_____

_____

inspired   _____

                  _____

                  _____

                  _____

approving   _____

                  _____

                  _____

                  _____

satisfied   _____

                  _____

                  _____

                  _____

_____   _____

(other)   _____

                  _____

                  _____

_____   _____

(other)   _____

                  _____

                  _____

2. Different people express their reactions differently; however, there are usually two or three main ways of expressing a reaction in any given culture. Look for the *main ways* reactions are commonly expressed, always bearing in mind the individual peculiarities of each of us.

3. Taking the same list of emotions, videotape yourself reacting to an imaginary person who is evoking that particular emotion. Observe whether or not your facial expressions and body language do indeed express the reaction you want them to express. Adjust your expressions and body language until you are confident of the effectiveness of your own reactions.

In reacting to a
situation, you feel:

Adjustments you need to make
to your facial expressions
and body language to effectively
communicate this reaction:

disappointed   _____

                              _____

                              _____

                              _____

disapproving   _____

                              _____

                              _____

                              _____

disgusted   _____

                              _____

                              _____

                              _____

sad   _____

                              _____

                              _____

                              _____

interested

_____

_____

_____

_____

intrigued

_____

_____

_____

curious

_____

_____

_____

suspicious

_____

_____

_____

annoyed

_____

_____

_____

righteously
   indignant

_____

_____

determined

_____

_____

inspired

_____

_____

_____

_____

approving

_____

_____

_____

_____

satisfied

_____

_____

_____

_____

_____

_____
(other)

_____

_____

_____

_____
(other)

_____

_____

_____

The Sixth Step:
*Persuade With Logic
and Reason*

Success in the courtroom is built on the twin poles of decision making: logic and emotion. Simply put, a lawyer can't win a trial unless he/she has been emotionally convincing enough to sway the jurors *and* has given the jurors enough facts to back up those emotions in their minds. As Gerry Spence eloquently states: "Facts! They are as essential to the rendering of justice as studs to the framing of a house, as bricks to the mortaring of a wall."[1]

WHAT LAWYERS KNOW ABOUT HOW LOGIC AND EMOTION INFLUENCE THE JURORS' DECISION-MAKING PROCESS

Successful trial lawyers know this and ardently seek the emotional truth of the case as well as its logical underpinnings. It does a lawyer no good to have a juror say of him/her during deliberation, for example; "I think defense ought to win because it feels right" and leave it at that. The juror must be able to say; "I think defense ought to win because of points one, two, and three." On the other hand, if the jurors can enumerate logical reasons supporting the lawyer's argument but have no feeling for the client or what's at stake, the jurors are likely to gravitate toward a more emotionally appealing client or cause. You cannot persuade others on the basis of logic alone or on the basis of emotions alone; they are interdependent forces and the decision-making process requires both.

Get What You Want by Using Logic and Reasoning

How, then, can you use each appropriately? It seems impossible to be both logical and emotional at the same time, and yet, in reality it can be done. The relationship between emotions and logic is much like that between skeleton and flesh in the human body. If you were trying to communicate to an alien being twenty light years away the nature of the human body and you were asked, "Is the human body hard?" you'd say, "Well, sort of, but not really," and if the being asked you, "Is the human body soft?" you'd also say "Well, sort of, but not really." If, exasperated, the being then asked, "Well then, which is it?" you would explain to the curious alien how some of the human body—the skeleton—is hard, and how some of it—the flesh—is soft. So it is with decision making. Logic is the skeleton of decision making: It is the core, the basis, the underlying structure and foundation. Emotions are the muscles and skin of decision making: They provide the allure, the pizzazz, the cosmetic overlay.

Case in Point

People rarely say of a beautiful woman, "What a terrific skeleton," but they do say, "She has good bones." They recognize that her beauty is supported by a well-defined structure. Her beauty, however, the part that attracts people's attention and appreciation, lies in her flesh: the shape of her lips, the color of her eyes.

Emotions persuade, but without strong underlying logic, that persuasiveness is momentary and does not lead to action. Combine emotions with logic, and action—a decision made in your favor—follows.

In the following chapter, we discuss the many techniques trial lawyers use to bring forth the emotional component of their cases; this chapter is devoted to how lawyers create a solid foundation to their persuasiveness through logic and reasoning.

Technique #69: Use structure to promote people's acceptance of what you have to say

What is the trial lawyer's objective? To get the jurors to see the case the way the lawyer does, to interpret the facts the way the *lawyer* wants the facts of the case interpreted, not haphazardly nor according to opposing counsel's point of view. In order to accomplish this objective, the lawyer must appeal to the jurors' logical mind, and that appeal basically relies on the use of *structure*.

The logical mind needs structure in order to function and if not provided with structure, will seek to create its own. We need structure to categorize and catalog information, to label and define it. Structure is the only way we can create order out of chaos, meaning out of senselessness. It is up to the lawyer, then, to provide the jurors with the structure that will enable them to adopt the lawyer's version of "order" and "meaning."

The lawyer has an additional challenge: If how the lawyer structures facts and information is not clear and easy to grasp, the jurors will turn toward opposing counsel. Similarly, if the way you structure your presentation isn't clear and easy to follow, those you are trying to persuade will "tune you out." The following techniques will help you structure your content as trial lawyers do so that your point of view is readily accepted.

Technique #70: Use a theme to structure your thoughts convincingly

The success or failure of a case often hinges on an organizing principle known as a "case theme." The case theme in the Menendez brothers' defense, for example, was "the abuse excuse": The brothers should be excused from murdering their parents because they had been severely abused. A primary case theme of the O. J. Simpson defense was "the cops messed up and planted evidence": O. J. Simpson's guilt could not be proven "beyond a reasonable doubt" because the evidence was spoiled and part of a frame-up.

Just as a skeleton has a distinct shape that is defined by clearly articulated elements that fit together coherently, so too does a case have a distinct shape. That shape is also defined by clearly articulated elements that fit together coherently. The trial lawyer's first task in creating a solid structure for his/her case is to define the overall shape of the case. This is the case theme. The lawyer will then organize the facts of the case so that they fit together coherently in the service of that theme. (See page 228.)

Any information you wish to present can be organized around a theme. Themes are simple, brief (one sentence!) statements that capture the essence of your argument. Themes have many advantages, the first and most important of which is that *you* control the lens through which the facts you present are going to be viewed. By setting a theme, you define the terrain, you set the boundaries. For the trial lawyer, this is absolutely critical. If the lawyer fails to set a case theme, the lawyer tac-

HOW THE DEADLY DOCTORING OF ELVIS PRESLEY BECAME THE TALE OF A GOOD SAMARITAN

Criminal defense attorney James F. Neal developed the following brilliant case theme in defending Dr. George Nichopoulos. Dr. Nichopoulos was accused of contributing to Elvis Presley's death by the criminal prescription of drugs. Originally, it looked as if there were no defense, no way to present a viable case theme. What case theme could be developed given that the medical review board had indeed suspended Dr. Nichopoulos for overprescribing drugs, prescribing them too frequently and for too long?

What Neal found, in examining the facts of the case more closely, was that Dr. Nichopoulos was, in fact, dealing with a number of addicted patients who were difficult and desperate. Dr. Nichopoulos was, in effect, attempting to wean these patients off drugs in controlled fashion, rather than cutting off their supply entirely and having them resort to possibly criminal means of feeding their addictions.

Out of these facts, Neal developed his defense. The theme of the "Good Samaritan" became his case theme. Here's how it played out in court: "Neal told the jury that Nichopoulos jeopardized his medical license to help all his addicted patients [including Presley] diminish their supply of drugs and cure their addictions. He did this when many other doctors turned these people away, explained Neal. Nichopoulos was the man who would take a chance and even practiced in what other doctors would see as an unorthodox way if he believed it would help—rather than turning his back and passing on, leaving these victims to the mercy of the street peddlers."[2] Neal then proceeded to present his facts so that they would support this one overriding case theme.

THE LINDBERGH BABY CASE: WHEN INNOCENCE JUST ISN'T ENOUGH

A historic example of what can happen when a trial lawyer doesn't develop a case theme is the trial of Bruno Hauptmann, accused of kidnapping the Lindbergh baby in 1932. The defense did not have a theme: The defense simply denied that Hauptmann committed the crime. Claims of innocence are not enough! Despite much controversial evidence and the moving emotional outcries of both Hauptmann and his wife throughout the trial, the defense lost, in large part because they abdicated control of their case by ignoring the critical importance of defining a case theme.[3]

itly gives opposing counsel the advantage. Whoever controls the definition of the case is inevitably the one with the power. (See page 228.)

A theme gives people a mental handle with which to understand your point of view. This is the first element of structure. If you don't provide people with a convenient mental handle, they will either provide their own, over which you have no control, or lean toward that of whoever else is around who does give them such a handle.

A mass of flesh without a skeleton is just a blob. Did you ever try to hold onto a blob? Information presented without a theme is too difficult for people to make sense of; they need something definite, something concrete to make order out of disparate facts. A theme gives people a central concept to grab onto, a generalizing principle around which they can organize the information given throughout your presentation.

THE $52,000,000 HANDSHAKE:
THE GOLDEN ARCHES LOSE SOME SERIOUS GLITTER

"In a case that I [Gerry Spence] argued for a small ice cream company against McDonald's, the hamburger corporation, which had breached an oral contract, I choose the *theme, Let's put honor back in the handshake*, the message, of course, being that a handshake deal should be fully honored by honest businesspeople. . . . The jury honored the theme and my client with its verdict: $52 million."[4]

Just as a theme gives those you are trying to persuade a generalizing principle around which information can be organized, so too does it give you one. The great trial lawyers emphasize the need for an overall strategy as well as day-to-day tactics. A case theme embodies a lawyer's overall strategy in a nutshell and helps him/her organize the case so that the lawyer stays on target. Use a theme to help you stay well and easily focused on the overall thrust of your presentation.

Every point you make should be made with one directive in mind: Does it advance my theme? Does this point fit coherently with other points I'm making, reinforcing my theme, or is it extraneous and therefore unimportant? If your skeleton is in the shape of a man, don't elaborate points that distort that shape: a foot that grows out of a man's thigh does not clarify the shape of the man; it confuses.

Jurors look for guidance through the morass of facts they are to evaluate and will take that guidance wherever they can get it. The successful trial attorney gives the jurors the guidance they need right from the beginning of the trial and all through the trial in the form of a case theme. If you have created a good theme and have organized your presentation succinctly and consistently around that theme, you will give those you wish to persuade an excellent guide through the information, which they can follow to the logical conclusion you wish them to reach.

THE HIGH COST OF CORPORATE GREED: A JURY'S $43,500,000 PRICE TAG

"In a recent case in which I sued an insurance company for its fraud against my quadriplegic client, a case in which I sought damages for his emotional pain and suffering, I created the *theme*, 'Human need versus corporate greed.' The jury responded with its human verdict: $33.5 million, to which a human judge added interest amounting to another $10 million."[5]

A good case theme has the added bonus of enhancing your credibility. When you establish a theme, you let people know that you have a well-defined and thought-out point of view. Such specificity adds to your perceived competence and trustworthiness. Successful trial lawyers are never wishy-washy.

Technique #71: Use the "Rule of Threes" to persuasively support your theme

Once you've established your theme, select no more than three main points or issues to substantiate it. Although psychological research has not yet understood the reasons behind this mechanism, it seems that information is most compelling when it is grouped in sets of three: three points, three arguments, three phrases.

CASE IN POINT

For example, notice the difference in impact between the following two different presentations of the same facts:

Poor Presentation:

Jane is a hardworking person. She is a real "winner," dedicated to the principles of the firm.

Good Presentation:

Jane is hardworking.

Jane is dedicated.
Jane is a winner.

The facts are identical in the two formats, but the three-point structure makes the second presentation truly dynamic. By structuring your presentation in terms of three main points, you access a powerful, albeit not-well-understood phenomenon of the human mind.

"NO SHOES, NO WEAPON, NO CLOTHES:" FREEING O. J. SIMPSON

"Cochran and Scheck pointed out to the jury that this was a case of circumstantial evidence, that is, no eyewitnesses, and Cochran added smugly, 'The prosecution has no shoes, no weapon, no clothes, . . .' "[6] "No shoes, no weapon, no clothes" became an easy and powerful refrain for the jurors to keep in mind as they sorted through the evidence.

In addition to the psychological impact of a set of three points, three seems to be the number of points the mind can absorb and manipulate easily. The jurors must not only retain the points the trial lawyer makes, they must also be able to manipulate them mentally; that is to say, compare them with opposing counsel's points and weigh their relative merit. When presented with more than three main issues, jurors are easily confused and cease to understand the case well enough to appreciate its strengths.

Be picky—choose those issues that most clearly focus the facts and evidence in support of your theme. Then use the following diagrammatic format I have taught to numerous lawyers to help you organize your facts around the three issues you've chosen:

	(Theme)	
(Point 1)	(Point 2)	(Point 3)
Facts supporting Point 1	Facts supporting Point 2	Facts supporting Point 3

When you organize your facts in this fashion, you give people clear guidelines by which to understand and evaluate your position. You can easily refute someone else's points by referring to your structure. A good trial lawyer will not allow opposing counsel to panic him/her into distorting his/her original case theme and three points. Remain just as firm with your theme: If a theme is strong and your three points logically support and enhance it, you have a winning structure—stick to it. When a lawyer changes his/her case theme or main issues midtrial, it's usually lethal.

THE BIG GUNS: DUN & BRADSTREET ON TRIAL

Fred H. Bartlit, Jr., a highly reputed and successful trial lawyer, used a case theme and three-point argument structure vigorously in defending Dun & Bradstreet in a major antitrust lawsuit brought against it by National Business Lists. In a nutshell, National Business Lists, whose business is mailing lists, accused Dun & Bradstreet of monopolizing the information needed for those lists. Rather than elaborating a defense that consisted of denying or in some way defending against the antitrust charges, Bartlit developed a totally different and original case theme, which he then proceeded to uphold. His theme, repeated over and over again, was that National Business Lists was essentially getting a "free ride" by copying information Dun & Bradstreet worked hard to obtain. Here's how he elaborated his three points during his opening statement to the jury:

"Now, what is the believable evidence going to show in this case? Well, there are three important things. The first important thing is that Mr. Gans, who is sitting over there on end in the first row, he is the man who runs National Business Lists. He will be the first witness. He started his business from the first day under false pretenses. The second important point is that for twenty-five years, twenty-five years, he has run his business with a free ride because these names you have heard about, an awful lot of them were copies from Dun and Bradstreet, copied. We got the names, not him, and he copied them.

"And the third point is that even after we told him in 1975 to stop copying because it is illegal, he just ignored that and kept right on."[7]

Notice how clearly Bartlit elaborates his three points. He even says, right at the beginning, "there are three important things" and then enumerates them: "The first important thing . . . the second important point . . . and the third point. . ." You cannot get lost in such a clear and concise framework. The jurors could easily remember and refer to those three points throughout the trial, as could Bartlit himself. The points are readily understandable, easy to follow, and directly relate to the case theme. From then on, Bartlit organized the evidence and facts around those three points in defense of his case theme, in consistent and repetitive fashion. Structure that strong is virtually unbeatable.

How do you know if you have a really good theme with solid supporting points? Run your theme and points by a relatively bright fifteen year old. As odd as that may sound, a relatively intelligent fifteen year old should be able to understand your theme and points and agree that your points fit coherently with and support that theme. This is not to say that the people you will be trying to persuade will have the mentality of fifteen year olds, only that your theme and points must be that clear and accessible for your foundation to be a good one. Bright fifteen year olds are nothing to sneeze at; they can be surprisingly right on target when it comes to pointing out areas of confusion.

Technique #72: Follow the "Law of Primacy" and the "Law of Recency" to order your points so that you are most persuasive

The "Law of Primacy" and the "Law of Recency," as defined by communications research, state that what you say first will be remembered best, what you say last will be remembered second best, and what you say in the middle will be remembered least well. Whether they are designing their opening statements, or deciding the order in which their witnesses are to appear, successful trial lawyers take the psychological effects of order into great consideration. A good lawyer will take care not to bury an important point in the middle of his/her opening statement, or an important witness in the middle of a long string of witnesses.

CASE IN POINT

In the Hauptmann case, mentioned earlier, a critical analysis by communication scholars Schuetz and Snedaker revealed that the defense not only failed to put forth a case theme, but also lacked coherent order in their presentation of witnesses.[8] The defense did not order witnesses so they corroborated Hauptmann's story, but rather skipped around from one set of evidence to another, without regard to a logical sequencing of witnesses, much less with regard to the rules of primacy and recency. Schuetz and Snedaker concluded: "Reclustering and reordering of the witnesses could have produced a more coherent order and hence a more persuasive defense narrative."[9]

Always put your most important points first and last, with your third point falling in the middle. Within the development of any given point, always put the most persuasive aspects of that point first and last.

As much as you can, respect the laws of primacy and recency to gain maximum benefit for your point of view.

Technique #73: Use an "umbrella statement" to provide an initial overview to guide people to your point of view

Once you've come up with your theme and the relevant points and you're ready to design the overall presentation of your material, the "umbrella statement" technique can prove to be an invaluable tool. The umbrella statement is a statement trial lawyers use to give the jurors an overview of what's coming, a preview of sorts that allows jurors to adjust their mind set so that it is receptive to the information about to come. Without the help of this overview, jurors do not know where the lawyer is headed, and, since the mind seeks structure when it is not provided, jurors focus their energy on trying to figure out where the lawyer is going. The result is the jurors are only partially attending to the point the lawyer is trying to make, as most of their mental space is occupied trying to find some structure that will facilitate organizing the information. Jurors pre-occupied with providing a context for themselves may miss the lawyer's substantive points entirely until this task is accomplished.

This quest for structure is not particular to jurors. We all do it, all the time. Here's an everyday example: You're in a restaurant and you over-hear a conversation at the next table. Notice how you listen for a while to figure out exactly what the people at the neighboring table are talking about, and during that time, notice how your mind is actively searching for a context, some structure with which to make sense of the information you are overhearing. The mind cannot deal effectively with disjointed facts.

CASE IN POINT

For example, in the case previously cited in which James F. Neal defended Dr. Nichopoulos, Neal used an umbrella statement in beginning his cross-examination of a witness: "I want to take you back to the life of Elvis Presley. Do you agree that you had conversations with Dr. Nichopoulos in which Dr. Nichopoulos referred to Elvis Presley as a problem patient?"[10]

The sentence "I want to take you back to the life of Elvis Presley" is an umbrella statement that told the jurors to ready themselves for infor-mation regarding Presley's life, rather than information regarding

THE JOHN DELOREAN CASE:
THE TRAP THAT CAUGHT THE HUNTERS AND LET THE PREY ESCAPE

In 1983, John DeLorean, the flamboyant, jet-setting automobile manufacturer, was charged with conspiring to sell and distribute $60 million of cocaine. The case was very complex and little understood by most of the public. In order to clarify issues for the jurors, DeLorean's defense counsel, Howard L. Weitzman, used umbrella statements to reintroduce material and, in the following example, remind jurors of an already existing framework in cross-examining a key witness:

Weitzman: Mr. Tisa, we were discussing I think October the nineteenth a little earlier this morning. The decision was made that John should be arrested before he came to Los Angeles, correct?

Tisa: Yes.

Once Weitzman had thus oriented the jurors with his umbrella statement, he proceeded with the substantive issue he wanted to develop:

Weitzman: When was that decision made?

Tisa: Sometime right just prior to the—I guess the eighteenth or nineteenth . . .

Weitzman: You had already concluded that he had been involved in and committed a crime, correct?

Tisa: Yes . . .

Weitzman: You will agree with me, won't you, that Mr. DeLorean did not know the cocaine was going to be in the room?

Tisa: Yes . . .

Weitzman: Regardless of how he reacted, he was going to be arrested anyway, wasn't he?

Tisa: Yes . . . [11]

Given the setup Mr. Weitzman provided the jurors with his umbrella statement, the jurors could easily follow Mr. Weitzman's line of questioning; consequently, his point was clearly and forcefully made. Mr. Weitzman was successful; DeLorean was acquitted. Good structure is truly the foundation for persuasiveness.

Nichopoulos's reputation, for example. Neal further refined the context within which Presley's life would be considered: " . . . conversations with Dr. Nichopoulos in which Dr. Nichopoulos referred to Elvis Presley as a problem patient?" Well provided with structure, the jurors could attend to what was most important: Neal's interpretation of the facts of the case.

When do you use an umbrella statement? Anytime you introduce a new idea. There is a concept in acting called a "beat." A beat is the organization of thoughts around one idea. A new beat begins every time you introduce a new idea, and the beat ends when you've exhausted your thought, for the moment at least, on that idea. Neal's umbrella statement ". . . conversations with Dr. Nichopoulos in which Dr. Nichopoulos referred to Elvis Presley as a problem patient?" began a new beat, which consisted of everything that would be said about the subject of these conversations until the subject was, at least for the moment, exhausted. A new beat would then begin, which would require a new umbrella statement.

In court, a lawyer deals with new beats constantly, introducing new evidence, witnesses, concepts, and exhibits throughout the trial. The jurors need some kind of structure to help them assimilate this new information in a way that is both comprehensible to them and compatible with the lawyer's definition of the case. The umbrella statement serves that purpose well. (See page 235.)

An umbrella statement is also useful when you need to reintroduce an old beat, for example, to further develop a subject or add new information. It helps people place the new information in an already existing framework and frequently serves to remind them "short form" of what had already been discussed.

Technique #74: Speak everyday language

The simplicity and clarity of your thought contribute greatly to your persuasiveness; anything that supports or enhances clear thinking contributes to the logic of your case. Stated simply: you can't persuade people if they are confused. Aristotle's recommendation is worth noting: "Think as wise men do, but speak as the common people do." In court, for example, verbosity, complex expressions, indirect questioning, and indirect responses are all confusing and offensive to jurors.

CASE IN POINT

During the Erik Menendez trial previously mentioned, Ms. Thornton, a juror, comments on Dr. Oziel's testimony. Dr. Oziel was a key witness for the prosecution. "I find the way he can't give a straight answer to be extremely irritating . . ."[12]

Someone who is irritated by your lack of clarity is unlikely to find your arguments persuasive. A good trial lawyer will fashion opening statements, for example, with direct and clear speech in mind, knowing that such a presentation is a powerful one.

A good trial lawyer doesn't confuse oral presentation with written matter. They really aren't the same thing. If people are busy trying to figure out what you mean because your words are unfamiliar to them, they're going to be missing your important points. When you want to convince someone, don't use fancy words. Persuasion was never bought with expensive "for the elite only" words. Good trial lawyers use ordinary vocabulary, words everyone understands and use commonly.

Technique #75: Use jargon, technical terms, and slang appropriately

Use jargon, technical terms, and slang only to the extent that they are readily understood by the people you are seeking to convince. Otherwise, your use of such terms makes the people you're trying to convince feel like outcasts—they're not part of your "in group." Jargon and slang must also be a part of the acceptable culture of the people you are addressing. Certainly, most people in the United States know what the f- - - word means, but it is not part of many people's "acceptable culture." Your whole object in relating to the people you want to convince is in making yourself familiar to them; don't destroy that with unfamiliar or objectionable vocabulary. Most terms can be expressed in language familiar and comfortable to those you are addressing with a minimum of effort.

CASE IN POINT

Jurors in the O. J. Simpson trial appreciated those experts who made technical terms accessible: "On the whole, I did not find DNA too complicated to grasp because Barry Scheck took time to explain it . . . You really don't have to be a chemist or a scientist to be oriented to the front part of something, especially if you're told step by step . . ."[13]

If part of your presentation requires you to use certain technical terms, explain those terms, as the top trial expert witnesses and lawyers do, as simply as possible and without talking down to those listening to you. Your attitude in describing technical terms should be, Here's how I came to understand it myself, and now I'm sharing that understanding with you. Not, OK, you dodos, listen up.

Technique #76: Phrase for clarity of thought

Phrasing can help you greatly in achieving clarity of thought. Phrase your ideas one thought at a time (as described in Chapter 3), pausing often between phrases if you're explaining a complicated concept. When you ask questions of people, be careful to ask only one item per question. Many trial lawyers have discovered, to their dismay, that a witness cannot respond properly if asked: "Did you take that route on a regular basis and were you driving it that Tuesday, June 10?" More important, the persons listening, in this instance, the jurors, wonder exactly what it is the lawyer is trying to get at. Is the lawyer attempting to determine whether this route is a regular one, and therefore a familiar one, or does the lawyer want to know where the witness was that Tuesday? Ask one question at a time; you'll seem more competent, and people will be much more able to respond accurately to your questions.

Technique #77: Get to the point

A good trial lawyer doesn't ask, "Would it be fair to say, perhaps, that you were on good terms with the deceased at the time?" A good trial lawyer will ask simply: "Did you get along well with Mr. Jones?" "Did you consider him a friend?" It is irritating and confusing to people when those addressing them fail to get to the point.

GET TO THE POINT! CONFUSED MENENDEZ JURORS FIND FOR THE DEFENSE

Jurors in the Menendez trial previously mentioned reacted predictably to prosecution's inability to clearly communicate its point: "A criminologist from the LA [Los Angeles] Sheriff Department brought a pair of bloodstained women's tennis shoes to court. I have no idea what the prosecution's point was, but the defense noted that the blood couldn't be typed due to age and poor preservation."[14] Since the jurors couldn't follow prosecution's point, they believed the point they could determine: that of defense.

When you don't get to the point, people can't follow your thought and therefore you are not convincing. Often, failure to get to the point is just the result of failing to think through what you have to say before you open your mouth. I have helped innumerable witnesses, preparing them for trial, give good testimony just with this suggestion alone: "Think before you speak." Much of our rambling and indirectness is the result of our thinking out loud. A good trial lawyer does not ramble. A good trial lawyer thinks first and then gets right to the point of whatever it is he/she has to say.

COCHRAN SCORES POINTS BY MAKING POINTS

"Cochran, surprisingly, was more specific in his summation than either Darden or Clark. He quoted the actual trial testimony much more than they, and wasn't saying 'I think' the way the prosecutors so often did. He came across as being more confident and knowledgeable about the facts of the case than the prosecutors . . . Though he could have gotten appreciably more out of many of his articulations on these points [problems with the prosecution's case], he was nonetheless effective since he *did* make the points . . ."[15] Sometimes all it takes to convince people is clearly making your points.

How do you know if you are getting to the point and using language that is clear and easy to understand? If it is appropriate (that is, does not violate confidentiality or someone's privacy), tape-record your presentation and ask a friend to listen to the recording. Ask for specific feedback; ask your friend to pay attention to such things as: Is your choice of vocabulary clear and easy to understand? Are you phrasing for sense or nonsense? Are your sentences too long, containing too many thoughts? Do your thoughts follow logically? Use the practice worksheet at the end of this chapter to help you design a presentation. You can significantly increase your ability to persuade simply by clarifying your speech.

THERE'S STRENGTH IN WEAKNESS: LEARN HOW LAWYERS INOCULATE JURORS AGAINST OPPOSING COUNSEL'S ARGUMENTS BY ADMITTING WEAKNESSES

It is tempting for lawyers to present only their side of the case. Though it is tempting, when a lawyer is impassioned by his/her interpretation of the facts, prides him/herself on the strength of his/her arguments, and is convinced that jurors, once they have heard that lawyer's argument, will be inevitably swayed by the lawyer's brilliance and will dismiss opposing counsel's testimony as a sham, he/she is making a fatal mistake.

MARCIA CLARK 'KO'ED BY THE FRAME-UP SHE FAILED TO KNOCK OUT: O.J. SIMPSON WINS ANOTHER ROUND

"Since it had been obvious to everyone for months, then, that a police conspiracy to frame Simpson was the essence of the defense, as the prosecutor don't you automatically sit down with your yellow pad and come up with seven, eight, or nine very powerful arguments why a frame-up in this case was ludicrous, and argue for at least an hour or two on this point alone? . . . Yet unbelievably, Clark, in her opening argument, *never uttered one single word to knock down the frame-up, conspiracy allegation.* She treated it like a nonissue."[16] Ms. Clark gave the jurors nothing solid with which to counter defense's arguments. When people are left empty-handed, they are likely to go toward whatever information allows them to grasp the situation, in this case, defense's interpretation of the facts.

Social psychologists have clearly demonstrated that a convincing one-sided communication presenting only positive arguments will indeed sway people toward the communicator's point of view; however, when the same people hear an opposing point of view, also supported by what seem to be valid arguments, they will now be influenced in the opposing direction.

This is not beneficial to you. You need people to be swayed by what you have to say in such a way that they *stay* swayed by your argument, regardless of what anybody else has to say. One way to accomplish this is through "inoculation."

Technique #78: How you can admit weaknesses in a way that strengthens your point

"Inoculating" a jury is similar to being inoculated against a disease: The lawyer presents the jurors with the weaknesses in his/her case and those of opposing counsel's arguments the lawyer believes are potentially damaging to the lawyer's case, *and the lawyer leads the jurors nonetheless to the lawyer's conclusion.* How does this work? The lawyer has now given the jurors a way to ignore or discount opposing counsel's arguments; the jurors have already heard those arguments and have been provided with reasons to dismiss them. Thus inoculated, the jurors are much more likely to retain the lawyer's interpretation of the facts.

PARDONABLE TRAITORS: HOW THE PROSECUTION WON THE JULIUS AND ETHEL ROSENBERG CASE

A classic example of the value of inoculation is found in the Julius and Ethel Rosenberg case. In his critical analysis of why the prosecuting attorney gave the better (and winning) argument, noted professor, author, and trial attorney J. Alexander Tanford shows how the prosecutor used admission of weaknesses to strengthen his case: "One example [of using two-sided communication admitting weaknesses] was his recognition that his witnesses were spies and traitors who were cooperating out of self-interest, but then using that to his advantage by comparing their apparent repentance and attempt to 'make amends for the hurt which has been done to our nation,' to the Rosenbergs' compounding of their betrayal with lies and deception. The defense used only one-sided communication, never admitting any weaknesses and addressing only the favorable evidence."[17]

Be strong enough to admit where you are weak. Be willing to show the "downside" of your arguments, showing how those downsides are not all that awful. By demonstrating that you are aware of another point of view, you let people know that you aren't just a zealot, single-mindedly homing in on one interpretation. On the contrary, by admitting weaknesses, you show how you have thought the matter through carefully, and have come up with a fair assessment of how things are. A good defense lawyer, for example, rather than adamantly rebutting every one of opposing counsel's arguments, will admit that opposing counsel has some good points and will then go on to show how defense's conclusion is valid anyway. People value and appreciate those who come to their position as a result of close and thorough scrutiny. Such an approach will significantly reduce the impact of any opposing argument, as well as strengthen your points.

Technique #79: How to disclose weaknesses to increase your trustworthiness

Your trustworthiness also increases as you show yourself willing to disclose weaknesses. People are willing to forgive human error and weakness; what they won't forgive is cover-ups.

HOW THE L.A.P.D. LOST THE O. J. SIMPSON JURORS' FAVOR: LOOKING BAD TRYING TO LOOK GOOD

In the O. J. Simpson trial, jurors commented how: "When the police were testifying there always seemed to be controversy over whatever they said or did . . . Case in point, Vannatter and the Fiato brothers and the issue of talking about the case. I mean, just say straight out, 'Yes, we talked about the case. It wasn't anything intentional. It was just something that happened to come up . . .' And, 'Yeah, I may have said he [O. J. Simpson] was a suspect because the husband is always a suspect.' Just be straight out instead of going back and forth. It was really no big deal, but the police made it a big deal, just trying to make themselves look good, and that's where they ran into problems. . . . and then he [Vannatter] was running around town with the blood vial rather than booking it in properly. Just be straight out and say you did it, say, 'I made a mistake. Through the excitement of this case, I just got wrapped up and made a mistake.' We are human. We can understand these human errors. . . ."[18] Oddly enough, in trying to look good, the L.A.P.D. actually ended up looking bad. It's always preferable to admit to the relevant flaws right up front, rather than hope that they somehow won't be discovered. They virtually always are.

There is something in all of us that loves a confession. When you are willing to disclose weaknesses, you will be perceived as fair and honest by those you are seeking to convince, and your point of view will more readily be accepted because of your "honesty."

THE ABSOLUTION OF LT. COL. OLIVER NORTH: CONFESSION IS GOOD FOR THE SOUL (AND FOR WINNERS)

Lt. Col. Oliver North was forthright in admitting to his mistakes: "I did probably the grossest misjudgment that I've made in my life. I then tried to paper over that whole thing [the funding of his security system] [with] two phony documents." (Newsweek, July 20, 1987, at 14.)

"Here is a flat-out admission of a mistake. Once North says this, there is little more anyone can say about this particular issue. It reflects back on the American theme of forgiving people if they come clean about their mistakes. What child was not told the story (true or not) of George Washington cutting down the cherry trees and then being forgiven because he confessed?"[19] Be willing to acknowledge your mistakes. People will forgive truth; what they will not accept is stealth and lies.

EDWARD BENNETT WILLIAMS: MASTER OF FAIR PLAY

Edward Bennett Williams, considered one of the "greats" by his trial-lawyer peers, spoke in his discussions with Norman Sheresky of how disclosure of weaknesses enhances trustworthiness: "Such a quality [the ability to seem sincere or truthful to a court or jury] requires the advocate to avoid overstating, and sometimes it requires him to do or say things that seem counterproductive to his interests. He has to tell the jury about the weaknesses of his case as well as the strength: [quoting Williams] 'You have to have all of the cosmetics of fair play, and I have found over a quarter of a century that, certainly, the best way to have all the cosmetics of fair play is to *do* fair play.' The jury will love you for it."[20]

Your audiences will love you for your "fair play." Presenting both sides of an argument, or presenting the downsides as well as the upsides of your position will impress those who listen to you with your honesty, with your willingness to take the risk of your position being rejected rather than hide something from those you seek to persuade.

Case in Point

Jurors in the Erik Menendez trial commented on a witness's testimony, Dr. Vicary, Erik Menendez's psychiatrist in jail: "I like Dr. V., not because I'd want to confide in him myself, but because he was very candid and admitted to things like the fact that this trial isn't making him any poorer and that he likes to control things (Eric was hard to control)."[21] There are few things more compelling than the truth.

How Lawyers Use Rhetorical Questions to Involve Jurors in Decision Making

The more you can get people involved in actively thinking about what you are saying, the better are your chances of convincing them. This is why successful trial lawyers use rhetorical questions frequently throughout their opening and closing statements. "What's the issue here?" "Why are we here?" "Do we ignore a person's mistake just because he/she is basically an honest person?" "How do we know it's Mr. Jones's fault?" These are typical examples of the rhetorical questions lawyers use to get jurors actively thinking along the same lines as the lawyer, thereby facilitating their acceptance of the lawyer's interpretation of the facts.

Technique #80: Use rhetorical questions to persuasively engage your listeners

A rhetorical question is simply a question to which *you* provide the answer as well as the question, as opposed to a normal question, in which you ask the question, but you expect the person to whom you are addressing the question to provide the answer. Because rhetorical questions automatically engage the mind of those listening to you, they are inherently more persuasive and engaging than direct statements.

"IF MR. SIMPSON DIDN'T COMMIT THESE MURDERS, THEN WHO?" A QUESTION ASKED AND ANSWERED

As part of his examination of why the prosecution fared so badly in the O. J. Simpson trial, Vincent Bugliosi rewrote the prosecution's closing argument. His summation is studded with rhetorical questions: "If Mr. Simpson didn't commit these murders, then who? Who else would have had any reason to commit these murders? We know Mr. Simpson beat his wife severely, to the point of the photos where she had to call the police *nine* times during their marriage . . . who else could have had the motive to kill these two young people [Ron Goldman and Nicole Simpson]? . . . . What is the likelihood that someone they knew would have had a reason to kill either one of them, much less both of them, and particularly in such a savage and brutal way? . . . Who in the lives of these young people would have had any reason to hire someone to kill either one of them? . . . I ask you once again to ask yourself this question back in the jury room— *who else* had any reason at all to kill Ron and Nicole, particularly in this way? There is simply no one except O. J. Simpson, the defendant in this case."[22] Notice how automatically your mind seeks to respond to Mr. Bugliosi's questions, even as he provides you with the answer he wants you to accept—O. J. Simpson's guilt.

Use rhetorical questions frequently: at the beginning of a new subject or thought, to change the pace, to wake people up, and to give your points impact.

SUCCESSFUL LAWYERS GET THEIR WAY BECAUSE THEY KNOW HOW TO ASK FOR WHAT THEY WANT

Logic is an attempt to bring order out of chaos. The more concrete and specific you are in your thinking, the easier it is to bring order out of chaos. It may seem elegant to argue a convincing case and then leave the conclusion up to the jury so as not to browbeat them or be heavy-handed; however, communications research shows that it is far more effective to state conclusions explicitly.

MISS WYOMING VS. *PENTHOUSE* MAGAZINE: HOW "A DOLLAR A RAPE" BECAME A $26,500,000 JURY VERDICT

Kim Pring was crowned the woman's grand National Baton Twirling Champion of 1978. From there she became Miss Wyoming and went on to represent Wyoming in the Miss America Pageant. A writer for *Penthouse* magazine saw Kim perform her magic with the baton, but the story that then appeared in *Penthouse* had nothing to do with her winning the talent award in the pageant that year. As Kim later tried to explain to the jury, in less than three thousand words *Penthouse* transformed her from the greatest baton twirler in the nation to the greatest blow-job artist in the history of the world. The story claimed Miss Wyoming was so good at oral sex she could actually levitate a man—all this without her permission and without even bothering to label the story as fiction. The indecent calls, obscenities shouted at her in public, messages left on her car, and other abuses devastated Kim.

Gerry Spence, Kim's attorney, used a powerful simile to explain to the jurors what happened to Kim: "It was as if she had been raped, because rape is when someone takes from you what you don't want to give, and what *Penthouse* had done to Kim was take her privacy and her good name, . . . and sold it to the 25 million men who, according to *Penthouse*, constituted the readership of that month's edition. . . . I argued that every time someone read that article, Kim was raped, and that the jury should punish *Penthouse* by charging them a mere dollar a rape," one dollar for each of the twenty-five million subscribers to that month's edition.

The jury returned a verdict of $26.5 million: $1.5 million as damages for Kim and $25 million to punish *Penthouse*.[23] What price the defamation of a young woman's good name and the consequent hardship in her life? Such things have no price. Spence helped the jurors figure out how to help Kim by being explicit in his demand: a dollar a rape.

A successful trial lawyer will guide the jurors in concrete and specific terms from opening statement right through to the end. The successful lawyer won't confuse the jurors by suddenly leaving it up to *them* to figure out what to do. For a lawyer to conclude with something to the effect of: "Listen and keep your minds open," or "Listen and do justice" is weak and ineffective. The jurors are thereby left without guidance: How are they supposed to translate "keep your minds open" and what does

PROSECUTION'S APOLOGY BECOMES DEFENSE'S TRIUMPH: HOW O. J. SIMPSON RODE OFF INTO THE SUNSET

Right from their opening statements, the prosecutors in the O. J. Simpson case confused the jurors by not stating clearly and directly what they wanted: ". . . in his opening argument . . . Darden had very unwisely told the jury that on the issue of whether Simpson was guilty or not guilty, 'the decision is yours, and I'm glad that it is not mine. . . .' "[24] "Marcia Clark, during jury selection, making one of the most ill-advised statements ever made to a jury by a prosecutor: 'You may not like me for bringing this case. I'm not winning any popularity contests for doing so.'

This trend continued into prosecution's closing arguments: "Chris Darden's almost equally incredible and ill-advised statement to the jury in his summation at the end of the case: 'Nobody wants to do anything to this man. We don't. There is nothing personal about this, but the law is the law.' (Can you imagine being almost apologetic to a jury when you believe the person you're prosecuting committed a brutal double murder?)"[25] How can people possibly be convinced by you if they don't know what you're trying to convince them of? Be clear and direct in asking for what you want, it will work for you as it did for O. J. Simpson's defense team.

Cochran, in his final summation, asks for exactly what he wants: "Who then police the police? You police the police. You police them by your verdict. You are the ones to send a message. Nobody else is going to do it in our society . . . nobody has the courage . . . Maybe you are the right people at the right time at the right place to say no more. We are not going to have this."

". . . it couldn't have been clearer from the context in which he [Cochran] made the remarks, as well as his entire argument, that he was telling the jury that *the facts and evidence in the Simpson case, and the law applicable thereto, required a non-guilty verdict.*"[26]

"do justice" mean? A good trial lawyer will tell the jurors directly what the lawyer wants: "guilty" or "not guilty."

Technique #81: How to use an explicit conclusion to get what you want

Don't confuse your listeners at the last minute. Both Marcia Clark and Chris Darden erred with the O. J. Simpson jurors by failing to give explicit clear and unmistakable conclusions.

Give the people you want to convince a concrete and specific outcome to focus on, one that can help them structure their thinking as they make their decision. Use verbs, which are the action part of a sentence, right at the beginning of your "demand" sentence to help people know immediately what action you want them to take.

THE CASE AGAINST A KILLER CONTRACEPTIVE: A JUDGE DEMANDS WHAT RIGHT THINKING COMMANDS

The Dalkon Shield was a contraceptive device that was known to have caused great harm to many women. The manufacturers, A. H. Robins, were trying to avoid recalling the shields for fear of more lawsuits. Judge Miles Lord, in directing the officers of A. H. Robins to take corporate responsibility for the damage done, was absolutely explicit in what he wanted. The power of his exhortation is undeniable:

"Under your direction, your company has continued to allow women, tens of thousands of them, to wear this device—a deadly depth charge in their wombs, ready to explode at any time. . . . The only conceivable reasons that you have not recalled this product are that it would hurt your balance sheet and alert women who have already been harmed that you may be liable for their injuries. . . . Confession is good for the soul, gentlemen. Face up to your misdeeds. Acknowledge the personal responsibility you have for the activities of those who work under you. Rectify this evil situation. Warn the potential victims and recompense those who have already been harmed."[27]

Judge Lord's use of verbs directing the corporate officers as to which actions to take is excellent: "face up," "acknowledge," "rectify," "warn," and "recompense" all provide clear and unmistakable guidelines for action. The officers may not want to follow these directives, but there is no mistaking what Judge Lord's directives are.

Ask directly and clearly for what you want. You are much more likely to get it.

Summary

A thorough knowledge of communication principles will greatly facilitate your success at getting your way. Understanding how both logic and emotion are necessary to the decision-making process will help you structure your presentations and arguments successfully. Techniques used in the service of logic are the theme, the three-point argument, order, the laws of primacy and recency, simplicity and clarity of speech, umbrella statements, inoculation, and the explicit conclusion. Once your substantive issues are structured such that your point of view has a solid, logical foundation, the emotional appeals you make will have validity. This is truly a winning combination.

WORKSHEETS
LOGIC AND STRUCTURE: CHECKLIST OF PSYCHOLOGICAL AND SOCIAL-PSYCHOLOGICAL TECHNIQUES DESIGNED TO INCREASE YOUR PERSUASIVENESS

Use this checklist to help you incorporate the techniques discussed in this chapter.

1. What is your case theme? _____

_____

_____

2. What are the three points supporting your case theme?

a. _____

_____

b. _____

_____

c. _____

_____

3. What are the facts supporting each of your three points?

Point #1: _____

_____

_____

_____

_____

_____

Point #2: _____

_____

_____

_____

_____

_____

Point #3: _____

_____

_____

_____

_____

_____

4. Observe your use of language:

   a.   Is it everyday language?

   b.   Is there any jargon or slang?

   c.   Do you clearly and simply explain technical or unfamiliar terms?

Technical/unfamiliar terms: Explanation:

#1 _____   _____

                                     _____

                                     _____

#2 _____   _____

                                     _____

                                     _____

#3 _____   _____

                                     _____

                                     _____

#4 _____   _____

_____

_____

#5 _____   _____

_____

_____

5. Observe your use of phrasing:
   a. Do you express one thought per phrase?
   b. Are your phrases to the point?
   c. Are your phrases clear and easy to understand?
   d. Do your thoughts follow logically?

6. Are your points ordered for effect? How? _____

_____

_____

_____

_____

7. Are any people or things you are presenting ordered for effect?
   How? _____

_____

_____

_____

_____

8. Have you provided umbrella statements to introduce topics? What are they?

_____

_____

_____

_____

_____

_____

9. Have you provided umbrella statements to reintroduce topics? What are they? _____

_____

_____

_____

_____

_____

10. Have you inoculated your audience against the other side's arguments or against different points of view? What weaknesses have you disclosed?

_____

_____

_____

_____

_____

11. Have you used rhetorical questions to involve your audience in your presentation? What are they? Can you use any more? _____

_____

_____

_____

_____

_____

12. Is your conclusion explicit? What is it? _____

_____

_____

_____

LOGIC AND STRUCTURE PRACTICE

Videotape or audiotape your presentation. Then listen to the replay of your statement and use the following checklist to assess your persuasiveness.

1. Do you have a case theme?   Yes ____   No ____

2. Are there three points supporting your case theme?

   Yes ____ No ____

3. Are there facts supporting each of your three points?

   Point #1: Yes ____   No ____   Not enough ____

   Point #2: Yes ____   No ____   Not enough ____

   Point #3: Yes ____   No ____   Not enough ____

4. Observe your use of language:

   a. Is it everyday language? Yes ___ No ___ Some ___

   b. Is there any jargon? Yes ___ No ___ Some ___

   c. Do you clearly and simply explain technical/unfamiliar terms? Yes ___ No___ Sometimes ___

5. Observe your use of phrasing:

   a. Do you express one thought per phrase?

       Yes ____ No ____ Sometimes ____

   b. Are your phrases to the point?

       Yes ____ No ____ Sometimes ____

   c. Are your phrases clear and easy to understand?

       Yes ____ No ____ Sometimes ____

   d. Do your thoughts follow logically?

       Yes ____ No ____ Sometimes ____

6. Are your points ordered for effect?

   Yes ____ No ____ Sometimes ____

7. Are the people or things you are presenting ordered for effect?

   Yes ____ No ____ Sometimes ____

8. Have you provided umbrella statements to introduce topics?

   Yes ____ No ____ Sometimes ____

9. Have you provided umbrella statements to reintroduce topics?

   Yes ____ No ____ Sometimes ____

10. Have you inoculated your audience against other arguments or different points of view? Disclosed weaknesses?

    Yes ____ No ____ Sometimes ____

11. Have you used rhetorical questions?

    Yes ____ No ____ Sometimes ____

12. Is your conclusion explicit?

    Yes ____ No ____ Sometimes ____

With the preceding observations in mind, note the corrections you feel are necessary to improve your use of logic and structure to persuade. Use the logic and structure techniques checklist to help you figure out how to make the necessary corrections.

The Seventh Step:
Win with Emotion

Emotions—you can't see them, taste them, touch them, or smell them, yet they are the single most powerful force of persuasion. Emotions—without them, there is no juice, no intensity to what you say. Your words are dull and lifeless.

PLODDING WORDS NEVER JUROR HEART WON: THE FATE OF THE O. J. SIMPSON PROSECUTION

Prosecution's case in the O. J. Simpson trial suffered seriously from lack of emotion: ". . . what was almost *totally lacking* from both prosecutors' [Marcia Clark and Christopher Darden] arguments was any imagination, or eloquence, or oratorical style. Nothing is more effective in driving home an important point than a colorful and well-chosen example, metaphor, or even a humorous story. The virtual absence of soaring oratory by the prosecutors—their very few attempts at a colorful example or parable . . . were banal and dull—showed that both had the mentality of journeyman lawyers, ill equipped to have been thrust on center stage in what the media called "the trial of the century."[1]

Emotions—with them, you can move mountains, conquer worlds, and convince others of whatever you want. Successful trial lawyers are those who know best how to stir up jurors' emotions, to touch their hearts and souls. The great trial lawyers know a trial is never won on the basis of pure logic; people need emotions to sway their minds.

257

CASE IN POINT

Former justice of the Pennsylvania Supreme Court, Michael Musmanno won sixty of his first sixty-four cases. Musmanno, widely respected among his peers, credited much of his success to his awareness of the emotional nature of people:

"More people "feel" their way than think their way through life. The basic emotions can never be obliterated or submerged, and to ignore them in a speech to the jury is to display an unawareness of reality; for every case is a slice of raw life boiled, broiled, and roasted over the fires which generate from the friction and clash between human hates and human loves."[2]

So why the six preceding chapters? If emotions are so powerful, why not cut to the chase? Because emotions are so powerful that only when respected, harnessed, and focused can you use them in service of your argument. It takes all the insights, skills, and techniques of the past chapters to provide a foundation solid enough for you to effectively work with emotions.

How Lawyers Use Emotion to Get the Jurors to Believe in the Rightness of Their Cause

The more strongly jurors believe in the rightness of a lawyer's cause, the more likely they are not only to reward the lawyer with a winning verdict, but to give that lawyer all he/she is asking for and then some. Knowing this, good trial lawyers realize it is imperative to engage the jurors' emotions. But how? How do you engage something so elusive?

If logic is the language of the conscious mind, emotions are the language of the unconscious mind. Emotions do not follow the laws of logic; emotions are predicated on subjective experiencing. Although subjective experiencing does not lend itself to reasoning, it is susceptible to a reliable set of techniques. These techniques facilitate the jury's subjective association with a lawyer's client or a witness's experience either by directly or indirectly engaging the jurors' own emotions. When the trial lawyer enables the jurors to feel the witness's pain as *their* pain, the witness's outrage as *their* outrage, the lawyer can now convince the jurors of the rightness of the lawyer's position. Gerry Spence speaks for many successful trial lawyers when he states: "To prepare mentally for it [a trial], I concentrate on the justice of my client's case, on my anger. I cherish it, contain it. Feel it . . . If lawyers cannot feel their own anger rising out of the injustice imposed upon their client, how can they expect the jury to feel it and to render justice? . . . The lawyer who *thinks* the words but does not *feel* the words will seem disingenuous to jurors who themselves feel, but who, despite his words, are able to sense that the lawyer does not."[3]

If a lawyer fails to engage the jurors' emotions, the jurors can easily remain uninvolved with the client's plight and therefore susceptible to opposing counsel's arguments.

Emotion, which comes from the Latin *emovere*, means to move away, or to move greatly. Given that decisions are first made emotionally, then backed up logically, your primary objective in getting your way is to literally move people away from their present point of view over to your point of view. To accomplish that, you must indeed move them greatly.

(MURDERING) FROGS INTO (SEXUALLY VICTIMIZED) PRINCES: THE WONDROUS TRANSFORMATION OF THE MENENDEZ BROTHERS

"Opening statements were as riveting as anything I've seen on TV. I was glued to the edge of my seat. I think I forgot to breathe for an hour and a half! Prosecuting attorney Lester Kuriyama didn't have anything surprising to say. His comments were brief and to the point about how cold and calculating and greedy he intended to prove the defendants were. But defense attorney Leslie Abramson spelled it right out, saying, 'The question isn't *who* murdered Jose and Mary Menendez, but *why* they were murdered.' She proceeded to give us quite a detailed description of the years of mental, emotional, physical, and sexual abuse supposedly suffered by the boys . . . for so many years that they felt they had no alternative in the end but to kill their parents in "self-defense."[4]

Defense lawyer Leslie Abramson engaged the jurors' emotions in creating her case theme, whereas prosecuting attorney Lester Kuriyama relied on a more prosaic presentation of the facts. It doesn't work! Emotions are integral to decision making.

It is easy to see how emotions are important and can be used effectively when a plaintiff's lawyer, for example, argues a personal injury case or a wrongful death action. A doctor mistakenly removing a healthy kidney from a man's body rather than the cancerous kidney evokes an immediate emotional reaction. Jurors can easily relate to and understand the man's distress. The importance of emotions and how to use them effectively is much less obvious in a case involving complex business law, a battle, say, between two corporations over a copyright infringement that involves millions of dollars but leaves the average juror cold. And that is indeed a problem. Leaving the juror cold will lose the case.

It is in the business situation and similar seemingly nonemotional types of situations that the use of emotions is the most crucial, because only by using emotions will you get people to relate to what you have to say in a meaningful way. Good trial lawyers are expert at transforming the most apparently bloodless business cases into stories about human beings with lots of emotional appeal.

A THIEF ON WALL STREET: THE CASE OF THE UNJUSTLY ACCUSED

Fred H. Bartlit, Jr., representing Dun & Bradstreet, Inc., in the previously mentioned antitrust lawsuit initiated by National Business Lists, gave a brilliant demonstration of the use of emotions in a business case. The antitrust arguments revolved around such issues as the definition of a competitive market in the areas of credit information and business lists. These are not areas that have emotional appeal for the vast majority of jurors.

Rather than argue the case in terms of such impersonal economic issues, Bartlit redefined this complex case into a simple formula with direct emotional appeal: that National Business Lists, had, in fact, been operating their business since its inception twenty-five years ago on information stolen from Dun & Bradstreet. The emotional message Bartlit reinforced over and over was: "So they've [National Business Lists] been stealing from us all these years and now they turn around and accuse us of being the bad guys? No way!"[5]

A jury can easily identify with the outrage of being unjustly accused. It's happened to every one of us at some point in our lives. Few jurors, however, can relate in any meaningful way to two major corporations battling over an antitrust issue. It is just too far away from the jurors' daily cares and personal concerns.

If people remain uninvolved and emotionally distanced from your concerns and issues, it will be extremely difficult for you to convince them. That is why no matter how difficult it may be to translate business and other such seemingly nonemotional issues into terms that can be subjectively experienced by the people you wish to persuade, it is vital to do so.

LEARN TO USE EMOTIONS AS LAWYERS DO: TO GAIN SYMPATHY FOR YOUR CAUSE

Emotions operate in two basic ways in trial work: they gain sympathy for the lawyer's client and/or his/her cause, and they enable jurors to experience the case in subjective fashion.

A note of caution: "Sympathy" in this context does not mean "feel sorry for"; rather it means to support, be in accord with, to approve of a person or his cause. Making people feel pity is not an effective persuasive technique: Getting them to approve your point of view is.

Emotions focus attention onto specific aspects of a situation rather than on others: emotions determine what people will take into account, and what they ignore.

CASE IN POINT

Every person is a combination of different aspects. A man may be, for example, attractive, intelligent, and witty, yet at the same time may be somewhat dishonest and often aggressive. If you like this person, for example, you notice his good points: how handsome he is, how intelligent, how witty, and you will dismiss his occasional dishonesty and frequent aggressivity as, "Oh, that's just Bob." If, however, you don't like Bob, his good points still exist, but your *attention* is focused so that it fits with your emotion; you primarily notice his dishonesty and his aggressivity, for example, and are quite oblivious to his looks, intelligence and wit: "So he's good-looking and smart, who cares? He's a flake and too pushy."

Emotions make some facts more salient than others. When jurors do not relate in sympathetic fashion to a lawyer's client or the cause, they will tend to notice arguments that support their negative feelings—and opposing counsel will win. Good trial lawyers make sure that the jurors relate emotionally and in sympathetic fashion to their client and cause. Jurors will then notice those facts and arguments that tend to support their positive feeling about the client and will dismiss those that are contrary to that feeling.

How do you get people to be sympathetic to your cause? Jury studies have clearly demonstrated that the most effective position for an advocate to demonstrate is allegiance and zeal for his/her client's cause.

CASE IN POINT

Mr. Cochran's zeal for his client was clear: "Johnnie Cochran's final summation to the jury was his best performance at the trial. Contrasted to the uninspiring and flat delivery of the two prosecutors, Cochran spoke with more style, flair, and, though the facts were against him . . . more passion."[6]

If you are to win people's approval of your cause, then *you* must approve of it. Jurors are favorably impressed by an attorney who is "demonstrably enthusiastic"[7]: a trial lawyer cannot be lukewarm about his/her case; if the lawyer is, the jurors will be too!

IGNITING THE FIRE: THE ROLE OF PASSION IN THE O. J. SIMPSON DEFENSE

In the O. J. Simpson trial, for example, prosecutors were altogether too lukewarm in their presentation of their case. This made it very difficult for the jurors to get sufficiently "fired up" to move over to prosecution's point of view: ". . . a lawyer cannot expect a jury to buy his cause if they detect that he does not believe in it *completely* himself. There is no question in my mind that Clark and Darden completely believed in their case. The problem is they didn't clearly show it to the jury. Both of them were far too laid-back and casual in their presentation. There was no fire, no passion, at all. Cochran and Scheck, the ones who should have had much more difficulty summoning up fire and passion (since their client was guilty and they had to know it), spoke with more flame than the two prosecutors. In fact, throughout the trial, the sad irony was that the defense attorneys seemed to be fighting harder for injustice than the prosecutors were for justice."[8]

Your passionate belief in your cause is what inspires others to believe. Studies in social power conclude that a person's ability to influence others increases with his/her increasing certainty in his/her own opinion.[9]

Technique #82: How to express sincerity to favorably influence people

There is a catch, however. The jurors must perceive the lawyer's belief in the client's cause as *sincere*. This is why a blatant emotional appeal does not work: It is not perceived as sincere. Times have changed; dramatic gestures and expressions of passionate belief are no longer accepted as sincere in the courtroom, largely due to the changes in the media. Film and television require more subdued playing than does theatre, due to the size of the images on the screen and the use of microphones. We have become accustomed to more restrained expression of emotion and are likely to be uncomfortable with grand gestures.

F. LEE BAILEY: TOO MANY TEARS FOR PATTY HEARST

Although F. Lee Bailey has certainly done well as a trial lawyer, his style may not be as persuasive now as it has been in the past: The jurors in the Patty Hearst trial (1976) "reported great displeasure with the dramatic and overbearing deportment of her attorney, F. Lee Bailey; in the end, Patty Hearst did not fare well in their verdicts."[10]

A trial lawyer walks a fine line: On the one hand, jurors do not approve of a reserved, passive approach, but neither do they appreciate a lawyer expressing commitment to the client in overly dramatic fashion.

Successful trial lawyers convey sincerity in a way jurors appreciate and understand by suiting their expression of emotion to the deed, as described in Chapter 3. This is how a trial lawyer avoids melodrama, all the while assuring an attitude of dedication and commitment to the client's cause.

Technique #83: How to use positive emotions to win people over

Positive emotions are much more attractive to a jury than negative emotions. A trial lawyer will effectively engender sympathetic feelings for his/her client and/or his/her cause by appealing to positive emotions such as love, pride, or devotion to an ideal. Appealing to negative or hostile emotions by attacking opposing counsel or their client or by sarcastically ripping to shreds opposing counsel's case do not engender sympathy for a lawyer's client and are generally avoided by good trial lawyers. Jury studies systematically show that jurors tend to be highly critical and disapproving of attorneys who indulge in such disparagement. Overaggressiveness has been repeatedly pointed out as the advocate's most common flaw.

This suggests a dangerous misunderstanding of the effect of negative emotions. Negative emotions rarely persuade; rather, negative emotions make people uncomfortable, and they tend to avoid them, especially when the negativity seems disproportionate.

A WITNESS BLOWS HIS COOL, BLOWS HIS TESTIMONY, AND BLOWS AWAY THE SIMPSON JURORS' APPROVAL

Ron Shipp, one of the prosecution's witnesses in the O. J. Simpson trial, talked about O. J. telling him about dreaming of killing Nicole. On cross-examination, Shipp got frustrated and angry. Juror Armanda Cooley said, "I'm watching this and thinking, *Don't blow it out of the water because we're listening to you. You're emotional now. Come on, what's the matter here? Are you telling us this just because you're mad at him now?*" Juror Carrie Bess concurred with "It looks like he's so angry that he'll say anything to get back at him. Like I'm saying, I was listening to each witness and thinking, *Where are you coming from? Are you going to discredit yourself in here?* . . . So I felt he was a liar."[11] Had Ron Shipp simply kept a more positive outlook through cross examination, he would have retained juror sympathy.

This is not to say, however, that a lawyer or witness will not have, for example, a moment of honest anger during a trial, or that the jurors will turn against a lawyer who indulges in an occasional sarcastic comment. Both these and other negative emotions have their place; they should not, however, constitute the main emotional thrust of your argument and must be used with great care.

THE POWER OF SHARED EXPERIENCE: HOW LAWYERS CREATE EMOTIONAL RAPPORT WITH THE JURORS AS A BASIS FOR PERSUASION AND HOW YOU CAN DO IT TOO

Good trial lawyers will not only establish rapport through body language, voice, and mirroring, they will also establish rapport emotionally. A trial lawyer seeks to create an emotional alignment between the client's cause and the jurors; the jurors must be able to empathize with the client's plight if they are to be receptive to the lawyer's arguments on his/her behalf.

How do you do it? Emotional rapport is created in much the same way that you created nonverbal rapport, by emphasizing similarities between yourself and those you seek to persuade. Remember the sequence: similarity, familiarity, rapport, trust. Emphasize the similarities between your cause and what goes on in the jurors' daily lives, between your concerns and their own concerns. People like what is similar to themselves; people feel comfortable with what is familiar to them. Speak to people of *shared experience*.

SATISFACTION (NOT) GUARANTEED: THE CITY OF NEW YORK AND THE DEFECTIVE SUBWAY CAR RIP-OFF

Arthur L. Liman, representing the New York City Transit Authority in their and the City of New York's action against Pullman Incorporated and Rockwell International Corporation over the purchase of defective subway cars, spoke of shared experience in explaining breach of warranty:

"Now, this is a case, as the court indicated, of breach of contract and breach of warranty. The term 'warranty' is familiar to anyone who has ever bought a refrigerator or a television set. Here we are dealing with warranties on a different type of product and a different consumer. Here the consumer was the City of New York and the Transit Authority, and the product was subway cars."[12]

By defining "warranty" in terms of refrigerators and television sets, Liman established the commonality between his client's concern and the jurors' daily concerns, he paved the way for a bond between his client and the jurors.

The emotional bond is developed roughly as follows: The juror thinks: "I got it; it's like when I buy a TV set, brand new, and it falls apart, and the guy won't fix it—even though I've got a warranty. OK, I know what that feels like—it feels like I've just been ripped off, I hate it. So this guy's subway cars broke, and the manufacturer won't fix them, even though he's got a warranty—that's awful!" Now you have emotional rapport, based simply on shared experience.

A trial lawyer will establish emotional rapport in an opening statement and will then continue to use shared experiences throughout the trial, both to keep the jurors reminded of their emotional tie to the client's cause and to get them back over to the lawyer's side anytime the lawyer feels the jurors are tuning in more to opposing counsel. If you are in a situation in which you are trying to uphold your point of view in the face of others expounding different points of view, people may drift away from your point of view as they are swayed by that of others. Use the technique of shared experiences anytime you need to hook those you are trying to convince back in emotionally. If you give people an emotional basis for relating to your cause, you'll find they are much more willing to let themselves be convinced by you.

LEARN TO USE STORY TELLING AS LAWYERS DO TO PERSUADE PEOPLE

Story telling is mentioned repeatedly by the great trial lawyers as a reliable and necessary technique to get jurors on their side. But why? What is it that you can accomplish so successfully through story telling, and why is it absolutely vital to convincing people?

Technique #84: How to capture people's attention

First of all, a story gets the jurors' attention. We all love a story; jurors are no exception. People are far more likely to sit up and listen to a story than to a Spartan listing of the facts. A story is more interesting. Story telling, which is an ancient art, has been reinforced significantly in this century by the media. Both television and film use story telling extensively as a way of communicating ideas. People are thus highly familiar with and accepting of the story format. Although story telling is used in its most elaborate form in opening statements, good trial lawyers will use story telling throughout a trial, in encapsulated form, whenever they sense the jurors' attention wandering. Capture your listeners' attention by telling them a story and keep their attention in the telling of it.

Technique #85: How to organize your facts in an emotionally meaningful way

Second, telling a story is a way trial lawyers use to organize what they have to say so that the jurors can make an emotional connection to it. Material that is not organized into story format is difficult to experience emotionally. For example, many people find avant garde music or art disconcerting because these media do not tell a story. People find it hard to

A KID'S BICYCLE TAKES A $8,235,000 SPILL: SCHAFFNER VS. THE SCHWINN BICYCLE COMPANY AND THE RAILROAD

Philip H. Corboy, one of the acknowledged "greats" of the courtroom, organized his facts into a meaningful emotional framework, a story, in a particularly moving opening statement. Corboy was representing Danny Schaffner, a young man who was permanently mentally and physically disabled as a result of a fall from a bicycle, in a suit against the Schwinn Bicycle Company and a railroad, the Chicago and North Western Transportation Company. The facts Corboy was presenting were that as Danny and his friends pedaled over a bumpy railroad crossing with which they were very familiar, the front wheel of Danny's bike came off; he flew off his bike and hit the pavement, and as a result was crippled for life. Here's how Corboy presented those facts:

"This is the story of a typical family, had its ups and had its downs, had its heartbreaks, it had its good times, and had its bad times. But it was a normal everyday American, mid-American type of family. Perry and Jean Schaffner met sometime before 1953 where they both lived in Chicago, both attended high school in Chicago. They fell in love, got married in 1953, and they started to raise a family. They moved in 1960 out to a far north suburb, as a matter of fact, even into a different county called Lake County, where they began to raise their children in Highland Park, Illinois. There were three children born of that marriage. Terry was born in 1956. James was born in 1958. And Daniel, the boy who has been injured was born in 1961, approximately a year after they moved out into the suburb."

Corboy continued, detailing the ordinary events of Danny's young life, until he got to the day of the fall. He told the jury in vivid and specific detail every moment of that day, taking them with him through his description down every street and through every turn the boys made as they bicycled along on their way to a Saturday afternoon movie, creating a virtual imaginary reenactment of that ride. Finally Corboy's story led him to the crucial moments: "As Danny got on to these tracks [at the railroad crossing], he started bouncing and his bike went out of control. All of a sudden he was bouncing and he eventually got to the other side of the tracks, and he was completely off the tracks when his bike disassembled and his bike came apart and he fell to the ground. When he fell to the ground it was immediately apparent to his pals who came up to him that he was hurt, and his pals asked him what had happened, and he does not respond as to what occurred on the crossing because he does not know. But he did say, "My shoulder hurts," and he said it loudly, and he was crying, and then he said, "My shoulder hurts," and it was lighter, and then he didn't talk anymore. He went into a coma."[13]

enjoy these art forms because they cannot connect to them on a feeling level. In the courtroom, there is a good deal more at stake than enjoyment. Much of the jury's decision will be based on purely emotional considerations, so it is critical that the lawyer make it easy for the jurors to connect with the client's cause. Help those you are trying to convince make the necessary emotional connections with what you have to say by organizing your facts into a story. (See page 267.)

Corboy skillfully organized the facts into a story framework with which the jurors could easily connect. He even stated right at the outset that this was a story, the story of an average American family. Notice how Danny's physical and mental condition assumes much more emotional relevance when it is described within the context of his life story. The jurors can readily identify with a young boy's growing up in normal suburbia and can feel the impact of his sudden impairment more vividly, placed as it is against the backdrop of that environment, than they could simply hearing it described in and of itself. Either way, the event is tragic, but Danny's fall is more *moving*, therefore more persuasive, when it is woven into a story format.

Just about any event can be placed into a story format, given your willingness to be imaginative and creative. The story's persuasive power is well worth the effort such an endeavor might take.

Technique #86: How to facilitate people's vivid, vicarious experiencing of an event or situation

The third function of story telling in the courtroom is to create a reenactment of any given event so rich in sensory detail that the jury literally sees, hears, and feels that event. The trial lawyer's goal is to make the description so vivid that the jurors feel the client's distress as their own and are moved by it. Given the intangibility of emotions, how is this done?

By addressing the senses. The senses, as we discussed in Chapter 3, are the gateway to the emotions. Story telling provides you with an excellent vehicle for accessing the emotions via the senses. Talk in terms of how things feel. What is your experience like? What is the nature of the thing that you want to convince others of? Is it warm, cold, soft, hard, calm, excited, dark, light? Is it sudden, slow, tearing, searing, harsh? What does it feel like, look like, taste like, smell like, sound like? Use the color words described in Chapter 3 to help you express how things feel.

Case in Point

Here's how a trial lawyer might use story-telling in presenting the following facts: "Dr. Peters, a thirty-two-year-old pediatrician, was run over and killed by a yellow Pontiac in the parking lot of the local hospital."

In and of themselves, the facts are sad, a life was lost, but they are not particularly heartrending. After all, we all have to die sometime. Now, reorganizing the facts into a story, using descriptive words to appeal to the senses, here's what the trial lawyer might make of the facts: "Dr. Peters, a thirty-two-year-old pediatrician, leaves her office, as usual, around 6:00 P.M. Friday evening. She strolls through the near-empty parking lot, pleased with the way her day has gone—her seven-year-old patient on Ward III is responding nicely to the new leukemia medication. Dr. Peters stops for a moment to chat with a colleague about the new medical center that's soon to be built and then continues to walk toward her car, feeling good, tired but happy, enjoying the warm August sun of late afternoon, when all of a sudden, seemingly out of nowhere, a yellow Pontiac comes hurtling straight at her and—that's all. No more Dr. Peters. Just a limp lifeless body lying bloody on the hard concrete of a parking lot."

That's a story. It has the emotional impact the trial lawyer needs to persuade. The lawyer has used descriptive words to engage the jurors' emotions via their senses, so that they feel Dr. Peter's experience, vicariously relive it, and are thus receptive to the lawyer's interpretation of the facts.

Facts in and of themselves rarely win anything. An emotional presentation of the facts does. The more concrete and specific your descriptive details, the more persuasive your story telling. People connect much more easily with concrete and specific details: Such details give immediacy and reality to your description. (See page 270.)

Williams's use of specific detail pulls the listener into the story, making it real, making it believable. He doesn't just say "the shore of Lake Orta," it's the *western* shore." The rain is not simply "torrential," it's "*driving torrential mountain* rain." The members of the mission were not simply "hidden in a church," they were hidden "*in a small hole in the roof underneath the ceiling.*" They didn't live over the very heads of the Nazi troops for "about a week," they lived there for "*five days and five nights.*"

All these details make it much easier for people to create visual and sensory experiences in their imaginations, allowing them to experience

NAZIS IN THE CHURCH: PROVING THE INNOCENCE OF LIEUTENANT ALDO ICARDI

Edward Williams, a venerable trial lawyer, could tell stories that would keep jurors spellbound. Williams's opening statement in the 1956 *U.S.* vs. *Icardi* case is a classic example of his story-telling prowess. In a nutshell, Lieutenant Aldo Icardi was accused of killing a Major William Holohan; both men were volunteers parachuted, with others, behind enemy lines in Italy during World War II on a special mission, called the "Chrysler Mission." In defending Icardi, Williams used story telling extensively. Notice the use of concrete, specific detail in the following passage, taken from the opening statement in which Williams is describing the events leading up to the time of Major Holohan's death:

"The next day they [the members of the Chrysler Mission] rowed back to the western shore of Lake Orta, because it had been shown to them that this was not a safe hiding place. They went up into the mountains and lay there one whole night in a driving torrential mountain rain. On November 1 they abandoned the mountains. They went to the city of Grassona and there one of the same priests hid them again. This time he hid them in his church in a small hole in the roof underneath the ceiling. After they were hidden some Nazi troops came into Grassona. They searched every nook and cranny, and forty of them lived in the church underneath the Americans for five days and five nights . . ."[14]

the event you are describing, the thing it is you want to persuade them of, as if they had been there, as if it had happened to them, as if it mattered to them. Such powerful emotional identification is truly persuasive.

Technique #87: How to use well-known myths and stories with built-in emotional appeal as "hooks"

You can organize a set of facts in an emotionally significant and meaningful way by placing those facts within the larger context of an individual's life, as in the examples previously given, or you can organize a set of facts to the same effect by casting them in the familiar and recognizable lines of a classic story or character.

Trial lawyers frequently use classic stories or characters to guide them in transforming their cases into riveting stories. David and Goliath, Cinderella, Beauty and the Beast, the story of Cain and Abel, the story of

Job, for example, are stories common to our culture, stories we grew up with and understand. On a deeper level, these stories and characters are archtypal; they represent prototypical experiences common to all humans and are to be found across cultures and across epochs. Such classic stories tap a profound emotional dimension that people respond to almost instinctively. People know, when they hear such a story, for example, who is the good guy and who is the bad guy; the moral of the story is built in, as it were.

CASE IN POINT

For example, James F. Neal's defense of Dr. George Nichopoulous, in the Elvis Presley case cited earlier, was based on the archetypal story of the Good Samaritan. By defining his case along archetypal story lines, Neal took advantage of already existing powerful emotional triggers. The Good Samaritan is a culturally and societally accepted "good guy"; Dr. Nichopolous became a "good guy" by association.

Structure your story so that it suggests archetypal characters or story lines. Identify your client's cause with that of the "good guys"; the justification for that definition will be inherent to the story.

Technique #88: Use analogies and similes to help people relate emotionally to your point

Analogies and similes are frequently used by trial lawyers to create links between ideas they want to get across and the jurors' life experience. Analogies compare ideas or situations that are identical in some ways but not in others; for example, cooperation on a surgical team may be compared to that on a baseball team. Most people are familiar with baseball; few are intimate with the details of surgery. The comparison between the familiar and the unfamiliar allows the unfamiliar to be understood, at least in terms of what is identical to the two situations, in this example—cooperation. (See page 272.)

Similes liken one thing to another using a comparative word such as "like" or "as." For example, a common simile for psychotherapy is: "Psychotherapy is like a bridge between where you are and where you want to be." Not everyone has personal knowledge of psychotherapy, but just about everybody knows what a bridge is. By comparing therapy to a

EXPOSING A NUCLEAR DEATHTRAP: SILKWOOD VS. KERR-MCGEE

Karen Silkwood, who worked with plutonium in a Kerr-McGee-owned plant, had been on the verge of disclosing the poor health and safety conditions at the plant, which put workers at great risk of contamination and of developing plutonium-induced cancer, when she was killed in an automobile accident. Karen's father, Bill Silkwood, brought suit against Kerr-McGee on behalf of his grandchildren. The true purpose of the suit was to win such a large award that such poor health conditions would never be allowed in any atomic facility ever again.

One of the key experts for the plaintiff was Dr. John Gofman. Dr. Gofman, a physician and nuclear chemist, had to explain to an Oklahoma City jury in terms they would clearly understand and could relate to how infinitesimal amounts of plutonium in the lungs causes lung cancer. "So, when people say a small amount of this won't hurt you [which Kerr-McGee had alleged], that is so absurd one wonders how anyone can think it. Expecting that an alpha particle will go through a cell and not do horrible damage is like ramming an ice pick through a fine Swiss watch, or shooting a machine gun through a television set and saying it will function just fine."[15] Plutonium and alpha particles are substances most people never encounter. Ice picks, fine watches, machine guns, and television sets are commonplace. Providing the jurors with such comparisons allowed them to fully appreciate and understand the damage radiation causes and therefore made it possible for them to find for the Silkwood family.

bridge, the therapist ties into common experience (the bridge) and makes it easier for the lay person to understand an otherwise complex idea (psychotherapy).

We use analogies and similes constantly in our daily life without thinking about them as specific communicative tools. All you have to do in order to use analogies and similes powerfully is use them deliberately. How? Take something from common experience and compare your specific fact to that common experience. For example, imagine your specific fact is represented by the word "it" in the following statements: "It's like casting pearls before swine," "It's the difference between night and day," "It's clear as day," "She took to it like a fish to water," "It's like a dog barking up the wrong tree," and so forth.

Analogies and similes are critical to successful trial work for the simple reason that jurors come from a variety of life situations and may or may not have had any experience with the issues in the case. Analogies and similes, by comparing the legal issue to something commonly understood and experienced, allow the jurors to relate and connect emotionally to the issue.

A HOLLYWOOD MOVIE SET ILLUMINATES THE TRUTH: HALLINAN VS. SAN FRANCISCO ET AL.

Terry Hallinan, one of San Francisco's most reputed trial lawyers, used an elaborate and compelling analogy in order to explain to the jury how to evaluate the conflicting contentions of eyewitnesses for the defense. Hallinan was representing the plaintiff, his son, in *Terence Hallinan v. Michael J. Brady, City and County of San Francisco, and Norbert Butierrez:*

"Some years ago I was in another city and a friend took me to an establishment that he deemed would be interesting. We walked down a curious kind of street with old-fashioned houses on each side and strange-looking, almost artificial-looking trees, and there was no life to it, no traffic along a cobbled street. No birds sang in the trees. There was no sound or sign of life behind the windows. And then we came to one of the houses about a block and a half down, and the door was open and behind it were struts, two-by-fours, holding up the wall. It wasn't a house at all. It was the facade of a house, a moving picture set. We were on a Hollywood lot. I didn't have to go back to the other houses to find out that they were facades, too. And you don't have to go back and examine everything that these men said to convince yourself that you can't put a moment's reliance on any single thing that they uttered."[16]

The comparison between a facade masquerading as a house and a verbal front masquerading as truth is a powerful one. Use analogies and similes to give those you are seeking to persuade a means of connecting emotionally to your points, by comparing those points to something commonly understood and experienced.

Technique #89: Use analogies and similes to give focus and impact to an issue

In addition, analogies and similes enable trial lawyers to focus an issue strongly so that their points are communicated effectively. (See page 274.)

The idea of necrophilia is horrific to most people. With this simple analogy, Ms. Fairstein was able to galvanize the jurors' emotions by con-

THE CASE OF THE NECROPHILIAC DENTIST

District Attorney Linda Fairstein, in prosecuting Marvin Teicher, a dentist accused of making a number of his women patients engage in sexual contact with him when they were in a helpless anesthesia-related drugged state, compared Dr. Teicher's actions to those of a necrophiliac—with the difference that in Dr. Teicher's case, the bodies were still warm.[17]

necting Dr. Teicher's behavior to something already established as nefarious in our culture. Her point was communicated most effectively.

When you use an analogy to help people identify with a point, in a sense, the analogy does the work of persuasion for you. People already have feelings hooked into the analogy: necrophiliacs are sick or bad people, houses on a movie set are without substance and therefore useless in the real world. Those feelings are transferred to your point, as long as your analogy is an accurate one.

> *Technique #90: Select analogies and similes that have emotional appeal for your specific listener*

Selecting appropriate analogies and similes can be delicate, especially when dealing with highly complicated technical issues.

A ROLLS ROYCE PROMISED, AN EDSEL DELIVERED: HOW ROCKWELL INTERNATIONAL LOST TO THE NEW YORK CITY TRANSIT AUTHORITY

Arthur L. Liman, in the previously cited case of the New York City Transit Authority against Rockwell International Corporation, chose his analogies and similes skillfully when he compared subway cars provided by Rockwell, which the Transit Authority claimed were defective, to Edsels:

"To give you the case in a nutshell, the proof here will show that when the defendants were selling and promoting the R-46 [subway car] to the city, they promoted it as if it were a Rolls Royce of the subway industry, fast, safe, quiet, and long-lasting. We will show you that they didn't deliver a Rolls Royce. They delivered an Edsel, a lemon, a car whose undercarriage is disintegrating, literally."[18]

Not only were the engineering matters discussed in regard to the subway cars difficult to understand, they were virtually impossible for the average person to connect to *emotionally*. How many of us can relate on a feeling level to a discussion of cracks in the transom arms of subway cars? The Rolls Royce and the Edsel, however, are commonly held cultural symbols of excellence and failure, respectively. *Excellence and failure* are easy to relate to on an emotional level.

Later, during the course of his closing argument for this case, Liman, who uses analogy and simile masterfully, compared the defenses given by Rockwell's attorneys to mechanical rabbits:

"I call them rabbits because they remind me of the mechanical rabbits that they have in tracks where they have dog races, and the dogs are let loose and they chase after the mechanical rabbit and they expend a lot of energy, and of course, they never catch it, and they come away very, very confused. And they have set a lot of rabbits loose in this courtroom and I intend now to deal with them and show that they are nothing more than that. They are nothing but phony alibis."[19]

The analogy of mechanical rabbits is wonderfully vivid and readily engages the senses. Because it refers to something most people in our culture understand and relate to, it gives emotional focus to the jurors as they deliberate, a focus directed by Liman himself. This is a sterling technique and one well worth developing.

Know your audience! Think about which analogies and similes will have greatest emotional appeal to those you are seeking to persuade. Beyond the cultural myths and stories we all understand and relate to emotionally, there are plenty of culturally shared experiences and situations to draw from, such as Liman's Edsel and mechanical rabbits. As you go about your daily life, build your personal "treasure chest" of emotionally powerful analogies and similes, ready to pull out right when you need them most.

Technique #91: Avoid the problems inherent in using analogies

As powerful as they are, there are problems in using analogies, as many a trial lawyer has found to his/her regret, and these must be addressed.

Make sure your analogy is accurate   First of all, if a trial lawyer's analogy isn't 100 percent accurate, opposing counsel can take the analogy and turn it against the lawyer. If you're using the analogy of a football team, for example, you would want to be aware that although a football team can be comprised of people who readily and willingly support one another through the game, it can also be composed of a "prima donna" quarterback and some disgruntled players.

Be sure you turn your analogy inside out before using it, verifying that no matter how it's turned around, it still works for you. A movie set can be nothing more than a facade, for example, no matter how you look at it. There are no redeeming aspects to an Edsel. These are good analogies given the context of the cases. Select your analogies with as much care.

Avoid overstatement   Second, a trial lawyer must be careful not to overstate or overemotionalize the case with the analogy; this serves only to give ammunition to opposing counsel. Be sure you can back up your analogy with a detailed factual argument. If Ms. Fairstein had not been able to present facts that genuinely upheld her analogy of necrophiliac, if, for example, the women Dr. Teicher had sex with were awake and aware, even if not consenting, such a comparison would have been ludicrous. A phony emotional hook is deadly.

Be sure your analogy suits the person you're trying to convince   Third, a trial lawyer always takes great care to suit the analogy to the specific jury he/she is currently addressing. If the person you want to convince is quite young, analogies from the Depression may have little impact; if a group you are addressing is primarily female, sports-oriented analogies may be worthless. Think carefully about what the life experiences of the person or group have been and choose analogies and similes from that life experience.

Choose analogies from your own experience   Last, choose analogies that make sense to *you*. You cannot be persuasive discussing something you know nothing about. Be sure the analogy is one you thoroughly understand and relate to. Don't use an analogy from baseball, for example, if you know nothing about the game. Bear in mind that your sincerity is a prime persuasive tool, and you must sincerely believe in the value of your analogy for it to be effective.

How You Can Use Repetition, Catch Phrases, and "Money Words" as Lawyers Do to Reinforce Your Points

Repetition, catch phrases, and "money words" are devices trial lawyers use to reinforce their points. You can't just state your position and expect people to connect emotionally with it on the spot; it won't happen. People need the connection to be reinforced many times and in many ways for it to be strong enough to hold through their decision making. The reason cultural myths, for example, have such power is that we have heard and seen them repeatedly throughout our lives, in a variety of expressive modes. David and Goliath, for example, is a theme repeated in literature, movies, popular songs, stories people tell, jokes, advertisements, and more. Reinforce the emotional connection you want people to make to your points by using the following valuable techniques.

Technique #92: How to use repetition

Repetition may seem like a simplistic technique, but it is a surprisingly effective one. Sheer repetition creates familiarity with an idea or event, and that familiarity leads to liking. We tend to interact often with people and situations we like and avoid those people and situations we dislike. Successful trial lawyers use repetition throughout trial work: repetition of themes, of points, of key arguments, and repetition of *catch phrases*.

Technique #93: How to use catch phrases

Catch phrases are phrases designed to capture the essence of an idea. They are then used over and over again. We are a nation of catch phrases. We tend to speak a great deal in catch phrases:

> We're Number 1.
> The Pepsi Generation.
> We shall overcome.
> Blondes have more fun.
> Buy now, pay later.
> The antidote to civilization.

And so on. It is no accident that advertisers use catch phrases as extensively as they do. Their research has shown how easily people respond to catch phrases and how well people remember a product when it is attached to a catch phrase. Catch phrases have a decidedly useful function: Once defined, everyone knows what they mean, and they can be repeated endlessly to reinforce an idea. (See page 278.)

When trial lawyers refer to their client as "the victim," they are using this technique. Repeated identification of the client as "the victim" will lead the jury to define the client, Mr. Smith, not as a whole person

THE GOOD, THE BAD, AND THE UGLY:
THE NATURE OF LT. COL. OLIVER NORTH'S TESTIMONY

Lt. Col. North used many catch phrases during his testimony, which greatly facilitated the favorable characterization of his actions; for example: "I came here to tell you the truth—the good, the bad and the ugly—and to accept responsibility for that which I did. I will not accept responsibility for that which I did not do."[20] When you find catch phrases to describe your points or ideas, you hook into a powerful ready-made persuasive device.

with a multitude of other roles (father, brother, banker, softball fanatic), but as one thing only: "the victim," which is exactly and precisely what the lawyer wants.

Catch phrases are essentially a way of labeling someone or something with a particular emotional bias so that the people will come to perceive it in the same way. In the aforementioned example, the lawyer labels the client "the victim" deliberately because it is to the lawyer's advantage for the jury to dwell on the *victimhood* of the client, not on his success as a banker or his reputation as a womanizer. Catch phrases can readily be developed out of whatever story you tell to reinforce that story as you continue your presentation, or out of whatever analogy you've used to reinforce that analogy.

CASE IN POINT

Every time Ms. Fairstein, in the previously cited case, referred to Mr. Teicher's sexual activities as "necrophilia," she reminded the jurors of the emotional bias with which she had tagged the sexual activity: completely unacceptable and nefarious. Eventually, it becomes difficult to separate the thing or behavior from the bias of the label.

The persuasiveness of this technique, however, relies on an accurate assessment of what might be a valid catch phrase. You can label to your heart's content; if there isn't enough documentation to substantiate the emotional bias you are trying to establish, the catch phrase either won't take hold or will work against you. It's not about inventing a catch phrase to somehow change things in your presentation to your advantage, but rather using the catch phrase as a way of expressing an emotional truth inherent to the situation or thing you are describing.

The trial lawyer's case theme can be thought of as a special kind of catch phrase. It is a catch phrase or slogan used over and over again which sums up what is going on in the case.

CASE IN POINT

Cochran was particularly gifted at finding and using catch phrases to bring home his case themes: "Right from Cochran's opening statement . . . , the defense said the prosecution's blood evidence was 'contaminated,' and hence their constant 'garbage in, garbage out' argument."[21]

"From Johnnie Cochran's opening statement through his closing argument, he kept telling the jury that in the LAPD's [Los Angeles Police Department] 'obsession to win' it had 'rushed to judgment' . . . The 'rush to judgment' argument was another big theme of the defense's case."[22]

"Cochran argued to the jury (concerning the failed glove demonstration), "If it doesn't fit, you must acquit. . . ."[23]

You can do the same thing with your theme. If you accurately capture the essence of what you are trying to convince others of in your theme and repeat it often, the people you are addressing will come to see the situation as you do, just by the familiarity you have thereby created.

Technique #94: How to use "money words"

In their research, in addition to the idea of catch phrases, advertisers have come up with a concept called "money words." A "money word" is a word that represents something of value for people in a given culture and that is therefore emotionally loaded. It is no accident, for example, that a popular credit card is called "Discover". "Discover" is a money word; discovering things and ideas has great meaning for Americans; we pride ourselves on discovering frontiers and miracle cures, great ballplayers, and missing children. (See page 280.)

The fact that such "money words" became attached to the defense lawyers greatly increased their chances of success: "Most of the Simpson jurors, of course, knew about the 'Dream Team' before they were selected to serve, and undoubtedly continued to hear of this nonsense through

A MYTH THAT BECAME REALITY: THE MAKING OF "THE DREAM TEAM"

"Dream Team" is the potent association of two money words: "dream" and "team." Both of these are concepts dear to the American heart, akin to Mom, country, and apple pie. The association of the two had previously been used only to describe incredibly gifted athletes: According to Vincent Bugliosi, "The term 'Dream Team' is only properly used to describe the best in the field, like the 1994 Olympic basketball Dream Team consisting of players like Michael Jordan, Larry Bird, and Magic Johnson. . . . The 1995 U.S. Davis Cup tennis team was called the Dream Team, but the team consisted of Pete Sampras and Andre Agassi, the two top tennis players in the world."

Bugliosi had his doubts that the defense lawyers constituted such a team (others had their doubts that the defense lawyers even constituted a team): "The question I had at the time—and the trial only confirmed my need to ask it—was, how do you take a lawyer who has never tried a murder case before [Shapiro], another who is not even primarily a criminal lawyer but a civil lawyer who may have never won a murder case before a jury in his career [Cochran], and another who lost the last big case he tried over twenty years ago, and convert them into the Dream Team, the best that money can buy?" Whether the defense lawyers constituted a veritable Dream Team or not, that is how they were perceived: "It had become holy writ—and to my knowledge, virtually all members of the media accepted the apparently unassailable verity—that Shapiro, Cochran, and Bailey were the very best lawyers in the country that money could buy. They were 'the Dream Team,' as almost all of the media started to call them, and no one was going to change that. It had become official."[24]

conjugal visits and, as I've suggested, osmosis. And consciously or unconsciously, people want to be on the side of the celebrity, the side of glamour. That's just the way it is. . . There's another related but more subtle phenomenon at play here, and it's that usually, people see what they expect to see or want to see, not what they are actually seeing."[25]

What you expect to see directly affects what you do indeed see. Expectation is such a strong factor in human perception that scientists have had to devise the "double blind" technique of experiments in order to nullify the power of a researcher's expectation. "How could this tendency to see what we expect to see contribute to the verdict in the Simpson case? It is likely that the Simpson jury perceived the courtroom performances of the defense attorneys as being more effective than they were because they saw what they expected to see. And what they expected to see was the defense lawyers scoring a lot of points in their questioning of witnesses (whether they were doing so or not) *because* they were the Dream Team. If they were the Dream Team, they must be scoring a lot of points, and this all helps add up to reasonable doubt."[26] Such is the immense power of money words.

People pay particular attention to money words: A money word alerts them to a situation or event that has emotional relevance for them. The money words useful to trial lawyers are discover, health, easy, proven, results, safety, love. You can find other money words by noticing the words advertisers tend to use repeatedly. Whenever it is possible for you to use one of these words rather than another similar word, use it. You are taking advantage of a word that already has intrinsic power, and you can make that power work in your favor.

How Lawyers Use Personalizations to Get a Juror or Witness to Relate Subjectively to a Point

The most valuable money words of all are "you," and a person's name. There really is no better attention-getter than a person's name. Try this with friends and family. Insert the other party's name every so often in the course of a conversation and notice how the person with whom you are conversing seems to perk up at those moments and pay more attention. Notice how *you* instantly perk up and pay attention when you hear your name called. The word "you" serves a similar function.

The word "you" or your name symbolizes yourself, your very being. The mention of either one of them demands attention, if only on a survival level. A good trial lawyer uses the word "you" or a person's name to personalize the proceedings, to make the presentation of the case more immediate, more relevant to the jurors. The lawyer is, in a sense, forcing jurors to assess not whether *X* statement is true for others (a thought that may or may not be of interest to a juror), but to assess whether statement *X* applies directly to them. For example, in questioning a prospective juror, saying, "People often feel hesitant about discussing such things" is much less effective than saying "You may feel hesitant about discussing such things—people often do." In the latter format, the lawyer takes the juror off the hook by generalizing the juror's feeling to a lot of people, but the lawyer has made the statement powerful by addressing the juror specifically and directly. Jurors cannot escape considering an issue that is directly aimed at them.

The word "you" is used most effectively when a trial lawyer wants the jurors to relate vividly and directly to the client's experience, as if it were their own. It draws the jurors in, maximizing emotional impact. Rather than relate the client's experience in the third person, the lawyer will relate the event as if it were happening to the jurors themselves.

CASE IN POINT

For instance, using our previous example of Dr. Peters, the fictitious thirty-two-year-old pediatrician killed by a yellow Pontiac in the parking lot of the local hospital, let's say that Dr. Peters was maimed for life, rather than killed. To assure maximum emotional impact, the lawyer restates the event in "you" form:

"Let's say you're going for a walk, oh, at around 6:00 P.M. on a Friday evening. You're pleased with the way your day went—one of those days when everything seemed to go right. Along your way you stroll through an almost empty parking lot, you stop for a moment to chat with a neighbor about a new building that's soon to be built in the neighborhood, and then continue to walk, feeling good, tired but happy, enjoying the warm August sun of late afternoon, when all of a sudden, seemingly out of nowhere, a yellow Pontiac comes barreling straight at you and—that's all. That's it. That's all you remember until you wake up in a hospital room, confused and in pain, and you try to get up, and then you realize you can't, you have no legs. And you have no idea how that happened. All you know is one moment you were a healthy functioning human being, and now something is terribly, terribly wrong. . . . That, ladies and gentlemen of the jury, is Dr. Peters's experience. And that is why we are here today."

The word "you" puts people on the spot. It forces them to identify directly with what is going on. It takes an active effort of will *not* to identify with "you" statements, and most people will not choose to exert that effort. Because the word "you" puts people on the spot and obliges them to identify with what is going on, it must not be used lightly. As with the other techniques taught throughout this book, use the word "you" in accord with your overall intent, not haphazardly, and be well aware of its power when you do so.

The more directly individuals have experienced an event or situation, the more meaning it has for them. People who lived through and suffered the effects of the concentration camps in World War II relate emotionally to the experience in a way no twenty year old ever could. The closer you can get people to feeling the emotions of the situation or event that makes you want to convince them of something, be that anger, despair, disappointment, joy, enthusiasm, or any other emotion, the more persuasive you will be.

Role-play is the single most powerful way to induce attitude change through vicarious experiencing. In an experiment designed to convince people to stop cigarette smoking, noted social psychologist Irving Janis had cigarette smokers role-play having lung cancer. The smokers play-acted reviewing X-rays, receiving the news that they had cancer, discussing the operation with the doctor, having the operation, and so forth. The number of smokers who stopped smoking following the experiment was significantly greater than those in a control group who had not participated in the role-play, and, more important for our purposes, the more *intensely* the smokers participated in the role-play, the greater the likelihood that they would stop smoking.[27] You are rarely in a position where you can get people to role-play an event, but the closer you can get to role-play, the better your chances of persuading others.

Engage those you are seeking to convince in the process of vicarious experiencing by personalizing events and situations vigorously. There are two ways to do this: (1) Directly engage them with the "you" format, recasting the event in personalized terms; and (2) translate the event or situation into terms directly taken from the personal experience of those you are addressing.

Technique #95: Get people directly engaged with the "you" format

With the simple use of the word "you," (see page 284) Darrow took the alien (for whites) experience of being black in 1926 and recast it in terms the jurors could relate to from intimate details of their own experience: What would it be like to have a different color of skin? Undoubtedly some of the jurors had had nightmares of being colored. By asking such direct, pointed questions, Darrow forced the jurors to put themselves in Sweet's shoes: This is a highly effective form of mental role-playing.

AN ALL-WHITE JURY FREES A BLACK MAN

No one used this technique more brilliantly than Clarence Darrow, in his brilliant defense of Henry Sweet in 1926, a time when segregation was the rule and African Americans were persecuted and vilified. Henry Sweet was one of eleven blacks arrested and charged with first-degree murder, shortly after Sweet and his family had moved into an all-white neighborhood in Detroit, Michigan:

"Ten colored men and one woman are in this indictment, tried by twelve jurors, gentlemen. Every one of you is white. At least you all think so. We haven't one colored man on this jury. We couldn't get one. One was called and he was disqualified. You twelve men are trying a colored man on race prejudice . . . You don't want him. Perhaps you don't want him next to you.

"Suppose you were colored. Did any of you ever wake up out of a nightmare dreaming that you were colored? Would you be willing to have my client's skin? Why? Just because somebody is prejudiced! Imagine yourself colored, gentlemen. Imagine yourselves back in the Sweet house on that fatal night. That is the only right way to treat this case, and the court will tell you so."[28]

The more you can, as Darrow did, make it easy for people to step into the situation you are trying to persuade them of, the more likely you are to make it easy for them to go along with you.

DEADLY DUST: THE CASE AGAINST ASBESTOS

When it became known that asbestos was linked with lung cancer, as well as with other diseases, there were a number of suits filed attempting to get corporations to take responsibility for the damage done. Milton Wheeler, who worked in a plant where the asbestos fiber was processed, testified to his experience. Notice how Mr. Wheeler's use of the word "you" pulls you into his experience, making it easy to feel what it was like. One of the machines raised so much of the deadly dust, Mr. Wheeler said, that "you couldn't see from one end of the machine to the other. You were covered with dust and the fibers . . . It would be in your ears, it would be in your nose, even through the mask. It would be under your pant legs, it would be inside your socks. You'd just be literally covered with it. You'd be blue."[29]

Technique #96: Translate the event or situation into terms taken from people's personal experience

Situations that are clearly meaningful to a lawyer often leave jurors emotionally cold and therefore unpersuadable. The net result is that opposing counsel thinks the lawyer has a heck of a good point, but the jurors couldn't care less. A good trial lawyer will not forget to establish an emotional connection to every key point so that the jurors really "get it."

AGONY ON THE STAND: THE COERCED CONFESSION

Rikki Klieman, a well-known criminal defense lawyer, gives an example worth noting. She takes the statement "It was a coerced confession," which is certainly significant to an attorney but has little *emotional* impact on a jury and translates it for the benefit of the jurors into relevant personal terms as follows:

"They brought him into the room at four o'clock in the morning. The room was eight by ten. It was like a large closet at best. It had one light bulb. He asked for something to eat. They didn't give him anything. They kept talking to him for hours and hours. He kept saying that he didn't know anything. He asked for something to drink. The temperature kept going down and they wouldn't give him a coat when he asked for a coat. In fact, later on, they told him to remove his sweater and next to remove his shirt. He had to remove his socks and his shoes. He was freezing."[30]

Klieman is in a sense obliging the jurors to experience the event from the client's point of view by reframing it in terms that the jurors can identify with. An abstract notion "coerced confession" has been made real by translating it into actual sensory details, with which the members of the jury can identify from their own experiences.

How can you work similar emotional "magic"? By remembering that the emotions are accessed through the *senses*. When you want to personalize an experience for others, ask yourself, "What does this experience *feel* like" and then ask yourself, "How do I have to describe this so the people listening to me feel it that way too?" A good trial lawyer would never simply state, for example, that the client, Mr. Jones, suffers pain from his injury. A good lawyer will translate that pain into personal details the jurors can experience vicariously. The lawyer will talk about how Mr. Jones has to get up an hour and a half earlier now to get to work on time, because it takes him twenty minutes to button his shirt, the pain is so bad in his damaged hands, and how it takes forever for him to work a zipper, it hurts so for him to put his fingers together to hold the zipper, and so on.

It is to your advantage to translate any technical terms into experiences those you want to persuade can relate to directly and immediately. Trial lawyers are constantly faced with the need to translate medical and technical terms into emotionally relevant phrases: a "tri-malleolar" fracture may mean a lot to a doctor, but little to a juror. A trial lawyer will translate a "tri-malleolar" fracture into something along the lines of: "There are three bones in the ankle. He broke all three bones. These bones connect the foot and the ankle. Now the foot and ankle are disconnected."[31] These statements give reality to the "tri-malleolar fracture"; the jurors can relate to their own feet and ankles and to how awful it must be to have those disconnected.

What is less obvious is that terms not generally thought of as technical, such as distance expressed in feet or temperature expressed in degrees, are not emotionally effective. Few people think in terms of twelve feet away, or nine inches apart; if you want people to connect with the emotional reality of these terms, make them real by either showing them on a diagram or pacing the distance off or showing what the distance is with your hands. Do whatever you have to do to translate the distance into experiential rather than conceptual terms. Don't talk, for example, about the plant workers having to deal with 102-degree heat; talk about it being so hot you can't breathe, and your sweat keeps dropping in your eyes. In a word, make it real. It's the only way you'll have the impact you need to persuade.

Successful Lawyers Always Choose a Case Theme that Sells!

How do the jurors select which version of the case they are going to believe? They select the version that interprets the facts in a way that is most consistent with the jurors' knowledge and experience of human behavior and that fits in with their understanding of the way the world works. Successful trial lawyers respect the fact that a basic human urge is to protect the weak against the strong, that jurors tend to do what is morally right, rather than what is technically correct. They will therefore case themes that address these concerns; successful trial lawyers always choose a case theme that sells.

BAD COPS IN SUMMERDALE

A good choice of case theme is given by Barney Sears in his prosecution of seven police officers from the Summerdale District of the Chicago Police Department, charged with conspiracy to commit burglary and receiving stolen property.[32] Sears defined the conspiracy as a violation of public trust and made the moral reprehensibility of such an act his case theme: In so doing, he appealed strongly and convincingly to the jurors' desire to do what is morally right.

Establish your cause as one that is morally just and you will immediately give yourself an advantage. People really do like to "do the right thing."

Technique #97: Get your way by elevating your theme to a higher cause

Often, to formulate a case theme that will be both meaningful to a given jury and persuasive, a trial lawyer must elevate the theme to a higher cause. A lawyer cannot engage a jury emotionally, for example, by simply arguing the details of whose car hit whose in an automobile personal injury case. If the lawyer wants to win a large award for the client, the lawyer will have to raise the theme to a larger issue—that of irresponsible drivers, for example, or of the state of automobile safety, issues with which the jurors can connect emotionally. The lawyer will open to the jurors the possibility of making their community safer for other drivers, of preventing many needless deaths, and will give them the opportunity to right some fundamental wrong. These are moving issues, persuasive issues, issues to which people can commit on a feeling level.

THE $200,000 AIRLINE TICKET: THE KLUCZYNSKIS VS. DELTA AIRLINES

An unexpected and spectacular elevation of a case theme was demonstrated by Philip Corboy, defending a well-off couple, the Kluczynskis, who had been bumped from a Delta Airlines flight and were thus inconvenienced on their way to a social weekend with friends. The suit was for $100,000. No one thought Corboy would win. His clients had been, at the most, slightly inconvenienced and, by an average citizen's definition, hardly inconvenienced at that.

Corboy raised the theme of the case to an unexpected level, that of the need to deter airlines from dealing lightly with people, pointing out how people miss important moments in their lives—marriages and funerals, business meetings, long-awaited encounters, reunions with loved ones—due to the irreverent attitude of airlines toward their patrons. By elevating the theme to this level, Corboy allowed the jurors to relate emotionally to the Kluczynskis's experience in terms that had meaning in their personal lives and appealed to the jurors' basic human desire to right a moral wrong. The jury not only returned a verdict in favor of the Kluczynskis, but awarded them twice the amount that had been asked for.[33]

It is especially important to raise your theme to a higher level when you know your position is counter-normative, that is to say, goes against the prevailing norms in the community.

"LIES VS. LIVES": HOW LT. COL. OLIVER NORTH JOINED THE RANKS OF THE RIGHTEOUS

Lying goes against community norms. Lying to entities such as Congress, even more so. Lt. Col. Oliver North successfully elevated his case theme to a higher level where lies would be acceptable, thereby transcending the sanctions normally occasioned by going against community norms.

Lt. Col. Oliver North was accused of lying to Congress regarding, among other things, the situation in the Honduras with Nicaraguan rebels and U.S. forces. He admitted to the lie, saying: "I did it because of what I have just described to you as our concerns, and I did it because we have had incredible leaks, from discussions with closed committees of the Congress."[34] North further stated that those leaks cost lives. North saw himself as having to choose between lying to Congress and violating higher goals: jeopardizing military operations and human lives.

This elevation of his case from "liar" to "lies versus lives" was brilliant. North captured the essence of his case theme in the phrase "lives and lies," which then became a catch phrase for the rest of the investigation, picked up by media and public alike. Lt. Col. North: "Lying does not come easy to me. But I think we all had to weigh in the balance the difference between lives and lies. It is not an easy thing to do."[35]

The farther away your position is from community norms, the more difficult it will be for you to persuade people from that community. Raising your case theme to an ideal that supersedes ordinary norms will overcome the difficulty. Carefully select your theme in order to guide those you wish to convince in a direction they will find acceptable.

CASE IN POINT

It is counter-normative to approve of a doctor who encourages and supports a patient's drug addiction. James Neal was perfectly aware of this when called upon to defend Dr. Nichopoulos in the case of Elvis Presley, cited previously. Mr. Neal chose, therefore, to raise the case theme to a higher level, that of the moral issue of doing whatever it takes to help someone, even if how you do it is unpopular and may be to your own detriment.

The theme of the Good Samaritan was very effective. The jurors were able to set aside conventional ways of dealing with the case and focus rather on the moral issues involved, guided as they were by Neal's case theme.

You set the emotional tone of your argument. The more you can connect your cause with people's highest values and beliefs, the more easily you can convince them of your position. Do be careful, though, that your theme is *solidly* connected to higher values. Just giving lip service to such values won't work.

HOW LAWYERS PUT EVENTS IN THE PAST OR PRESENT TENSE TO SWAY JURORS' EMOTIONS

Everything a successful trial lawyer says in a courtroom is designed to, in some way, sway the jurors to his/her interpretation of the facts. Just because something happened a number of years ago does not dictate that the lawyer will recount those events in the past tense. Good trial lawyers use present and past tense as they do all the other techniques in this book—to convince jurors. When trial lawyers use the present tense and when they use the past tense in presenting a situation is entirely predicated on whether they want the jurors to feel as if the event were happening "here, now," or if they want the jurors to feel distanced from the event, as if it happened "out there, at some time."

> *Technique #98: Use the present tense to help people relate*
> *intensely to an event or situation*

If a trial lawyer wants jurors to connect emotionally to those events and circumstances that brought the client to court, the lawyer must move the jurors across space and time. The lawyer must somehow make jurors feel that the event is happening *now*, not at some time in the remote past, because the farther away an event is in time, the less urgency is felt around its occurrence. The song "Time Heals Everything" is apt. For most people, time is indeed a great healer. Time puts things in perspective; time cushions the raw feelings that erupt at the time of a traumatic event.

The lawyer needs jurors to experience something that happened to someone else in the past with the same intensity as if it were happening to them, personally, in the present. The use of the word "you" and per-

RIGHT PATIENT, WRONG KIDNEY: JORDAN VS. LONG BEACH COMMUNITY HOSPITAL

Attorney David M. Harney's direct examination of an expert witness, Dr. John S. Wilson, provides a clear example. Mr. Harney represented Harry Jordan in a suit brought against the Long Beach Community Hospital and all the doctors involved. Mr. Jordan's healthy right kidney was removed, rather than his cancerous left kidney, which was the kidney targeted for surgery. This left Mr. Jordan in very poor health with multiple physical and financial problems. Part of Mr. Harney's direct examination went as follows:

"In other words, doing an X-ray review for impending major surgery with the urologist, without talking to a radiologist who is within a few feet of this box, within a few feet, and he doesn't talk to the radiologist. He spends five to fifteen seconds talking to a urologist who has the films in backwards, where he, Dr. Waters himself, has them in backward. Now, is that below the standard?"[36]

Let's restate that passage in the past tense, which would be more accurate in terms of reality, and see what it does to the intensity of the experience:

"In other words, having done an X-ray review for impending major surgery with the urologist, without having talked to a radiologist who was within a few feet of this box, within a few feet, and he didn't talk to the radiologist. He spent five to fifteen seconds talking to the urologist who had the films in backwards, where he, Dr. Waters himself, had them in backward. Now, was that below the standard?"

sonalization, as described earlier, is how lawyers get jurors to identify emotionally with the client's circumstances as if they were the jurors' circumstances. The use of the present tense in describing the circumstances is how lawyers get the jurors to feel the event as if it were happening *now*. Use the present tense any time you want people to "feel it now." (See page 290.)

Notice how, stated in the past tense, the experience does not have the same vividness as when the experience is stated in the present tense, and vividness is what appeals to the *emotions*. The experience has been made more comfortable, more removed, and therefore less intense. But for the jurors to really identify with Mr. Harney's point, the substandard level of care, they had to feel that lack of care now, feel outraged here in the present moment, not comfortably removed from the experience at some distant point in the past.

The principle, then, is as follows: Any time you want to re-create an event or situation vividly and emotionally for people, state it in the present tense.

Technique #99: Use the past tense to distance people emotionally from an event or situation

This principle also works in reverse. In other words, if you want an event to seem less immediate, less important, put it in the past tense. When a trial lawyer talks about the opposition's distress, for example, the lawyer will put that distress in the past tense; it won't seem quite so real.

Distance those you seek to persuade from an experience by recasting it as something that happened in a dim and less important past. You will lessen the impact of the event subtly and effectively.

Keep People's Focus Where You Want It as Lawyers Do by Using the Positive or Negative Forms of Speech

The positive and negative forms of speech are little recognized but are powerful techniques of influence. A lawyer can easily keep the jury's attention on a certain point by stating the point in the positive and can distract attention by stating the point in the negative.

For example, if someone says "Don't think of a pink elephant," 99 percent of us will immediately think of a pink elephant. The mind does not distinguish between "do" and "do not" as it sorts through your memory to bring all relevant material to your attention. Your mind simply attempts to bring to consciousness *all* elements included in the statement. If you say, "I want this meeting to run smoothly and well," chances are everyone will think "OK" internally. The mind picks up information pertaining to "meeting run smoothly and well." If, however, you say "I don't want this meeting to get out of control," the mind picks up information on "meeting go out of control," and you have just unwittingly introduced the possibility that the meeting could get out of control.

Technique #100: Keep people on track with you by using the positive form of speech

When a trial lawyer wants to keep a juror's or witness's mind attending to certain issues and not to others, the lawyer will phrase statements positively to keep the jurors' minds on a certain track.

CASE IN POINT

In the course of voir dire, for example, a lawyer might say: "Is there any reason why, if *you* were on trial, you would not want eight jurors just like yourself?" Asked this way, the prospective juror's mind will immediately come up with twenty reasons why he/she would *not* want eight jurors just like him/herself. If this is not the desired result, the lawyer will phrase the question positively: "Would you, if *you* were on trial, *be satisfied* with eight jurors just like yourself?" Phrased like this, the mind will not hunt for negatives: It will "go with the flow," and the juror will respond "yes."

Technique #101: Sow doubt by using the negative form of speech

Using the negative form of speech is a highly effective way trial lawyers sow doubt in the jurors' minds.

CASE IN POINT

To get an idea of how this works, let's take the case mentioned earlier against Long Beach Community Hospital once more as an example and study Mr. Harney's direct examination of the expert witness: "In other words, doing an X-ray review for impending major surgery with the urologist, *without talking* to a radiologist who is within a few feet of this box, within a few feet, and he *doesn't talk* to the radiologist. He spends five to fifteen seconds talking to a urologist who has the films in backwards, where he, Dr. Waters himself, has them in backward. Now, is that below the standard?" The italicized phrases are in the negative form.

Confronted with "without talking," the mind immediately jumps to "should have talked"; "doesn't talk" leads the mind to "could have talked," and so forth. In addition, faced with "doesn't talk," the mind instantly asks "why not?" This is the very effect Mr. Harney desired.

Now let's look at what happens when the same question is posed in positive form: "In other words, a radiologist is within a few feet of this box, within a few feet, doing an X-ray review for impending major surgery; *he talks with the urologist.* He spends five to fifteen seconds talking to a urologist who has the films in backwards, where he, Dr. Waters himself, has them in backward. Now, is that below the standard?"

Notice how using the positive form greatly dilutes the emotional impact of what happened, and yet emotional impact is what you need in order to persuade people, as Mr. Harney persuaded the jurors in this case of the outrageousness of the substandard care.

Why is this? In the positive form, the mind does not instantly pose probing questions. The positiveness of a statement puts the mind on a comfortable emotional track; it lulls the mind into emotional comfort, which then makes the mind slower to probe for the possible negatives in the situation. It requires mental effort for the mind to pick up on the incongruity of the doctor speaking only with the urologist in a situation in which speaking with the radiologist would be most effective. People are generally unwilling to make that kind of effort unless they are suffering from some sort of discomfort. Phrasing ideas in the negative is an excellent way to generate the emotional discomfort necessary to lead people to probe and question areas you want them to think about.

Learn To Choose Your Words as Lawyers Do: to Influence People's Thinking

Words have great impact. Words not only communicate meaning, words also have emotional connotations. People relate to different words differently. Good trial lawyers select the words they use with great care, knowing how powerfully words can elicit jurors' emotions.

Technique #102: Choose words that hold powerful subconscious images

A lawyer, to describe the client's suffering, will refer to the client as a "neck cripple." This is much more powerful than saying that the client "suffers from whiplash." The idea of "cripple" holds a more intense subconscious image than the idea of whiplash. An "accident" elicits a much different emotional reaction than does a "wreck," "pile-up," or "smash."

To appeal to people's emotional level, select words that have vivid appeal to the subconscious mind, words with strong emotional connotations. Use words with enough impact to get your idea across clearly and effectively. Avoid melodrama by making word choices that genuinely reflect the situation and can be substantiated.

CASE IN POINT

Two of the cases cited earlier illustrate this point particularly well. Ms. Fairstein's choice of the word "necrophilia" in her analogy characterizing Dr. Teicher's sexual behavior in the case cited earlier is an excellent example of the power of appropriate word choice. Dr. Teicher was interacting sexually with nonconsenting women in a drugged condition; nonconsenting and drugged is very close to dead when it comes to sexual relations. The word "necrophilia" was thus appropriate. The power of the word is clear: Most people have a powerful emotional revulsion to sexual relations with a dead body.

Mr. Liman's choices of Rolls Royce and Edsel in the New York City Transit Authority case are equally powerful. Cadillac and Pinto would not have had the same impact. Rolls Royce has come to be culturally defined as the summum bonum of automobiles, and although the Pinto has had problems, it does not have the generally recognized association with total debacle that Edsel has.

The reverse of the preceding principle is, of course, also true. If plaintiff's lawyer, for example, persists in labeling a client's broken leg "a mangled limb," defense lawyer can counter the emotional impact of "mangled" by relabeling the leg as "merely broken." If plaintiff's lawyer refers to the accident as a "wreck," defense lawyer can relabel it an "accident." This will greatly diminish the impact of plaintiff lawyer's terms.

If you seek to diminish the impact of terms used by someone holding a different viewpoint from your own, use this technique. You will be successful in relabeling the other person's terms, however, only if he/she has made inappropriate, that is to say basically exaggerated or overstated, terms. Since anyone can obviously turn around and do the same to you, be careful that your word choices do reflect your facts and express the reality vividly, not in overstated fashion.

Technique #103: Choose words that encourage people to think the way you want them to

Word choice is not important only to trial lawyers as they seek to persuade the jurors, it is also critical to directing witnesses' answers to attorney questions in a favorable direction. How you design your questions has a great deal to do with how they are answered. Psychological research has clearly demonstrated that people respond very differently, for example, when asked to estimate a person's height depending on whether the question asked is "How tall is he?" versus "How short is he?" When asked the height of a basketball player, those asked "How tall?" answered on the average, seventy-nine inches. When the question posed was, "How short is he?" of the same player, subjects answered on the average, sixty-nine inches. That's a difference of almost a foot![37]

Generally speaking, your choice of words determines greatly how people will think about things. Trial lawyers are aware of this and will carefully choose words such as "fast" when they want to suggest speed, "far" to suggest distance, "tall" if they want to emphasize height, and "short" to minimize it. Such words have a definite effect on how people respond. "How fast was the car going?" suggests high speed. "At what speed was the car traveling?" suggests more moderate speed. "How far was the intersection?" suggests that the intersection was far away. "How near was the intersection?" suggests the opposite. Trial lawyers choose the word that *presupposes* their desired answer. If they want the intersection to have been closer, they will use "How near?" If the lawyer wants the intersection to have been farther away, he/she will use "How far?"

Be aware of the differential meanings of such words as "a" and "the." "A" and "the" may seem interchangeable, but they are not; they imply very different things. "A" refers generically to an undefined object. "The" refers specifically to a defined object. "Did you see *a* man with *a* limp?" does not focus a person's attention in the same way as "Did you see *the* man with *the* limp?" does. The use of "the" presupposes that the man exists, the limp exists, and that the only question is whether or not the person saw the man. Thus people will search their memory more assiduously given the unconscious message that the man with the limp exists than if asked whether they saw "a man with a limp," which contains no such presupposition.

Similarly, notice the different impact of such words as "frequently," "occasionally," "sometimes," and "often." Subjects in the research cited here, when asked if they had headaches "frequently" and how often, replied, on the average, having had 2.2 headaches per week. Subjects asked if they had headaches "occasionally" stated, on the average, that they suffered from headaches 0.7 times per week. The power of such words to elicit different responses is considerable. Don't throw this power away by using words in haphazard fashion. Choose those words that reveal most clearly your point of view.

Use Visual Aids as Lawyers Do: as Often as Humanly Possible

People remember best and are most impacted by that which is presented visually to them as well as auditorily. Movies, videos, and television have long left radio in the dust as the foremost source of influence on people because of that phenomenon. Top trial lawyers are quick to use visual aids of all kinds as much and as often as is appropriate to the case and is allowed by the judge.

What is a visual aid? Anything from a simple blackboard diagram or scrawled writing on a piece of butcher paper to a full-color computer simulation projected onto a three-part six-by-six foot screen. Virtual reality simulations are even being used now in some courtrooms. A visual aid can be as complex or as simple as budget and opportunity allow; it hardly matters. What matters is that you use them.

Visual aids have a number of specific functions in the courtroom that can serve you well in your efforts to persuade.

Technique #104: Use visual aids
to clarify your points

There is nothing quite like a chart with your case theme as a heading and your three points listed as "#1, #2, #3" below it to keep your audience on track. Such a simple chart makes it easy for those you wish to convince to remember and internalize your points. They can come back to the chart over and over again. You can refer physically to each point by pointing to your chart as you further describe the issues involved in each point.

Graphs, charts, diagrams, and photographs are all wonderful ways of visually representing your ideas in simple, readily understandable form. They are the easiest way to achieve clarity.

During deliberations, the Menendez jurors tried to make sense of what they had heard during the trial: "Here is a teeny, tiny example of the millions of little details that we [the jurors in deliberation] have been arguing about for three weeks now. . . . On X-exam he [Lyle] said he heard them [Kitty and Erik] screaming 'from the main house,' which, to me, could mean from clear *inside* the main house or simply from the *direction* of the main house as they were running outside toward the guest house."[38] A simple drawing of the house, indicating where the screams came from, could have prevented such confusion.

The more you can physically illustrate your points, be that with the simplest of line drawings or the most sophisticated of virtual reality "trips," the more clarity you will bring to those who listen to you and the more easily they can therefore be persuaded.

Technique #105: Use visual aids to focus people's attention

Visual aids help keep the jury awake and interested in the proceedings. They break up the monotony of words. I do not mean to imply that trial lawyers' words are monotonous, only that any experience repeated over long periods of time becomes monotonous. Though a lawyer may be the most dynamic attorney in the courts, there are still many long, tedious moments in a trial. Given that the adult attention span is only eighteen minutes long, visual aids are useful in providing a different stimulus every so often to keep the proceedings lively. People can be emotionally swayed much more easily if they are alert and interested in what is going on.

There are always moments when the jurors are distracted or bored. Their attention will inevitably wander at different points during the trial, and smart trial lawyers will use visual aids in a way that encourages the jurors to be favorably distracted. If, for example, the lawyer has various visual displays in the courtroom, the jurors will naturally tend to look at those displays during those times when their attention is wandering. When you use visual aids in this way, you direct people's attention even when those you are trying to convince are seemingly distracted.

Technique #106: Use visual aids to access
the visual perceptual mode

Visual aids are also useful in accessing the visual mode of perception discussed in Chapter 4. Since many people are highly visual, illustrating important points or explaining complex points with the use of visual aids makes a significant difference to the trial lawyer's ability to communicate those points. The use of different colors in graphics permits the influence of those colors at an unconscious level and again serves to liven things up.

Red, for example, is a great attention getter. A simple blowup of an important point, with the key words circled in red, is a terrifically influential visual aid. Full-color photographs and illustrations tend to hold people's attention more readily than do black-and-white photographs. Notice the graphics and commercial art, such as advertisements, that capture your attention. Use these to help guide you to an effective use of visual aids in accessing people's visual perception.

Technique #107: Use visual aids to get people to experience events
and concepts as real

Using visual aids makes things more real. The old saying "A picture is worth a thousand words" truly applies in the courtroom.

CASE IN POINT

Sometimes a picture is not only worth a thousand words, but costs many sleepless nights: "The autopsy photos [of Nicole Brown and Ronald Goldman] were terrible. That was enough to send everybody out to lunch. Afterward, we had nightmares about them. I couldn't sleep."[39]

A photograph of an accident, a blowup of a document with a contested signature on it—these are infinitely more effective than the simple *telling* of the incident.

CASE IN POINT

As Gerry Spence recommends: ". . . avoid the abstract that tells so little. When people explain things to me in the abstract, I grow impatient. Give me an example . . . Show me how you do it. Don't tell me. Draw me a map. Draw me an illustration, a chart. Show me a time line of the events that have occurred. Let me *see* what happened and when. Don't tell me the man was hurt and suffered a broken femur. Show me a picture of his broken leg."[40]

Trial lawyers are well aware that we are a visual generation. Television and film have largely replaced the written word for most people as a mode of communication. We are used to *seeing* events more than we are to simply hearing about them. Use this reality to your advantage in order to influence people through a medium that they are used to and that is familiar to them.

If you elect to use visual aids, be sure you work with them *before* you attempt to do so in front of those you are seeking to persuade.

HOW THE PROSECUTORS ALLOWED O. J. SIMPSON TO WRIGGLE FREE: THE BLOODY GLOVE FIASCO

Perhaps one of the biggest mistakes the prosecution made in the O. J. Simpson case was to fail to work with the famous "bloody glove" before presenting it to Mr. Simpson to try on. "The glove demonstration . . . Many feel it was the pivotal point in the trial, from which the prosecution never recovered." This, from the June 26, 1995, edition of *Newsweek*: "It was either one of the greatest acting jobs of all time (by an actor of limited skills), or one of the biggest bungles ever committed by a district attorney's office. Or it may be both. But last week . . . as O. J. Simpson poked and wormed his hands into the infamous bloody gloves . . . he seemed to wiggle his way a bit closer to being a free man."

"Too tight" (some newspapers reported the words were "They don't fit"), Simpson said loudly enough for the jury to hear as he *seemingly* struggled to tug the leather gloves over his broad palms.[41]

The jurors couldn't believe what they were seeing. They recognized immediately how inept it was of the prosecution not to work with the gloves before presenting them to Mr. Simpson: "Now, when I saw that demonstration, I thought, *Why in the hell didn't the prosecution try that glove on somebody else that had the same size hands as O. J. before they allowed him to get out here and do this?* [try the glove on]. I was sick when I saw they didn't fit because I just thought for sure they were going to fit."[42] Prosecution's failure to be well prepared for this demonstration was a serious blow to its case.

Don't make the same mistake as the prosecutors in this case. Prepare yourself sufficiently so that you work with your visual aids easily and comfortably. Then you will truly have the impact you seek.

For example, a lawyer will have witnesses work with charts before a trial. The lawyer will have a diagram of the location of an incident drawn up, for instance, and then have the witness go over and mark where what happened: "This is where I stood, this is where my car was, this is where the man was when he threw the bottle at me, this is where I fell." The impact of the witness's story is far more tangible and more emotionally relevant when presented in this fashion than if the witness simply stated, "He threw the bottle at me from ten feet away."

Technique #108: Use visual aids to emotionally reinforce a point

Perhaps the most critical effect of visual aids, however, is to reinforce your point in a highly charged, emotional way. The great trial lawyers are tuned in to the emotional power such visual aids have on jurors.

CONVICTED BY A BROOM HANDLE AND A BASEBALL BAT: SOMETIMES GOOD-LOOKING RAPISTS DO GO TO JAIL

"In a recent case in Glen Ridge, New Jersey, a group of young men lured a mentally retarded woman into a cellar where, using the promise of a date with one of them, they subjected her to a number of sexual assaults. The ordeal was climaxed by inserting a broom handle and a baseball bat into her vagina.

"In the trial, the defense dressed the young men up in suits and ties to present a picture of sturdy, middle-class youngsters, credits to the community and high school athletes. It helped that they were all good looking, clear-eyed and well-behaved in court.

"The prosecution brought the broom handle and the baseball bat into court! . . . No matter what was said in the boys-will-be-boys defense, the . . . instruments and the aura around them told their own story."[43] Sometimes good-looking rapists do go to jail. But it took the visual impact of such hideous instruments of rape to overcome the young men's clean and credible appearance.

Never underestimate the power of the visual! Good lawyers don't.

CASE IN POINT

In the previously cited case, for example, in which Philip H. Corboy represented Danny Schaffner, the fifteen-year-old boy crippled as the result of a bicycle mishap, Corboy entered the broken bike as his first exhibit. That broken bicycle remained in the courtroom for the duration of the trial, an immensely powerful silent witness to the drama of this boy's life.

The emotional impact of that bicycle was tremendous. Clearly, you may not always have a similarly compelling object with which to support your presentation. Still photographs, however, have a similar effect. A still photograph of something that in some way supports your position allows people's imagination to wander, to try to figure out more about what is portrayed in the photograph. It draws people's attention back to a certain moment or situation again and again, reinforcing the emotional impact. Sometimes, for sheer dramatic value, a black-and-white photograph is tremendously eloquent. In court, still photographs are often left for the jurors to view as long as possible to have the desired emotional effect.

LAWYERS' HANDLING OF EVIDENCE IS POWERFUL

How a trial lawyer handles the evidence, physically, is just as important as *what* evidence he/she introduces. Trial lawyers think of physical evidence as props, physical elements designed to enhance their interpretation of the facts, just as stage props enhance the reality of a performance, and use them accordingly.

Technique #109: How you can influence people's thinking by the way you handle objects

If you want those you are trying to influence to dislike an object, for it to seem abhorrent, for example, handle the object gingerly and with some measure of distaste. Your body language will express your feelings more effectively than words ever could. (See page 302.)

By handling the gun as if it were a toy, Klieman diminished the emotional impact attempted by the prosecution of "third most powerful handgun in the world." Don't ignore the effect your handling of objects has on the people you're seeking to convince. Everything you do in the presence of those people adds up to either increase or to diminish your persuasiveness.

HOW A .357 MAGNUM WAS REDUCED TO A MERE CAP GUN: IT'S ALL IN THE WRIST

Rikki Klieman, a criminal defense lawyer, was wonderfully astute in how she affected the meaning attributed to a piece of evidence in her defense of a man charged with manslaughter: "In Michael's case, the .357 Magnum, an incredibly powerful gun, will be treated by the prosecutor (if he or she is good) as if it were a cannon. I once saw a prosecutor literally put a pen through the part where the trigger was and hold it by the pen as if he were afraid of the gun. That gun became huge. . . . I used the gun in my opening and treated it like a Roy Rogers or Dale Evans pistol. I played with it so that it looked like a cap gun. No matter how many times the government tried to portray it as the 'third most powerful handgun in the world,' somehow my picture, because I am a small woman, created a different image."[44]

Technique #110: How to convince people by physically *demonstrating your point*

Earlier in this chapter, I discussed how role-play is the single most effective way to accomplish attitude change. The closer you can get to role-play, the better your chances of persuasion. A good trial lawyer will actually handle evidence in order to encourage the jurors to identify with the lawyer and to mentally handle the evidence themselves.

When you handle an object, the clearer your body language is, the more accurately it expresses how you feel about that evidence, the easier it is for those listening to you to emotionally connect with you and experience the object in a similar way. Illustrating a point physically is effective for the same reason.

CASE IN POINT

David Harney's cross-examination of an expert witness during the trial in which he represented Harry Jordan, whose healthy kidney, rather than his diseased cancerous kidney, had been removed by mistake, included some masterful physical demonstration of a point:

Harney: And how could he [the operating surgeon] ever get a game plan [for surgery] if he never found out which side the tumor was on?

Karlan: He was told which side the tumor was on.

Harney: [holding a ball in his right hand and showing it to Karlan] Which hand is this ball in?

Karlan: Mr. Harney, if you told me that ball was in your left hand, I would have the utmost respect for you and say it is in your left hand.

Harney: Sir, which hand has the ball in it?"[45]

The expert witness could repeat all day how the assistant surgeon must respect what the head surgeon says is truth; the jurors are going to be swayed by that common-sense demonstration.

Physically demonstrating a point is always more powerful than verbally explaining the same point. Use your creativity and imagination to come up with lots of ways to physically demonstrate your points. Your persuasive power will increase tenfold.

Summary

Influence the decision-making process where it starts—at the emotional level. Through this chapter, we've looked at a number of ways to do that. By using the techniques of instant rapport, story telling, analogies and similes, catch phrases and repetition, money words, personalization, present tense and positivity, word choice and visual aids, you will be able to speak directly to the emotions, where you can be most persuasive.

WORKSHEETS
EMOTIONS: CHECKLIST OF PSYCHOLOGICAL AND SOCIAL PSYCHOLOGICAL TECHNIQUES DESIGNED TO INCREASE YOUR *PERSUASIVENESS*

This checklist may be thought of as a "think list." It is designed to encourage you to actively *think* about how to be emotionally persuasive in some specific ways. You may choose, in function of your legal expertise, to use all, some, or none of the items in this checklist, but the important part is that you know *why* you choose to include or discard any of the items listed.

1. Are you sincere in your presentation?

   Yes _____ No _____

   If No, what can you do to increase the sincerity of your presentation? _____

   _____

   _____

2. Do you emphasize the positive emotions in your presentation?

   If yes, which ones? If no, why not? _____

   _____

   _____

   _____

   _____

   _____

3. Have you created emotional rapport with those who will be listening to you? Have you spoken to them of shared experience? If yes, how? If no, why not?_____

   _____

   _____

   _____

   _____

   _____

4. Have you organized your facts into a story? If yes, how? If no, why not? _____

_____

_____

_____

_____

_____

5. Is your story telling descriptive and rich in sensory detail? If yes, how? If no, why not? _____

_____

_____

_____

_____

_____

6. Are you availing yourself of the power of emotional archtypes? If yes, how? If no, why not? _____

_____

_____

_____

_____

_____

7 Have you included analogies and similes in your presentation to help people relate emotionally to your points? If yes, how? If no, why not?

_____

_____

_____

_____

_____

8. Are your analogies and similes accurate? If yes, how? If no, why not? _____

_____

_____

_____

_____

9. Do you avoid overstatement?

If yes, how? If no, why not? _____

_____

_____

_____

_____

10. Are your analogies and similes from your own experience?

If yes, how? If no, why not? _____

_____

_____

_____

_____

11. Do you use repetition for effect? If yes, how? If no, why not?

_____

_____

_____

_____

_____

12. Have you included catch phrases in your presentation? If yes, how? If no, why not?_____

_____

_____

_____

_____

13. Have you included "money words" in your presentation? If yes, how? If no, why not?_____

_____

_____

_____

_____

14. Have you used personalizations to help people relate directly to situations and events? If yes, how? If no, why not?

_____

_____

_____

_____

_____

15. Have you translated events and situations into terms directly taken from people's personal experience? If yes, how? If no, why not?

_____

_____

_____

_____

_____

16. Does your case theme sell? If yes, how? If no, why not?

_____

_____

_____

_____

_____

17. Would it be useful to elevate your case theme to a higher cause? If so, how would you do it? _____

_____

_____

_____

_____

18. Have you used the present tense when you want to make an experience immediate and vivid? If yes, how? If no, why not?

_____

_____

_____

_____

19. Have you used the past tense when you want to diminish the impact of an experience? If yes, how? If no, why not?

_____

_____

_____

_____

20. Have you used the positive form of speech when you want to keep your audience on a certain track? If yes, how? If no, why not? _____

_____

_____

_____

_____

_____

21. Have you used the negative form of speech when you want to sow doubt in people's minds? If yes, how? If no, why not?

_____

_____

_____

_____

_____

22. Have you carefully chosen your words for maximum effect? If yes, how? If no, why not? _____

_____

_____

_____

_____

_____

23. Have you included the use of visual aids as an emotional hook for your audience? If yes, how? If no, why not?

_____

_____

_____

_____

_____

24. Have you considered how to demonstrate certain points physically in order to help people connect emotionally to those points? If yes, how? If no, why not? _____

_____

_____

_____

_____

25. Have you considered how you will handle any objects you wish to present so that you give the objects certain distinct emotional connotations? If yes, how? If no, why not? _____

_____

_____

_____

_____

_____

Out of the Courtroom, into Your Life

As should be clear from the preceding seven chapters, persuasion is not about arguing, at least not in the sense most people think of arguing: two people pitted against each other, each trying to impose his/her differing points of view. Persuasion is about carefully designing and expressing your point of view in a way that wins people over without "arguing" in the traditional sense of the term.

Persuasion is a strategy. The seven steps provide you with a clear and easy way to determine the strategy that will be most effective in getting you what you want in each particular situation. Persuasion takes the willingness to think ahead and be creative, two areas in which winning trial lawyers excel. The techniques given here show you how you, too, can excel in these areas. The rest of this chapter is devoted to showing you how to use the techniques through a series of practical examples. The examples are chosen from various aspects of daily life: at work, at home, and in the public eye.

For purposes of clarity, the seven steps are applied sequentially in each example. In reality, however, the seven steps are often used concurrently or in a different order. What matters most isn't whether you separate, for example, your use of logic and emotion, but that you use both logic and emotion in designing your strategy. The order of the steps is most relevant when you are trying to understand how persuasion works: Each step rests and builds upon the step before it, and they must all be present for you to win.

A worksheet is provided at the end of the chapter to remind you of the various techniques that are available to you within each step. As you will see from the examples, some of the techniques are important every time you set out to be persuasive; others are valuable depending on the situation at hand. Use your common sense and understanding of the techniques to know which to use when, and you will indeed come out a winner!

Example #1: Persuading Your Budget-Conscious Boss to Give you the Raise *You* Feel You Deserve

You are a loan officer at the local branch office of a major bank. Although you receive performance reviews every three months, this is the "big one," the annual review that determines whether or not you'll get a raise. You are confident that your review will be pretty good, given your performance over the year and your interim evaluations, so you are confident that you will get a raise. However, you've heard from others who have already had their performance reviews that raises are few and far between this year, and so far, all raises have been limited to cost-of-living type increases.

You want more.

Step #1: Credibility (Techniques #1–#14)

Your performance review is with not only your supervisor, but the field manager, who answers to corporate headquarters and who visits the different bank locations only periodically. You have come to the meeting prepared with what you want and how you intend to get it, thus you have an air of quiet self-confidence about you. You accentuate your positive self-image by a clean and neat appearance. You wear an outfit that fits you well, is appropriate to the circumstances, and in which you feel comfortable. You've checked your outfit, shoes, and any accessories so that they are all in good condition. You even remembered to clean your glasses (ordinarily sporting a few thumb prints and other smudges). You are in pretty good shape, so you trust your energy will be "alive," but you do a moderate workout that morning anyway, just to feel your own energy.

When you arrive at the meeting, you take the time to greet everyone, looking directly at each person as you do. You then take your seat and compose yourself, taking a breath to make sure you stay moderately relaxed. As each person speaks to you, you look at him/her clearly. You are respectful of the occasion by being on time and of the people involved by being polite and being pleasantly serious. This isn't the time to relate that absolutely hysterical story about your dog and the leg good old Spot mistook for a fire hydrant.

Your attitude fits the situation: You are awake and alert, interested, focused on what your supervisor and the field manager have to say. Your focus is positive; regardless of what is said, you know you have a way to see your desire through. You internally look forward to a successful result, and this makes it easy for you to be committed to your cause.

Step #2: Body Language (Techniques #15–#37)

You took a square position on sitting down, making sure your back is erect. You know you have a tendency to cock your head to the right: That's where you hold the phone, between your right ear and your right shoulder. You've worked with yourself to correct this, but you still check your head placement every once in a while. Since the annual performance review at this bank is a formal procedure, you don't relax much into a different position, but maintain good posture throughout.

As you listen, you keep an interested look on your face (you've practiced this enough so it's fairly automatic), and you remind yourself not to tap your foot as you get nervous.

Step #3: Be Persuasive With Your Voice (Techniques #38–#47)

When it comes time for you to make your case for a more substantial raise, you make sure your voice is placed on the low end of your pitch, so as to give your voice more authority and counterbalance the nervousness that you know shoots your voice skyward. You regulate your pace so you are easily and clearly understood (you have a tendency to speak too fast), and you phrase what you say so only one thought at a time comes out. You've rehearsed what you have to say sufficiently so that you use pauses, color, peaks, and valleys to give your words life without having to exaggerate or use inappropriate emotion. Your emotional choices are of excitement and enthusiasm for what you are proposing. You figure (correctly) that your enthusiasm will help engage your supervisor and field manager's enthusiasm.

Step #4: Rapport (Techniques #48–#53)

Your supervisor wears bold, flamboyant, very trendy clothes, but the field manager tends toward conservative outfits. Establishing common ground with dress is a challenge, but you are undeterred: You wear a conservative outfit with a single trendy accessory. You're pleasantly surprised at how your choice of apparel boosts your confidence level, in addition to what you know it will do for rapport.

Both your supervisor and field manager are rather laid back individuals, so you rein in your usual wired-off-the-wall energy somewhat. They are both also fond of jargon and "bank talk." This makes mirroring their vocabulary and vocal style easy; you simply pepper your proposal with such terms.

In terms of perceptual modes, you're less sure of how to connect. Oh, certainly, you know your supervisor's mode: highly visual with some leaning toward the kinesthetic, but the field manager? Mr. Harper is a mystery. You've seen him at a distance going in to meetings, but you've never said a word to him or heard him speak. So now what? You design your proposal with lots of visual words for the benefit of your supervisor and decide to adjust your presentation to take Mr. Harper's perceptual mode into account once you're in the situation.

And there you are, listening to your supervisor and Mr. Harper going over your performance review. You get "good" ratings in terms of doing your work, how few mistakes you make, and your turnaround time on getting work off your desk and to the right departments. You get only "average" ratings in terms of your administrative duties. This does not surprise you, as filling out forms ranks with cleaning bathrooms on your list of "fun things to do." You get, however "excellent" ratings in the area of customer relations. You are offered a cost-of-living-type raise, with much talk about how "the economy has been rough" and "we're offering raises only to a very few select employees."

This is your chance, and you go for it—first taking a deep breath to relax and center yourself. You start pacing by acknowledging that, yes, the economy has hit the business world hard (by now you've figured out Mr. Harper's perceptual mode is kinesthetic, so you are using kinesthetic as well as visual terms) and that it must be rough for the bank to keep growing and developing in such a climate.

Step #5: Creative Listening (Techniques #54–#68)

You maintain good eye contact with each of them, but focus more often on looking directly at Mr. Harper since you know he is the primary decision maker in the room. Your supervisor is simply watching you, one brow up reflecting her curiosity. You are usually fairly quiet in these situations, and you figure your supervisor wonders what's coming. You observe Mr. Harper nod in agreement as he listens to you. You decide your pacing is successful and go on to lead with your proposal.

Step #6: Logic and Reason (Techniques #69–#81)

You knew you were going to have to get creative if you were going to pitch for a decent raise. The bank is truly not in a money-spending mode. You figure, however, if you can show the bank a way to make a lot more money by just spending a little more money (your raise) you may have a way in to their pocketbooks.

You've picked a theme of "Spend a little money to make a lot of money." You've extensively reviewed the customer survey of loan operations the bank had conducted earlier that year. The survey concluded that increased customer satisfaction would significantly increase revenues from loan operations. So far, no one has done anything with this information because the only recommendation the survey firm came up with was "retrain your whole staff in client relations," which clearly was not in anybody's budget.

You tell your supervisor and Mr. Harper of your research. They are surprised and more than a little intrigued: For someone to do such investigation on their own time and without compensation is unheard of. You start your lead: "I care about this bank. I really enjoy working here, and I want to see the bank grow and become ever more successful. And I have an idea about how to do that [umbrella statement]."

Your proactive approach (such positivity!) and your preparedness are serving you well. You continue to observe body language cues to make sure you're on the right track, then continue: "What did the survey point out as the number one thing we could do to increase revenues in the loan department [rhetorical question]? Increase customer satisfaction. And I think I have figured out a way to do that very inexpensively."

You hand Mr. Harper a neatly typed sheet of paper that outlines your three ideas (three points) on "how to increase customer satisfaction" (handing things to kinesthetic people makes them more real for such individuals), and then give one to your supervisor. You have included a neatly drawn graph (visual aid) showing how your ideas translate into dollars. You pause briefly and are still while they look over the sheet, letting the information sink in, then continue with your explanation. You talk about how, given your greater abilities in the area of customer relations, you'd like to restructure your job so that you concentrate your efforts on customer satisfaction. You show, on paper again, clearly and with diagrams, how the work can be distributed so that the job functions you are not very good at can be assigned to those who do them well (admitting weaknesses in a way that strengthens your point and increases your trustworthiness), while you take over what you are best at, customer relations. In return for the increased responsibility and higher level of work you will be performing, you ask for a different salary, one that is more in line with these functions (explicit conclusion, elevating the issue from a "raise" to a "different salary in line with new functions"). You maintain your outward cool and confidence as your wildly beating heart thuds under your shirt. Are you really going to pull this off?

Step #7: Emotion (Techniques #82–#110)

You have been sincere in your presentation and have maintained an upbeat and positive approach. You've used the positive form of speech as much as possible, talking about how this benefits the bank, how this plan increases revenues, and you have steered well away from a negative "if you don't do this, I'll quit/you'll lose money" type of argument. You have captured Mr. Harper's attention and interest by focusing on what is good for the bank, not just what is good for you. "Increased revenues for the bank" is a powerful catch phrase that you use generously (repetition) as you speak. You personalize the event for Mr. Harper by telling him, "And frankly, Mr. Harper, it's your excellent foresight in commissioning the customer satisfaction survey that got me started thinking this way. I kept thinking, 'There's got to be a way to put this costly research to work for us.' Customer satisfaction is the going trend, as you have pointed out many a time."

Because you say this sincerely and have backed it up with facts and figures, Mr. Harper can accept the flattery. Besides you've just shown him a way to make himself look better with the higher-ups. Your supervisor is impressed; she didn't know you had it in you. Nor did you, for that matter, but you keep watching body language cues, and it seems you're doing OK.

Mr. Harper looks over at your supervisor, nods, then looks over to you. "I'm going to take this up with headquarters," he says. "It might just work." You refrain from yelling "YES!" at the top of your lungs, and just smile, saying, "Thank you." "In the meantime," Mr. Harper says, "Why don't you write up a proposal of everything you just told us and send it over to me." "Got it right here," you say, pulling a neatly typed prospectus out of your file. "Hmmm," says Mr. Harper as you hand it to him, "you do mean business, don't you?" "Yes, I do," you say (preparedness counts!).

And there it is—you did it! Now all you have to do is follow through with the same creativity and zeal that got you this far and that raise (plus a job you will definitely enjoy more) will be yours.

EXAMPLE #2: GETTING YOUR STUBBORN "MY-WAY-OR-THE-HIGHWAY" SPOUSE TO GO ALONG WITH YOUR VACATION PREFERENCE

You get only two weeks a year off, and both of you had to plan well ahead to get the time together. You really don't want to take separate vacations: That doesn't sound in the least bit attractive. Your husband's way of taking a break from his desk job is vigorous exercise, and he has lots of good energy. You are so tired of running around, between your sales job, your commitment to various community organizations, and the usual running around of everyday life, that the idea of a vacation involving any physical activity greater than putting on a bathing suit is enough to make you cringe.

Somehow you have to make it to that beach . . .

Step #1: Credibility (Techniques #1–#14)

When your husband first brought up his vacation idea of bicycling through France, fortunately you were at the stove at the time with your back turned to him, so when you screamed, you could just say "It's nothing, I just touched the hot pan." You need to buy time here. You need a strategy if you're going to succeed in getting your St. John vacation, so for now, all you say in response to your husband is, "Hmm . . . sounds interesting, I'll have to give it some thought," with a nice smile, as you then rapidly change the subject.

You realize that if you are to sway your husband over to your point of view, you will have to build up your credibility in the area of "negotiated agreements are truly win-win." You also are totally unprepared to speak with any authority and as of now have a totally negative focus, vociferously expressed (to yourself, in the shower, with the water running), expletives not deleted.

You give yourself a week to build up credibility. You orchestrate a series of small decisions to be made, along the lines of "Which movie to see?" "Where to have dinner?" "Who will pick up the cleaning?" "Spend time with the in-laws?" and you make sure that you remain calm, logical, and pleasant through the making of all these decisions. You make sure these decisions are all *negotiated* (meaning involve movement from each of your original positions) and that they all "work," meaning they are satisfactory to both of you. Now you have a credible track record in the area of negotiation agreements. You are ready to go for something bigger.

Since you are dedicated and committed to the success of your plan, you respect your husband by choosing a time and place that will be conducive to his being able to listen to you. You don't barge in when he's trying to work out, you don't ask him to sacrifice his "card night with the guys," you don't start talking when you're in a public place where he might feel "trapped." You decide to make a nice dinner at home and, since you know doing things one at a time works better, wait until you've had dinner to talk. You have maintained good outward focus toward your husband and have put yourself in a situation in which you are moderately relaxed.

Step #2: Body Language (Techniques #15–#37)

You are both sitting on the couch; you sit so you can easily engage eye focus with your husband. You maintain good eye contact throughout and keep a pleasant expression on your face, reflecting your inner excitement at the story you are about to tell.

Step #3: Be Persuasive With Your Voice (Techniques #38–#47)

Since this is an intimate situation, you suit your voice to your subject. You keep your volume somewhat low and use lots of color, peaks, and valleys to illustrate your "story." You keep your voice sounding rich and warm, remembering the power of words to tantalize. You engage your husband's senses by using lots of words that appeal to the senses.

Step #4: Rapport (Techniques #48–#53)

You are very familiar with your husband's perceptual mode. He is primarily visual, secondarily kinesthetic, so you use lots of both types of words. During dinner, you created rapport by remembering and talking about some of the special experiences you've had together. Now you're ready to pace and lead: "Honey," you ask quietly, "what is it about bicycling through France that particularly intrigues you?" You've worked all week on asking this question without a shred of sarcasm coming through, and you're very proud of managing to have it come out ingenuously now. "Huh," he answers, "I don't know." You don't jump on him as you usually would, "What do you mean, you don't know?!" Instead, you pace: "It's hard for you to put into words," you say after a moment. "Well, yes and no," he says, your pace enabling him to open up and express himself. "I guess what I like is the freedom—it feels great to just ride and ride and not have to worry about where I am when, no time schedules, no deadlines, no phones ringing. Plus, I like to be out in nature, not in a stuffy room with fluorescent lighting." "It's great not to have to worry about anything, just be carefree and out in the sun and all," you pace, mirroring both his tone and energy level as you speak. He nods.

You get ready to lead: "I'm really looking forward to a couple of weeks of that kind of freedom—no phones, no hassle, being out in nature." You are creating rapport even as you start to lead, speaking of shared experience. "Yeah?" your husband asks, looking at you in surprise, "I thought you hated this outdoors stuff."

Step #5: Creative Listening (Techniques #54–#68)

As you speak, you observe your husband's body language, knowing if he tenses up at any point, you'll have to back off and try another tactic. But so far, he's with you. He seems very comfortable, very relaxed.

Step #6: Logic and Reason (Techniques #69–#81)

Rather than respond directly to his statement, you say to your husband, lowering your voice a little to emphasize the closeness between you: "What if there were a place where we could both have all the freedom and peace and quiet and nature we each wanted, in the way we wanted, and have plenty of time together as well [umbrella statement posed as a rhetorical question]?" He looks intrigued. "Go on," he says.

You continue building on your chosen theme—"and a good time was had by all." "What if," you say, "there were a place where you could bicycle from dawn to sunset in the most beautiful tropical forest imaginable and through funky little villages and all sorts of other interesting places, and then you could come back to the resort in time for a long soak in a quiet lagoon as the sun sets, sipping a frosty piña colada, and then we could have dinner and dance under a soft, velvet, star-studded sky [three points, all phrased as a rhetorical question]?" He looks at you, amazed; you've never waxed so poetic (color words, engaging the senses).

"And where are you while I'm doing all this bicycling?" he asks. "Doing my version of freedom and nature loving by lying on the beach, resting up for your return," you reply, sweetly and seductively (appropriate use of emotion). "Hmm," he says, "so you wouldn't need me to do the lying-on-the-beach part with you?" "No," you reply, "I can do that all by myself, no problem." "It's awfully hot in those tropical places, isn't it?" your husband asks, concerned. "Not at the time of year that we're going," you say, now whipping out the brochures and pamphlets you have on St. John, showing temperature ranges and some marvelous pictures of bike paths (visual aids). You did have to hunt to find those, but hey, preparedness counts!

Step #7: Emotion (Techniques #82–#110)

Since you've built up your credibility through the week regarding win-win negotiations, your husband is emotionally prepared to be convinced by you. You have proved your trustworthiness, and now you are demonstrating your expertness (knowing your facts).

You've been appealing to your husband's emotions throughout your presentation. You elevated the issue to a higher cause. You took the decision out of the realm of "your way versus my way" and put it into the larger context of "and a good time was had by all," which at the same time, is a positive focus. You are clearly seeking to accommodate each of your preferences in a way that both of you will equally enjoy. You have personalized and engaged your husband directly with the "you" format and with a form of story telling (as you related his "vacation day").

Your husband is clearly impressed. "You've done a lot of homework on this," he says. "I really want for both of us to be happy," you say, seriously and sincerely; "it matters a lot to me that *you* have a really good time—and that *I* do. And I think this is a way we can do that together. [explicit conclusion, getting to the point]." Your sincerity and commitment to your cause is convincing. Your husband smiles, "St. John, huh? let me see those brochures again." You smile. You can almost smell the suntan oil.

*E*XAMPLE #3: PERSUADING YOUR DIE HARD "I-NEVER-CHANGE-A-GRADE-ONCE-I'VE-GIVEN-IT" PROFESSOR TO DO JUST THAT

You're aspiring to grad school. You've managed to maintain a good GPA throughout your freshman, sophomore, and junior years, but senior year is really tough. You've had to take on some extra classes you didn't know you needed, your "part-time" job seems to be burgeoning into "full time," and although you desperately need the money, you're awfully crunched for study time. . . .

You got a C on your economics class midterm—you're panicked. You have to maintain a B average or better in all your classes or your chances of final acceptance into the Master's program you really need if you're going to have a decent opportunity in the job market are going to go down the tubes. Professor Brown is known to be a stickler for grades, always going "by the book," and never taking students' life situations into account. As far as he's concerned, "Your studies come first, and if you don't know your priorities, get out of my class."

Great . . .

Step #1: Credibility (Techniques #1–#14)

You come in well prepared. You've taken the time to review your test and make note of where you went wrong. You've figured out what the right answers would be. You are sincere about wanting to do well in this course, and your sincerity shows. You guard against giving the impression of being in the class just "for the grade." This does not fit the stereotyped image of a "good student."

When you go to your appointment with Professor Brown, you pay attention to your attractiveness. You make sure your person and your clothes are clean and neat, that they fit, and that there aren't any holes anywhere. You've kept your accessories (earrings, necklaces, bracelets, head gear, and so forth) down to an absolute minimum (much as it pains you) and made sure what you wear is in good condition. Since you're not in the world's best shape, you give your body the benefit of a little aerobic activity before going in to your appointment so as to have good energy. You've found that walking briskly up a flight of stairs three or four times will always work when you don't have time for anything else.

When you arrive at Professor Brown's office, you take a moment to check your appearance before going in. You take a deep breath to settle yourself, then knock and enter. You remember to do things one at a time. You greet the Professor, *then* close the door behind you, *then* walk over to the chair he indicates, sit down, *then* set your things down, *then* adjust your posture, engage good clear eye focus, and then and only *then*, make your request.

While the good professor responds, you are still. You focus on listening to Professor Brown intently, which helps you from indulging in your habitual fidgeting. Listening intently also helps you convey respect, even though you're totally bored by what the professor is saying. Lectures on priorities you don't need, but since he's giving you one, you listen. You don't interrupt. You are polite. You call him "Professor" since that's what he likes to be called.

You do your best to be interested in what the good professor has to say. You try not to be so attached to your point of view that you forget to focus out. You are committed to presenting yourself and your request in a winning fashion. You cultivate a positive focus: No matter what Professor Brown is saying, you think to yourself, "There's a way to win this. I know I can do it." You are at ease and comfortable with yourself, knowing you can succeed as long as you stay calm within and remain confident that you have the necessary skills. When you find yourself drifting or getting anxious, you take a deep breath, exhale quietly through your nose, and allow yourself to relax.

Step #2: Body Language (Techniques #15–#37)

When you first walk in the door, you walk in with good posture, your head erect and straight forward. When you sit, you sit "square" and maintain good posture. You don't shift around in your seat or pick at your nails; you stay relatively still and focused. You have by now become aware of your useless mannerisms, so you no longer idly pull at your earlobe (even when nervous), and you've learned to gesture to make a point, rather than just flail your arms around. You keep good eye focus throughout. You maintain an expression of serious concern on your face even as Professor Brown is going off on one of his long-winded tangents about how you are wasting precious years by being so undisciplined with your study time. You don't allow your frustration or boredom to seep through to your face.

Step #3: Be Persuasive With Your Voice (Techniques #38–#47)

You're pretty satisfied with your basic vocal pace and pitch, so you just remember to articulate well because it's a known fact that Professor Brown absolutely hates mumblers. You adjust your volume so that you're loud enough for Professor Brown to hear you across the desk, yet you are not blasting him out. You restrain yourself from blurting out your "spiel" in one great gush; instead, you phrase your thoughts, taking pauses in between each one. You let your voice reflect the truth of your words. For example, when you say: "I really want to do better in this course," you stretch the word "want" to give it color and emphasize its importance. Use of color, peaks, and valleys will convey the sincerity of your words to Professor Brown.

Step #4: Rapport (Techniques #48–#53)

You cringe at the thought of developing a relationship with Professor Brown. What are you going to have to do? Dress in a brown suit with a polka dot bow tie and speak in the imperial "we"? Hardly. Creating relationship is about establishing common ground, right? The operative word is "common." So, no, you tell yourself, you don't have to go the brown-suit-polka-dot-bow-tie route. Instead, you find commonalities, use mirroring, perceptual modes, pace and lead.

You think about what you know about Professor Brown. Well, you know he hates clutter and disorganization, he is always prompt and hates late comers to class, he abhors typos and poorly written papers, and he complains loudly about the general laziness of "young people today." With these insights in mind, you create rapport by being on time, having everything about your person uncluttered, and having both your papers and your thoughts well organized. The professor is one of the few faculty members who always wears a jacket and tie to class, so you dress conservatively, in something your family likes but your friends think looks "dorky."

When you sit across the desk from the professor, you observe he sits back in his chair and pretty much stays there; you mirror him by doing the same. Professor Brown speaks slowly and very articulately, so you adjust your pace and level of articulation a little to be closer to his. The professor's energy is strong but contained; you refrain from exuberant bursts of any kind but keep your internal energy high.

You've noticed from class that the professor is very visually oriented, and so you use visual terms as you present your cause as much as possible. You've carefully typed up (no typos) the correct answers to the questions you missed on the exam, and you give this to the professor, to engage his visual perception. You've also typed up your "strategy" (more on this in Step #6) neatly and give this to the professor at the appropriate moment.

And then you "pace and lead." When the professor starts to read you the riot act on how lax you have been in your studies and how disappointed he is in someone with your potential just drifting along and not taking your studies seriously, you don't get defensive, taciturn, or make objections. To the professor's complete stupefaction, you nod your head and say (pacing): "It must be very hard to want us to do really well and know we can do it and watch us fall short." When this sort of stops the professor in his tracks, you go on to lead: "Well, I'm disappointed too. I'm disappointed in myself. I'm falling short of me. And that's why I'm here. I want to live up to my expectations of myself and [you pause here, for effect] to your teaching." You now have the professor's complete attention.

Step #5: Creative Listening (Techniques #54–#68)

You watch the professor's body language for clues as to how you are doing. When he visibly relaxes after you've conducted the above pace and lead, you know you're on the right track. Especially when his brows shot up after your first "pace," that's when you knew you'd started to get him off his track, making him more willing to follow you to yours. You notice his voice is softening a little now, not as hard and attacking in tone as it was previously. You make sure you consistently acknowledge what the professor says with head nods and "uh-huhs".

You realize this is the turning point. You keep your eye focus very steady and your body still as you present your cause.

Step #6: Logic and Reason (Techniques #69–#81)

You know from your friends that Professor Brown is a hard sell. He is completely immune to pleas such as "My sister's in the hospital having her leg/arm/head amputated," or "I've had to work nights at the local fish market to support my ailing mother and fifteen younger brothers and sisters." He certainly isn't open to the truth: You were too busy with other things to study enough and frankly thought you could get away with whatever you remembered from class and a cursory review of your notes. The professor is likely to see this as typical student arrogance and lack of respect for his class, not as a winning disclosure of weakness.

You have to come up with something the professor can relate to and will approve of, so you structure your thoughts around the theme of "The Tortoise and the Hare." You start with an umbrella statement: "I've been a slow starter in this class, Professor. I haven't been able to see the concepts clearly, and it's only now that they are crystallizing for me (you're using all the visual terms you can as you go, remembering the professor's visual perceptual mode). I realize I did poorly in the test. It's an accurate reflection of where I was with understanding the concepts. (You disclose your weaknesses in a way that strengthens your point.) What do I want now? (Rhetorical question and getting to the point.) "I want an opportunity to demonstrate that I truly have understood the material, either by doing some research for you, writing a paper, or taking another exam (suggestion given in three points). If I do so to your satisfaction, then I respectfully ask that you do not penalize me for being a slow starter, but consider changing my grade to more accurately reflect my true understanding of the concepts [explicit conclusion]."

Step #7: Emotion (Technique #82–#110)

You've selected your theme so it "sells." There is a world of difference between a slow starter and a lazy student who is looking for a way to shirk work. You've resisted pleading, begging, and crying (negative emotions) and instead are appealing to positive emotions: an opportunity to demonstrate increased understanding. "More accurately reflect" and "true understanding" are money words for a person invested in science and learning (professor of economics). These are ideas that the professor can easily connect with and appreciate.

You then hand the professor your corrected version of your test. Such a visual aid reinforces your stated willingness to do more work and shows the professor that you indeed do now understand the concepts better. You then also hand him your "strategy" sheet with the three points neatly outlined: "Do research to assist professor," "Write a paper," and "Take another exam," with three ideas under the "research" and "paper" items for topics. Your preparedness and commitment to bettering your grade impresses the professor.

And now you listen. You listen carefully to what the professor says; you stay focused, and you don't lose your cool. You stay committed to the outcome; you are willing. You do a lot more listening than talking. And you follow through! When the professor finally says, "All right. It's not my general practice to do so, but you seem unusually dedicated and committed. I'll give you the benefit of the doubt. You may write a paper on . . ." (He scans your list of [3] ideas for papers and picks one, modifying it just a little.) You thank him, leave, and you make sure that paper is on his desk on time, well and thoroughly written (no typos). You won!

EXAMPLE #4. CONVINCING YOUR OPINIONATED FRIENDS THAT YOURS IS THE BETTER RESTAURANT CHOICE

You are with your friends, Sue and John. You've all met at your place so as to go out to dinner together. Sue says she wants Indian food. You hate Indian food—it's too hot and spicy and your stomach moans for days afterwards. John looks at Sue with a "What are you, crazy?" look and says, "I want to eat Mexican." You groan inwardly—all those beans! And more of that hot stuff. No thanks. Somehow you have to convince the two of these strong and determined individuals that your way is the way to go.

Step #1: Credibility (Techniques #1–#14)

You resist the urge to loudly proclaim your preference (Italian). You simply sit down, observe the other two (eye focus gives value), and just stay quiet. Both John and Sue, having harangued each other sufficiently and gotten nowhere, notice that you haven't said a word.

"Are you sick?" Sue asks. "Yeah, you haven't said anything—usually by now you'd be yelling and screaming," John comments. You refrain from saying something sarcastic (your usual retort) and, instead, work on your credibility. "I was listening to you," you say in a pleasantly serious voice (conveying respect, focusing out toward your friends, having a positive focus, and being moderately relaxed). "Oh," they say, almost in unison.

Step #2: Body Language (Techniques #15–#37)

"And I've been thinking," you continue, dropping your head for a moment, as if in serious thought, taking a pause to mark the point. You raise your head, look directly at your friends (eye focus), and say: "Why are we getting together tonight [rhetorical question]?" As you continue, you keep your body relatively still, gesturing occasionally to emphasize a point, but concentrating primarily on keeping good eye focus. You have learned to quiet your mannerisms and do so now. Even though these are your friends and it probably wouldn't influence their decision if you cracked your gum or rubbed your chin, you have more impact as you keep your body free of such extraneous movement.

Step #3: Be Persuasive With Your Voice (Techniques #38–#47)

As you continue your presentation, you use good vocal techniques, modulating your voice so you speak with good energy, appropriate volume, and especially good phrasing and well-placed pauses. You keep your tone sincere and somewhat serious, in line with your theme. You see a nifty opportunity to try out a build-drop, so you ask the second part of your rhetorical question on a rising pitch, and drop the answer: "Why are we getting together tonight? Just to eat [said with rising pitch]? No [the drop], to be together, share time together, enjoy the pleasure of one another's company." You give lots of warmth (color) to the phrases "be together," "share time together," "enjoy the pleasure of one another's company."

Step #4: Rapport (Techniques #48–#53)

Those phrases are also great rapport builders. You are stressing the shared part of the experiences. You are reminding the others of the relationship you experience together and what that means. You've deliberately used kinesthetic terms such as "be together," "share time," and "enjoy pleasure," because you know that both your friends are primarily kinesthetic. Now you are ready to pace and lead. "John," you say, "what is it about Mexican food that is appealing to you tonight?" You nod in acknowledgment as John tells you all about the wonders of rich flavorful thick sauces and cheese, and then pace him: "It's really nice to have all that wonderful thick sauce and gooey cheese and all." Turning to Sue, engaging good eye focus and clearly wanting to hear what she has to say, you ask "How about you, Sue, what is it about Indian food that turns you on?" "The spices!" she exclaims, "I love all that hot stuff—makes me sweat in a good way." "All those spices bubbling in your blood—feels good," you pace, smiling as you mirror her up-energy (rapport).

Step #5: Creative Listening (Techniques #54–#68)

As you've paced each of your friends, you've watched carefully to see what their body language tells you. John's face is still quizzical; he's crossed his arms over his chest. From your experience of John, you know this type of body language means he has some doubts, in this case about what you are doing here; you'll have to work harder to convince him. Sue seems to be enjoying the "game"; she's smiling and looking at you openly, her body language undefended.

Step #6: Logic and Reason (Techniques #69–#81)

You have chosen a theme of "the value of friendship." You've already given your umbrella statement with your rhetorical question and its answer.

You use your lead to back up your position: "What if we could find a type of food that would give us all what we want? Thick, gooey, cheesy sauces for John, hot, spicy food for Sue, and something lighter and less 'hot' for me?" You watch (creative listening). Sue is smiling, John's brow goes up. "Yeah," John says, "like what?" "Like Italian [explicit conclusion]," you say. "You can definitely get thick, gooey, cheesy food there, John, and you can get spicy sauces with lots of that hot red-pepper stuff, Sue, and I can get something that suits me too [three points to back it up and personalizing the experience for your listeners]. Then we all get to eat something we like, and more important, we get to put our attention on being *together* and having a good time *together*, which is why we get *together* in the first place [getting to the point, repetition of money word, development of theme in three points]."

Step #7: Emotion (Techniques #82–#110)

Sue is already clearly won over, amused and impressed by your approach, "I'm game," she says. "Besides, I can always go eat Indian on my own." John has uncrossed his arms, so you know you've gotten somewhere with him; he stands, hands on hips now, which although not a totally "with you" body position, is less defended and more accessible. "When did you get so philosophical?" snorts John. "When I realized how much I value us being friends and how I don't want anything to get in the way of that," you reply, seriously and sincerely. You've clearly elevated the issue of "what are we eating?" to the higher cause of "the value of friendship." Your theme is a positive one. It emphasizes the positive aspects of being together, rather than, for example, a theme of "why does it always have to be your way?" which would be negative and not likely to work.

The "value of friendship" is a hard theme for John to object to. It is a theme with strong emotional underpinnings, especially since you are maintaining a sincere emotional tone, putting caring through your voice. And you do believe what you say; such sincerity cannot be faked. It's just that before learning persuasive skills, you wouldn't have thought to negotiate "where we are going to dinner" from such a perspective. Bottom line, though: It is true. And that is what is making your argument persuasive.

John drops his arms off his hips and grabs his windbreaker. "OK, you win," he says, "let's go. Luigi's?" "OK," says Sue. "Luigi's," you concur. Luigi's was your second choice, but heck, you got Italian, and you can always go to Mario's some other time.

EXAMPLE #5: CONVINCING YOUR BOSS TO LET YOU TAKE THAT EXTENDED LEAVE OF ABSENCE AND GUARANTEE YOUR JOB UPON YOUR RETURN

Your company recently merged with another company. Although in the long run, this will be a great move for both companies, in the short run it meant that all the employees, yourself included, have been working on double and triple overtime. Plus you have some family problems to deal with that you can't seem to get resolved, your cat just died, you have a constant headache—all in all it's been a really difficult six months. You need a break. You figure if you could just get about two months off, you could sort out your family problems, get your health back on track, and get some decent rest. Your boss, however, is a great proponent of "When the going gets tough, the tough get going," and his idea of a "break" is a three-day camping stint. You don't want to lose your job; what do you do?

Step #1: Credibility (Techniques #1–#14)

You ground your credibility by being very prepared before you go in to talk with your boss: You literally become an expert in what you are about to propose. Although you are basically a reliable and dependable person on the job, you make sure you are even more so in the day or two it takes you to figure out your strategy of persuasion.

Once you're ready, you don't just walk into your boss's office and start talking; you ask for an appointment. He grumbles "You don't need an appointment; what's on your mind?" "I do need an appointment," you say, smiling. "I need an uninterrupted twenty-minutes of your time, which I'll never get with the phones ringing. How about tomorrow morning before work?" Your self-assurance as you stand up for what you need reinforces your credibility. You get your appointment.

You arrive at your appointment on time, conveying respect for your boss's time. You knock, walk in, close the door, sit down, and engage your boss's eye focus before you say a word. Doing things one thing at a time gives you an aura of self-confidence and helps you actually feel that way, too.

Step #2: Body Language (Techniques #15–#37)

You sit square, with good posture and good energy. You pay special attention to not do your usual fidgeting, shifting, and shuffling. Even though you are burnt out, you keep a positive focus, both mentally and physically. Whiners don't win; positive people do.

Step #3: Be Persuasive With Your Voice (Techniques #38–#47)

You use good, clear articulation, since your boss often says to you "Speak up, why are you mumbling?" and you phrase what you have to say in distinct short sentences, knowing that is your boss's preference. You use peaks and valleys to emphasize your points rather than color (which plays to the emotions), since your boss prides himself on being a rational (read "nonemotional") man—which is utter rot, since he gets frustrated and yells a lot, but for some reason he qualifies that as "not being emotional," and you're not here to change him, but to convince him. . . .

Step #4: Rapport (Techniques #48–#53)

So, you use logic itself as a cornerstone of rapport building. Your boss understands and values logic, and what you have to say is very amenable to logic. You mirror your boss's vocabulary and vocal style by using simple, clear language and short phrases. You also adopt an energetic, direct, no-nonsense approach, which mirrors your boss's direct no-nonsense approach and his typical level of high personal energy.

Step #5: Creative Listening (Techniques #54–#68)

Throughout, you pay careful attention to your boss's words as well as to his body language. You've observed him closely over the past few days, noticing what are body indicators of his interest versus disinterest in things, approval versus disapproval. You learn that much of what your boss thinks can be "read" in his eye focus. You watch most particularly for when his eye focus becomes very intense, which you know to be a sign of great interest on his part, and when it drifts off, which tells you you may have lost him. You are also aware that your boss's primary perceptual mode is visual, and you intend to capitalize on that knowledge.

Step #6: Logic and Reason (Techniques #69–#81)

When you're ready to start, you take a deep breath (quietly, so your boss doesn't notice) to ground yourself. You engage good eye focus and say, "What would you say if I told you I've come up with a way to save the company money and increase productivity [getting to the point, umbrella statement, and theme]?" Then you wait.

You have your boss's undivided attention. You've used two terrific business catch phrases/money words: "save money" and "increase productivity." "I'd say, 'Go on,' " your boss replies.

"I love what I do," you continue, "The company is great to work for, I am happy to work here—and I am totally burnt out. The last six months have taken their toll. I cannot give what I have to give to this job without taking a serious break to renew myself [admitting to weaknesses in a way that strengthens your point]." Your boss frowns, confused, "I thought you were going to tell me about how to save money and increase productivity?" "You are confused," you say, pacing, "because it doesn't sound like that's what I'm talking about." "You're right," your boss says, feeling better now that his confusion has been acknowledged. "But saving money and increasing productivity is exactly what I'm talking about," you say, leading, "and here's how."

Step #7: Emotion (Techniques #82–#110)

You now take out the graphs and charts you have been putting together over the past couple of days (visual aids). You show your boss statistics and government charts on decreased productivity resulting from employee burnout (bless your local library's reference librarian for finding these for you). You tell your boss this is where you are inevitably headed for. You contrast this with your plan of attack. You call it that, knowing these are words that have meaning to your boss (ex-military that he is).

You continue developing your theme, "Save money and increase productivity," which raises the issue from "I want a break" to the more boss-acceptable theme of "This will be good for the company." You show him (graphically, he's visually oriented) your three (highly logical) points: (1) You can set up your work so that all ongoing projects continue to be handled with employees who will be willing to cover for you in your absence, and there will be no need to hire a temp; (2) you show him with figures that the time and money it would take to hire and train a new person into your position, able to perform at your level (you show him your excellent production quotas and performance reviews for the past year), would be much greater than simply continuing your salary for two months; and (3) you show him with government statistics (of which he is fond) the results of preventative measures against burnout: increased productivity and decreased absenteeism.

You explain how two months off the job will give you the opportunity to really refresh and renew yourself so your productivity will soar upon your return. You tell him again (repetition) how much you value and enjoy your work, how well you want to perform for the company, and therefore how you want this opportunity to "retool" yourself (using an analogy your boss will understand) and come back fresh (three points again!). You want two months off, with pay, and a guarantee that your job will be there when you get back (explicit conclusion).

Throughout, you have been sincere and committed to your cause. You have maintained a positive focus, emphasizing the benefits of this plan rather than your burnout. You have spoken at all times with confidence, equal to equal, educating your boss to burnout and its consequences simply as a fact of life. You resist the impulse to let him see just how pathetic you feel right now. You refuse to pull a victim ploy on him.

"You've got moxie; I'll give you that," your boss says, grudgingly. "You really think people will take over your work for you?" "Guaranteed," you say, knowing you can work it out. "I can't have everybody doing this, you understand," your boss says. "I have no need to talk about my employment conditions with anyone," you say, respecting his position. "I'll take this upstairs," he says. "When do you want to leave?" You gulp, this is it! "Tomorrow?" you venture. "Tomorrow, schmorrow—you leave on the fifteenth. We'll call it sick leave," he says, asserting his bosshood. "Done deal—and thank you," you say. "Get outta here—I got work to do," he says.

You leave the office, shutting the door behind you. You lean against if for a moment. You did it! You can hardly believe it. Now, if you could just persuade the kids to pick up after themselves . . .

EXAMPLE #6: MOTIVATING YOUR LAID-BACK EMPLOYEES TO THE SUPERB PERFORMANCE THAT WILL GET YOU YOUR SPECIAL BONUS

You're a shop foreman, and your employees are basically a pretty good bunch, but they've been spoiled by your somewhat casual "buddy" approach to management, and they just barely make the company quota every month. You hate confrontations, and you don't want to hassle them, but your manager has just informed you that if you meet a certain production quota within the next six weeks, you'll get a nice bonus. You could really use the money: You found out yesterday your kid needs braces, and the transmission just fell out of the Trans-Am.

Step #1: Credibility (Techniques #1–#14)

You figure if you want the shop to operate more efficiently, you'd better start with shaping up your own image. You start paying more attention to how you dress, making sure your clothes are pressed and go together. You start favoring shirts over T-shirts and making an effort not to slop coffee on your desk. You get to work early (preparedness), and congratulate those of your staff who are on time (conveying respect), bringing them a cup of coffee or making doughnuts available. This encourages those who tend to be late to get there on time without your having to say anything; after all, when they drag in late, the doughnuts are already gone, and that's no fun.

Your outward and positive focus pleases your employees, although they are somewhat surprised by this change in your behavior. You are chipper and pleasant as you greet your workers and have a definite "getting down to business" attitude about you.

Step #2: Body Language (Techniques #15–#37)

You practice walking with more energy, a bounce to your step, and take to jogging in the morning so that you actually have some energy through the day. You look at your employees directly in the eye and take a moment to greet each of them, being still and listening attentively with your eyes as well as your ears to their response. Your body language gives each of your employees importance and value.

After a week of preparing the way, you're ready. You call a meeting of all your employees. You have a plan, and you're raring to go.

Step #3: Be Persuasive With Your Voice (Techniques #38–#47)

As you talk to your employees, you speak with good volume, plenty of energy, much enthusiasm and gusto. You speak in short sentences with lots of punch, to help get your workers motivated.

Step #4: Rapport (Techniques #48–#53)

You've got plenty of good rapport going with your workers already, so your main focus is to present your plan in a way that will use the advantage that good rapport gives you. You begin by telling them that "we've got a problem [accentuating the already existent rapport by associating yourself as sharing the experience with them]. Our production quotas just aren't what they should be. I know a lot of that is my fault. I really like you all. I know you do good work, and I don't like to get on your backs, what do you need that for [admitting weakness in a way that increases your trustworthiness]? But I gotta fix this problem. So I ask myself, 'Is there a way we can up the production quotas without my getting on everyone's back' [umbrella statement formulated as a rhetorical question]? And I think about it and worry about it and think about it some more [using a story format to engage your listeners' attention], and finally I think, of course, there is. All I have to do is ask everybody 'what's in the way?' Since I know you are all good employees, and I know you're doing the best you can, then if we're not meeting quotas, there's something in the way. So now I put it to you, 'what's in the way?' "

Step #5: Creative Listening (Techniques #54–#68)

Now, as you're talking, you are observing your employees' reactions via their body language. You note how their bodies got tense as you talked about a problem and how their bodies relaxed as you took them off the hook with your *theme* of "what's in the way?" You continue to monitor your employees' body language to let you know how you are doing and from whom you are likely to get resistance.

Step #6: Logic and Reason (Techniques #69–#81)

You deliberately chose a theme that didn't assign blame to your employees. People are rarely motivated to do better by being beaten up. You then proceed to develop your theme into a three-point program, in which you really get to the point, giving an explicit conclusion: "Here's what I suggest we do: (1) I want you all to give some thought to what stands in the way in each of your jobs to delivering a higher production quota and to write that down for me so I can collect your notes at the end of the day today. It doesn't have to be neat or anything, just so I can read it; (2) I'll be going around to each of your stations today, just to observe how everything's working, to see if there's something tripping you up you haven't thought of that I might spot; (3) let's meet again tomorrow morning, right when you clock in, for a quick thirty minutes to review what came out of today's observations and figure out what to do from there. Whatever's in the way, let's get rid of it so we can really make some progress here. OK?"

Step #7: Emotion (Techniques #82–#110)

You've successfully kept a positive focus going, resisting the assignment of blame (negative emotion) and instead have engaged your employees' help on a fact-finding mission. You've expressed yourself sincerely and have clearly shown your dedication and commitment to helping everyone do better. You've conveyed your respect and caring for your employees by not blaming them.

On to step two. You go around to each person's station as promised and observe carefully how everything works. You see many ways you can streamline the work: simple rearrangements of equipment and people in order to eliminate wasted time and motion. You collect notes from all your employees at the end of the day, thanking them sincerely for their input.

The next morning, you come to the meeting armed with doughnuts and a set of charts. You didn't sleep much last night, but if this works, your kid will have braces and the Trans-Am a new transmission. You maintain good eye contact and strong voice throughout your presentation (body language and credibility). You stay standing for your presentation, so as to be able to use movement for emphasis, and you point to your charts as necessary (body language). You've drawn up a chart for every job position, taking both the worker's and your observations into account (visual aids). You thank your employees for their input and do so sincerely, emphasizing how this is a group effort and how important and valuable their contribution is (rapport building). You review how to step up production in each job position by following the directives on each chart.

You observe body language and ask for comments; whenever you see or hear an inconsistency or defensiveness, you probe to find out what's troubling that particular worker (creative listening). You make it obvious that this is a "together" effort (rapport) and keep hammering home your theme, "what's in the way? I know we can do this, what's in the way?" working and reworking the charts until both your employees and you are satisfied with the new plan. The meeting took up the whole morning, but you have something both you and your workers believe is doable.

At the end, you present your reward: "If we do this, if we up the production quotas to X in six weeks and show management we're not the dodos they've come to think of us as, I'm treating all of us to a party at Billy Bob's [the local bar and dancing hangout all the employees favor on the weekends]." Your workers are delighted, "All right!" they shout. You're reemphasizing the rapport between you and your employees by making the reward a shared experience of something they like and are continuing your positive focus with the offer of a reward as opposed to a negative focus (threat of punishment for work not done). You know the party at Billy Bob's (which serves only beer) will run you a couple of hundred dollars, but will be money well spent, since the bonus you will receive as a result of your employees' improved production will be large enough to cover the braces and the transmission as well as the party.

You realize you have to follow through, helping your employees to stay on track on a daily basis, continuing to listen to them, value them, be positive with and toward them (credibility), but heck, that's a small price to pay. You can almost see those braces shining . . .

Example #7: Convincing Your Old-Fashioned Traditionalist Boss to Allow You the Unthinkable: Flexible Work Arrangement

You've had a baby, your first, and suddenly you realize there is a world of difference between the fantasy of having a baby and the reality of an infant in the home. It doesn't matter how many books you read and how many of your girl friends you observed, there's still a vast difference. You don't want to be away from your child, not for an instant. You recognize you're not going to be able to stay with your baby twenty-four hours a day and still put food on the table, so you come up with the following: You'll work two days in the office and three days at home.

You know you can get your work done just as well with this arrangement, but the thought of approaching your boss with such a plan makes you shudder. Your boss is a fifty-four-year-old woman who raised three children on her own and never missed a day of work. Of course, she did have her mother living with her to help take care of the children for free, but you're not at all sure how you can use that to your advantage. Plus, your boss runs her department "by the book." There is no such thing as flexible hours, and "working out of my home" will probably sound to her like an excuse to goof off and get paid "good company money" for it. No one else in the department does it. How in the world are you going to swing this one?

Step #1: Credibility (Techniques #1–#14)

You know that credibility is going to matter a lot with your boss, so you prepare with the thoroughness of a general on the eve of a major confrontation. You schedule an appointment with your boss the week before you are due back from maternity leave. You resume moderate workouts so you'll get yourself back in shape. You know you'll need the energy.

You arrive early, truly dressed for the occasion. You've ascertained that your boss's primary perceptual mode is visual, so you've paid particular attention to how you look. Your outfit mirrors your boss's: clean, neat, and eminently sensible. A nice charcoal-gray suit that fits you well without showing off your figure, the skirt covering the knees, and flat pumps. Hair in place, conservatively styled (no wisps), tiny pearl stud earrings, just a little lipstick. You sit straight in your chair as you wait in the hall, trying to remember to breathe at least once in a while. You've prepared all the materials you will need in a neat file folder that you've slipped into a professional-looking attache case (borrowed from your best girl friend for the occasion), everything in duplicate.

You've arranged for a dear friend whom you really trust to stay with your baby while you take this appointment (the first time you've been away from your child since the birth), which at least allows you to be decently focused on the situation at hand and moderately relaxed. You are most certainly dedicated and committed to your cause and feel well prepared, which supports your feeling of self-confidence.

Step #2: Body Language (Techniques #15–#37)

When you're summoned in for your appointment, you take a deep breath, stand up, and walk with good posture, a straight head, and a decisive step into your boss's office. You engage good eye focus, shake hands firmly to mirror your boss's firm handshake, then sit down where indicated, sitting square, your ankles neatly tucked. You never had many mannerisms to start with, so you're not concerned on that score. You tend to freeze rather than fidget, so you simply try to keep breathing, which usually helps you stay more relaxed.

Step #3: Be Persuasive With Your Voice (Techniques #38–#47)

You know you are so nervous your voice is going to come out in a squeal, so you say "now" internally to make sure you speak rather than squeak once you open your mouth. You also make sure you speak slowly throughout, knowing your tendency is to "rush" when nervous. You take frequent pauses and articulate well, mirroring your boss's excellent articulation.

Step #4: Rapport (Techniques #48–#53)

Your boss starts off by asking you how you are and how the baby is. You answer that you are fine, the baby is well, and you seize the opportunity to build rapport by telling her you are eager to get back to work. This pleases your boss, with her unmistakeable dedication to the work ethic. She shifts back in her chair a little, leaning to one side, and you slowly mirror your boss's body language, to further estalish rapport.

"And that's why I've come to you," you say, "I want to talk to you about work. Is there a way, I've been asking myself during my maternity leave, to maintain or improve my productivity, while caring for my child [rhetorical question which serves as the umbrella statement]? Both are valuable, both are important, and both take time and energy—as you well know," you say with a serious expression on your face, hoping to further develop a sense of shared experience by mirroring your boss's values.

Step #5: Creative Listening (Techniques #54–#68)

"What do you have in mind?" your boss asks. As you continue, you observe her body shifts and facial expressions. Her emotional tone behind her words right now is somewhat wary, so you know you have an uphill battle. That's all right; you came prepared.

Step #6: Logic and Reason (Techniques #69–#81)

"I've been reviewing the company statistics on absenteeism and time lost from work due to parents' obligations to their children. I was appalled to see just how much the proper care of children ends up costing the company." You show your boss neatly drawn graphs (she's visually oriented) proving your point. "I realized," you continue, "that I was likely to become such a liability to the company also, and I don't want that [revealing weaknesses in a way that strengthens your point and your trustworthiness]. I love my work, I love my job, and I believe in this company. I want to be an asset to the company." "Go on," your boss says, still wary.

"I figured out that if I worked in the office two days a week and out of my home three days a week, I would have the flexibility that would allow me to take proper care of my child while getting my work done, since I wouldn't be tied down to specific hours and could just work until the job was done [explicit conclusion and getting to the point]."

"That's ridiculous," your boss scoffs. "No one has ever done that in this department; everybody just manages! I can't have employees all over the place not knowing where they are! How would I be able to supervise their work and assure that everything is getting done properly and on time?!"

You pace like crazy (verbally, not physically). You're ready for this one, you've role-played it with your girl friend half a dozen times. "It has never been done in this department, and of course you don't want employees all over the place. It's very important that you assure yourself that all the work is getting done as it should." This pacing quiets down your boss. You've taken her objection seriously and acknowledged the worthiness of her position. You take advantage of the lull to lead.

"Here's how this has worked in other companies," you say, showing her government reports, graphs, and summaries that demonstrate how other companies have significantly decreased absenteeism and increased productivity by offering such flexible work arrangements to parents. "That's the first point," you tell her. "It's been done before, and it's been done successfully. Second," you say, as you hand your boss a neatly typed sheet that outlines your points, even as you talk them through: "I am willing to be the guinea pig for a flex-time program that will greatly benefit the company. There is no cost to the company. I already have my own fax machine and computer, and I'm willing to pay for the hook-up to the company computer. Third, this could be a great PR move on the part of this department. Headquarters is always looking for new ways to make headlines; this would be right in line with the current business trends" (three points). You then conclude with your *theme:* "There is everything for the company to gain here, and nothing to lose."

Step #7: Emotion (Techniques #82–#110)

You stop, letting what you've said sink in. You've expressed concern and dedication as you've spoken, using positive emotions of caring about your job and your child and looking to ways to satisfy the demands of both (positive focus). You've transformed the issue from one of your individual need to be with your child to the more company-oriented focus of "benefits to the company." Your theme emphasizes a no-risk advantage to the company. "No-risk" is a much-loved money word in business, as, of course, are "decreased absenteeism" and "increased productivity." Your third point has given your boss an opportunity to shine. This is an emotional hook-in she can easily appreciate.

"Everything to gain and nothing to lose," your boss repeats (catch phrase) quietly to herself as she looks over your charts and outline. You know the fact that you came so well prepared matters greatly to your boss. "Nothing to lose," you say (repetition). "We could try it on a probationary basis, have me work two days in and three days at home for three months and evaluate the results at that time. I'm certainly willing." "Yes, I see that you are," your boss says. "All right, I'll give it some serious thought and get back to you. These are all recent statistics?" she asks. "Yes, they are," you reply, and resist the urge to ask, "Do you want more?"

The hardest part is to trust you've done enough. You have. You've opened your boss's eyes to a totally different way of thinking, one that may prove valuable to the company and to herself in the company's eyes. Your creative approach to getting what you want is truly persuasive.

EXAMPLE #8: GETTING YOUR "SOMETIME-NEXT-YEAR" CONTRACTOR TO FINISH THE JOB BY YOUR DEADLINE

Yes, you'd heard all the horror stories about contractors taking years off your life as well as years to finish a job, but you'd steeled yourself for the experience. You were faced with either selling off one of the kids, building an addition to the house, or moving to a bigger home. For some unfathomable reason, the rest of the family wouldn't let you sell off a kid, and moving to a bigger place just wasn't economically feasible. So, construction it was. The work was supposed to be done by the beginning of October. It is now the end of October. You thought you'd allotted plenty of extra time for delays, and so forth, but you're almost bumping into the holidays, which means your in-laws and other assorted family will be visiting, and the work is still just dragging along. You have nightmares of your in-laws criticizing every inch of work, yelling at the laborers, and in general making your life utterly miserable. You have to get the work completed, but don't want to get the contractor so mad he walks off the job. What do you do?

Step #1: Credibility (Techniques #1–#14)

Credibility is not synonymous with panic. There's a way here; just take it success-step by success-step. First of all, remember that a goodly chunk of your credibility is already in place: You have been paying the contractor on time and not one of your checks has bounced. Your trustworthiness is assured. You can build your expertness (preparedness) with one quick trip to the local library. Ask the reference librarian for a "construction made easy" type book that will tell you what are the different elements that go into building a house addition. Your common sense tells you there is a foundation, a frame, internal and external walls, plaster, plumbing, electricity, doors and windows, but you feel more confident if you can get some specific information. You're not looking to become a contractor, just to be able to speak with some degree of authority.

You respect your contractor's time by calling and asking when he next expects to be on site. You arrange to meet him at that time.

You adopt a positive attitude. You are outwardly focused toward your contractor, you are committed to getting your house ready for the holiday activities, and you remain confident that you can see this through. You've found that repeating to yourself "I can do this" numerous times through the day is a deceptively simple yet effective way to affirm your sense of your own power.

When you're ready to interact with your contractor (notice I did not say confront—this is not a battle, this is an interaction designed for your success), you dress appropriately for walking around the site, but you make sure your clothes are neat and clean nonetheless. You try to stay moderately relaxed and keep breathing.

Step #2: Body Language (Techniques #15–#37)

You greet your contractor with good eye contact, a genuine smile, and a firm handshake. You assume by your bearing and manner that this meeting will be a successful one.

Step #3: Be Persuasive With Your Voice (Techniques #38–#47)

You ask genuinely, "How's it been going?" and really listen to and acknowledge what your contractor says. You keep your voice pleasant, direct, and easy. You somehow manage to avoid any signs of anxiety such as "uhs" and other extraneous noises.

Step #4: Rapport (Techniques #48–#53)

You mirror your contractor's body language and general style (energy and vocal tone), but only as is comfortable for you and in keeping with your need to remain confident and straightforward. You ask your contractor to take you on a "tour" of the work done. You compliment him on whatever looks well and properly done (positive focus). When he presents you with the difficulties he's encountered in getting different parts of the work done, you pace him accordingly: "It's hard when workers don't come through for you."

You're ready to lead. You invite your contractor into the main part of the house for a cup of coffee. You don't want to put him in a potentially uncomfortable position with his workers by talking to him in front of them (respect).

Step #5: Creative Listening (Techniques #54–#68)

You've paid close attention to your contractor's body language as he took you on the "tour." You think you've been able to assess pretty well which of his stories of "it's the workers' fault" were true and which were stretching the truth from your observation of the inconsistencies between his words and his body language. You continue to monitor his body language response to your words as you speak.

Step #6: Logic and Reason (Techniques #69–#81)

You pour your contractor a cup of coffee and sit down. You engage good eye focus, and then you begin (doing things one thing at a time). "You've done some really good work," you say (positive focus), pausing to let it sink in, "but it doesn't look to me like you're going to be done anytime soon." You pause. Your contractor makes some noises about difficulties, problems, unforeseen circumstances. You nod, acknowledge, and pace appropriately, always maintaining good eye focus. You do not scream, pound your fists on the table, or hit your contractor upside the head, although the temptation to do so is extreme.

"Well, we have a situation here," you say, calmly and evenly. "My in-laws are coming out for their annual visit, and they expect to stay with us. Their arrival was planned and scheduled according to the date you originally gave me as to when the work would be done. Now, I'm confident that if we think together on this, we can come up with a plan that'll get the construction finished in time for their arrival [theme 'two heads are better than one,' positive focus, umbrella statement, explicit conclusion]. Here's what I've figured out on my own."

Step #7: Emotion (Techniques #82–#110)

Without giving your contractor time to say or do anything at this point, you whip out a well-prepared sheet of paper that lists what needs to be done in a usual house addition (ah, how good research and preparedness pays off!), and you now proceed to go over this list with your contractor: "Where are we on the framing? Is there anything left to do?" "Where are we on interior walls? Is there anything we still need to do here?" and you write down carefully what he says as to the status and "need to do" on each item. You do so dispassionately, without showing surprise, horror, or shock even though your stomach keeps turning over at the size of each "need to do." You simply ask, "Where are we at?" and write down the answer.

You keep nodding, acknowledging and pacing all the way through. You verify that you've covered all the areas.

You steadfastly deal in businesslike fashion with a business problem. You maintain emotional rapport with your contractor and a positive focus by using the word "we," rather than the accusatory "you." Much as it is desirable to use "you" to directly involve people and personalize issues, in this case personalizing the issue will only make your contractor defensive. It will also not be in line with your "two heads are better than one" theme. "We" supports that theme.

Then you go over each unfinished item, one at a time, and ask the contractor what he suggests (respect and maintaining rapport): "What do you suggest we do here? How can we get this part finished quickly?" You help your contractor think. Two heads really are better than one in many cases. As long as you maintain a genuine positive attitude of wanting to work this out, as opposed to the negative attitude of wanting to blame, you will succeed. You have plenty of common sense: Sometimes a person outside a given profession will be able to come up with original solutions to problems just because he/she isn't so close to the situation.

Your contractor is pleasantly surprised. "I knew we were running late on this job," he says, "and I fully expected you to take me to task about it. I appreciate that you didn't. Look, I'll do my best to get to these items right away. We might have to work Sundays. Will that disturb your family?" You could cry with relief. Will that disturb your family? you think to yourself—he clearly doesn't know your family; the likelier scenario is that your family will disturb him!

EXAMPLE #9: GETTING AN UNBUDGEABLE SELLER TO BUDGE AND SELL YOU THE HOUSE YOU LONG TO CALL HOME AT *YOUR* PRICE

You and your spouse have been looking at houses to buy—and looking, and looking . . . You finally find the perfect place for you, your spouse, three kids, two dogs, and one gerbil to call home—only the price is over your budget. The real estate agent goes back and forth between you and the seller, but the seller refuses to budge. The price is the price, and that's it. You and your spouse agonize over what to do. You look around for another place to live, but find nothing that even comes close to what you want, and finally you decide OK, if you can get the seller to throw in the washer and dryer, the customized curtains and cabinets not originally in the deal, you could stretch your budget to afford the house. Swell idea, but how do you get the unbudgeable seller to budge and see things your way?

Step #1: Credibility (Techniques #1–#14)

Preparedness is very important in this situation. You realize that you need to know what kind of person the seller is in order to convince him. You let your real estate agent in on what you're trying to do and ask her to gather as much information as she can about the seller. The first thing you find out is that the "him" isn't a "him"—the seller is a married couple, Mr. and Mrs. Cooper, retired, old-fashioned, somewhat staid, with a couple of grown children and several grandchildren scattered about the country. The Coopers are financially comfortable, and are only selling their home because it seems big to them now that the children are gone. They are in no particular hurry to sell, which now makes their "unbudgeability" understandable to you. The couple has been active in community affairs over the years, and with the help of the local librarian, you find a few articles where their good deeds are mentioned, along with some photographs. Great! Now you have something on which to base your credibility, as well as your overall strategy.

You tell your real estate agent that you are ready to make a serious offer, but want to do so in person. Your agent arranges for a face to face meeting with the Coopers in their home. Rather than arrive, as you usually would, in jeans and sweats, with all three children flying about you and the two dogs barking away in the car, you and your spouse dress neatly and conservatively (out of respect for the Cooper's traditional values), and ask only your most well-behaved five year old daughter to accompany you (out of respect for the Cooper's age and old-fashioned ways: "Children are to be seen and not heard"). You leave the other two kids, the dogs, and the gerbil under the watchful eye of a baby-sitter. You even have the car washed, just in case the Coopers should see your eight-year old Ford as you drive up.

You and your spouse leave yourselves plenty of time to get to your appointment, and make sure that your hair and attire are all in place when you arrive, in good time. You sit a moment in the car before getting out, and take a few breaths to calm your nervously beating heart (will this work, won't it?), knowing how important it is to be moderately relaxed. You remind each other to stay outwardly focused towards the sellers, and to stay positive in your approach. Your daughter knows she is taking part in something important and is being a perfect little angel (pray that it lasts!)

Step #2: Body Language (Techniques #15–#37)

You ring the doorbell, and when Mr. Cooper opens the door, you engage good eye focus, smile sincerely, and shake Mr. Cooper's outstretched hand firmly as you introduce yourself, and then your spouse and child. You maintain good posture as you walk into the living room, by your stance letting the Coopers know that you are confident and energized. You wait until you and your family are seated and the initial chit-chat of social amenities has taken place before you open the discussion (doing things one thing at a time). You maintain good eye focus throughout, and resist your usual nervous habits of running your hand through your hair or clearing your throat.

Step #3: Be Persuasive With Your Voice (Techniques #38–#47)

You remind yourself to use good articulation in speaking with the Coopers, and to keep your vocal tone calm and steady, so as not to betray your inner anxiety. Knowing that your tendency when anxious is to pitch your voice above its normal confident register, you make sure you take a deep breath to place your voice before you actually speak.

Step #4: Rapport (Techniques #48–#53)

In the process of establishing your credibility, you have been using your knowledge of mirroring to mirror the Cooper's somewhat old-fashioned and traditional style, both in your manner and dress. You now mirror also with your vocal patterns, allowing your speech to reflect the slower pace and somewhat formal vocabulary of the Coopers, increasingly creating rapport non-verbally as you prepare to create rapport with your words.

You take a deep breath, this "pace and lead" thing is new to you, but you're bound and determined to get this house, so you're willing to give it a try. You begin your pace with a clear and unequivocal acceptance of the Cooper's famed "unbudgeability."

"We're not going to ask you to come down on your price," you say, "that's not what this is about." The Coopers look at each other in surprise. This is not what they expected. "Your house is just beautiful," you say, continuing, "and worth every dime you are asking for it. But to us, you see, buying a house isn't like buying cereal. It's important to us to have some sense of the history of the house and what it's been like for you to live here. If you don't mind, we'd like you to take us on a tour, tell us a little about what you've done to the house, what some of the special features are, and what you've especially enjoyed about living here. Things like that," you say, calmly and pleasantly.

Once again, the Coopers look at each other, and Mr. Cooper says "Sure, why not."

Step #5: Creative Listening (Techniques #54–#68)

As the Coopers take you and your family around the house, you discover that Mr. Cooper's avocation is carpentry, that he finished many of the furniture pieces, and that he installed a number of the cabinets. Mrs. Cooper, you find out as the tour continues, has a love of fabrics, and chose the materials for the curtains and bedspreads with much care and attention to detail. You pay attention to the Coopers' body language and facial expressions as they describe different features of the house. You respond particularly warmly to those features that elicit pleasant expressions and vocal tones from the Coopers as they speak of them. You realize how important the warmth of a home has been to the Coopers, how the couple transformed a structure of wood and plaster into something much more meaningful, a safe and comfortable haven for their family to live in and be together. You increase rapport by sharing with the Coopers how important that is to you, with your family. You are generous with your acknowledgments both in body language and "uh-huhs."

Your daughter comes alive when she sees the room the Cooper's refer to as the "grandkids' room." There's a dollhouse Mr. Cooper put together with his grandchildren, bookcases built "child-height" and many other wonderful special features. You see the Cooper's delight in your daughter's reaction and figure this is a great time to start your lead.

Step #6: Logic and Reason (Techniques #69–#81)

Back in the living room once again, you ask the Coopers "What did you want to take with you? I know you were thinking about taking the washer-dryer, what else?" The Coopers proceed to enumerate the items they want to take, you nod, and write it all down, item by item. "That's pretty much what I thought," you say, "I'd like to show you something I figured out." You take out a neatly written up sheet of figures, written somewhat large (older people often prefer larger writing) on clean white paper (visual aid). "May I?" you ask, coming over to their side, sitting by them on their living room couch (by your body language, allying yourself with them, rather than sitting across from them, which implies being against them).

"I figured out," you say, "about what it was going to cost you to have the washer-dryer, the curtains and cabinets removed and stored." And sure enough, there on your paper you've listed approximate cost of removal and storage. "Huh," says Mr. Cooper, "let me see that." He peers at it for a moment, and asks "That much, huh? Who drew this up?" "I asked Bill, down at the hardware store to help me figure it out," you reply, knowing that Bill has served as handyman for the local people and figuring (correctly) that Bill probably served as such for the Coopers. "Oh, Bill," says Mr. Cooper, "good man." "And why did you do this?" Mrs. Cooper asks. "Well, Mrs. Cooper, we can't really afford this place," you say, advancing your theme of 'honesty is the best policy,' "but my family and I really love it, so we thought maybe we could find a way that we could afford it, if you were willing to work with us a bit on it."

Because you have taken the time and been thorough in your development of rapport, creating and reinforcing common ground, with your appreciation of those things which have value for the Coopers, Mr. and Mrs. Cooper are willing to listen to you. They do not reject your suggestion out of hand. "Mmph," says Mr. Cooper, waiting. "Well," you say starting your lead, this being do or die time, "it's going to cost you X dollars to remove and store the things you want to take, plus another X dollars to fix the holes and repaint where you remove the cabinets. I mean," you say to his surprised look, "How likely is it that you'll find someone who wants to buy your house at the price you're asking for it if it has a bunch of holes and mismatched paint in it (rhetorical question)?" "Mmph," Mr. Cooper repeats, "hadn't thought of that." "Essentially," you say, plowing on and showing the Coopers the bottom line on your visual aid, "that reduces your price on the house to X dollars." Staying true to your 'honesty is the best policy theme,' you then outline for the Coopers how, if they are willing to simply leave the washer-dryer and other items in the house, you and your family can stretch your budget to meeting their asking price, because you won't have to buy a new washer-dryer and so forth for quite a while. And with the money the Coopers save on not removing/storing/fixing (three points), they can buy things for whatever new home they find for themselves which will fit that new place wonderfully.

You have used sound logic to back up your desire for the house. You have given the Coopers tangible reasons how your desire could benefit them. You have gotten to the point quickly and effectively. Even when people are comfortable financially, "save money" are (literal!) money-words, especially to older people, who even when well-off are frequently living on a fixed income. You have impressed the Coopers with your willingness to do the work involved in figuring out the costs to them, and furthered rapport by figuring those costs with someone familiar to them (Bill).

Now comes the hard part. You close your mouth and wait. You would love to keep talking until the Coopers give up and go "yes, OK, fine, take the house," but you know such outbursts happen only on Perry Mason reruns, so you wait. You give the Coopers the space to think, you respect their process of decision-making.

Step #7: Emotions (Techniques #82–#110)

You have been honest in your praise and comments. You are genuinely interested in the work the Coopers have lovingly put into their home, and you have only made statements which reflect your truth. You have not tried to manipulate or emotionally 'con' the Coopers by devaluing their home to reduce the price. You are completely sincere in your 'honesty is the best policy' approach. Your genuineness shows through, and you are believable.

The Coopers look at each other again. "We need to think about this," they say. You nod. "OK," you say, "I'll just leave this here (referring to your page of numbers), I have a copy at home (leaving the visual aid as a reinforcer to your point of view)." You can't believe it—they didn't say "no"! They are actually considering your offer! Your agent tells you as she escorts you to your car that this is amazing, she's never seen the Coopers take to people as they seem to have taken to you and your family. You try very hard to stay calm and composed . . . until later that night, when your agent calls and says "Guess what, you got the house!" when you let out a whooping hoot-and-a-holler, and dance merrily about your (soon to be old) house with your spouse, three kids, two dogs and the gerbil.

Example #10: Getting Your Competitive "Me First" Colleagues to Back Your Project Rather Than Their Own

You work for a toy manufacturer. You are part of a team that develops new toys. Each member of the team works independently in coming up with ideas for new toys, but any toy that is actually to be produced must be accepted by the whole team since the team will work together to develop the finished product. You have come up with what you think is truly the next best-selling toy for three to five year olds in America. You are well aware, however, that at least three of the eight-person team are also currently working on their own toy projects and will be only too eager to shoot down your idea. You really believe in this toy! How do you persuade your team to accept your idea as "the" next toy to produce?

Step #1: Credibility (Techniques #1–#14)

Your credibility, generally speaking, is solid with your team. You've always supported other team members' projects to your fullest ability and have done your share of the work on time and without complaining. Appearance matters little at the plant and certainly won't impact your credibility, except for the "neat and clean" part, which you always are anyway. You figure the one area of credibility you can really work on is "expertness." You decide to prepare with rare dedication so that you will be ready to address every possible issue your colleagues are likely to raise. You review old notes to see the types of comments made and questions asked in the past on various toy proposals. You *really* want this toy to see the light of day!

When the day of the meeting on your toy comes up, you ready yourself with the charts and illustrations you've drawn up, plus the hand-outs you've put together for each team member. You then prep your attitude, reminding yourself to focus out toward your team members and to remain positive throughout. You are dedicated, that's for sure. "Moderately relaxed" is a challenge, but at least you didn't compound your nervousness with extra coffee this morning, and you did take an extra-long shower to help you relax. You are, as always, on time for the meeting (respect).

Step #2: Body Language (Techniques #15–#37)

After the usual meeting preliminaries, it's your turn to present your toy. You stand up (for better energy and a more authoritative presentation) and walk over to where you've placed the easels to hold your charts. Your energy is good, your step confident, your head level, and your facial expression reflects your inner excitement and enthusiasm. You remind yourself to make eye focus with each of the team members, going from one to another at different points during your presentation. You begin now by looking directly at each of your team members in turn and then, finally, begin to speak (doing things one thing at a time).

You gesture effectively to make your points, but other than that, you keep your body relatively still. You've practiced making this presentation in front of a videocamera, so you're comfortable about how you look and come across. You discovered some unpleasant mannerisms in the process, which you were only too happy to dispense with.

Step #3: Be Persuasive With Your Voice (Techniques #38–#47)

You speak clearly and articulately, in short sentences, using pauses to accentuate your points. You let your voice carry your enthusiasm and excitement about the product through color, peaks, and valleys, being careful not to rush or hurry what you have to say.

Step #4: Rapport (Techniques #48–#53)

You create rapport with your colleagues by mirroring their general tone and style, something you already do quite naturally. Most of your colleagues are perceptually visually oriented, with a secondary emphasis on the kinesthetic perceptual mode. You've made sure to include words, expressions, and demonstrations from both perceptual modes in your presentation.

Step #5: Creative Listening (Techniques #54–#68)

As you speak, you observe your colleague's body language to keep you on track, altering your presentation to either emphasize or illustrate a point when you notice body language that seems closed or defensive. You listen attentively to the objections your colleagues raise, so that you can pace them accurately.

Step #6: Logic and Reason (Techniques #69–#81)

You begin your presentation in silence, by unveiling your first chart (visual aid), which is an accurate artist's rendering of your new toy. As the others look at the rendering and comment on it, you walk silently around the table, distributing your handouts. You return to your original position and wait a moment before speaking (one thing at a time, stillness for effect before saying something important), then say: "Introducing—Schnuffy! You'll find a photocopy of this artist's rendition along with all the manufacturing specs for Schnuffy in the demo kit I just handed each of you." Your colleagues are impressed. No one has ever prepared *handouts* before: they've all just winged these meetings and sort of hashed everything out as they went.

Step #7: Emotion (Techniques #82–#110)

You now unveil your second chart: "The motto for this toy [rhetorical question]? 'Safe Toys for a Safe America' [money words]': this toy is (1) child safe, (2) environmentally safe, and (3) promotes learning about safety [your toy motto elaborated in three points, all of which are highly emotionally charged positive concepts]." The motto with its attendant three points is written on your chart as well as in each team member's handout (visual reinforcement). "What's in it for the company [rhetorical question, getting to the point]? A lotta bang for a little buck [theme, concept with emotional significance to the company]." Your colleagues howl with glee, "What the heck is that supposed to mean?" they ask.

"Thought you'd never ask," you say, grinning, mirroring their mirth (rapport). You unveil another chart that graphically illustrates the three points supporting your theme: "Number 1: This toy can be manufactured using existing molds for all the frame and structural components. The only new components are outer covering and padding. That saves us a bundle on manufacturing costs. Number 2: We can use public-service announcements and other such venues promoting safety to piggyback the product, so we save a great deal in advertising and marketing expense as well as get terrific exposure. Number 3: This toy with its 'safety' campaign will help rejuvenate the company and give it a much needed facelift in line with public demand for nonviolent toys." Your points address the primary issues each toy idea must take into account satisfactorily: manufacturing cost, advertising and marketing cost, and PR possibilities (matters of emotional relevance to your team).

"How are you going to sell that to corporate?" asks one of the members. "The question is," you reply, "how are we going to sell this to corporate [encouraging rapport]. I just have to sell you on this; we can brainstorm together on how to convince corporate." Your colleagues laugh. You ask for questions, and proceed to pace and lead systematically to your theme and three points. You've done your preparation work well. As simple as your presentation is, it covers all the relevant points thoroughly.

You've stayed calm and centered throughout, demonstrating sincere dedication to your product, allowing your enthusiasm and excitement to shine through (appropriate emotional choices). You've resisted pushing the panic button whenever someone asked a question, and you've relied on pacing and leading to see you through. You've maintained a sense of humor throughout your presentation (rapport) and presented your product in positive terms. You're still nervous as can be when the team takes a vote, and it's only once they say "OK, you're on," that you take your first full breath of the morning.

The others congratulate you, you sit down at your usual place at the table, and one of the members turns to the others and says: "OK, so how are we going to sell this to corporate?" Oh my, but success is sweet.

Example #11: Buying Your First New Car Without Being Swindled

You're buying your first new car—finally! You're absolutely thrilled. Your only experience with buying (used) cars, however, has been with individuals. You've heard all those awful stories about car salespersons, and you're afraid that given your inexperience, you are going to be nailed as an "easy mark" within the first ten seconds you walk onto the showroom floor. You don't want to seem naive (which you are) or overeager (which you are). How do you pull it off and drive out with the car of your dreams without indenturing yourself for life to pay it off?

Step #1: Credibility (Techniques #1–#14)

Well, for starters, if you don't look like an easy mark, you probably won't get taken for an easy mark. Establishing credibility is high on the list of "what to do" in this situation. The "expertness" or preparedness portion of credibility is critical to your success.

You figure out what car you want to buy. You talk to friends, you read *Consumer Reports*-type magazines, you ask your reference librarian for sources of reliable information on new cars. Once you know the make, model, and various extras you want on the car, you look in your local paper for how dealers are pricing the car. You then target three dealerships that appear to have a large selection and the best advertised prices. Then you locate one more dealership that is in an expensive area and that seems "pricier" than your three targeted dealerships. Here is where you are going to do all your field research, anonymously, giving yourself permission to look totally goofy and inept since you are not going to buy the car at this clearly too-expensive dealership.

You go to the expensive dealership, where you look the car over, ask a million questions, are willing to appear totally naive and uncar-educated, get a test drive, find out what documents would be needed to apply for a car loan, what the interest rates are, what the down should be, how much insurance costs, and so on and so on. You do all this basic groundwork (preparedness) under some fictitious name, so it doesn't matter.

Then you go home, and given what you learned today, you figure out exactly what you want on the car (a CD player? air conditioning? rich Corinthian leather?), a top-dollar amount you are willing to pay (at the most, $X), how much you are willing to put down and how much you want to pay per month, and then pull together the necessary documents you'll need to get loan approval.

You may not be the most "expert" potential car buyer out there, but you are now armed with a great deal more credibility than you had before you did your research.

It's time to attend to your physical credibility. You dress so that you look professional, conservative and no-nonsense. As always, you are clean, neat, and tidy about your person. You keep your accessories down to a minimum. You wear your hair in a neat professional style. When you walk in to the first of your three targeted dealerships, you make sure that your eye focus is clear and direct, your attitude positive (knowing inside that you are well equipped to make this transaction helps a lot), and that you are fully committed to driving off in your new car (!) today.

Step #2: Body Language (Techniques #15–#37)

Your posture is good, you have good energy (preferably courtesy of your moderate workout, not due to three cups of espresso), and you take a nice, comfortable, neutral stance to talk with the salesperson. You maintain good eye focus, a pleasant expression on your face, and you do not shift, fidget, or fuss. Your relative stillness speaks volumes about your confidence and self-assurance.

Step #3: Be Persuasive With Your Voice (Techniques #38–#47)

For once, you are more silent than talkative. What you have to say, you say clearly, directly, and with good energy. You drop all signs of indecisiveness or nervousness such as "uh," "I think," "I believe," or those nervous giggles that sometimes afflict you at the most inconvenient times.

You've practiced saying your "intro" line to a friend until you can say it easily and without stumbling: "I'd like to see an X model Z car, please."

Step #4: Rapport (Techniques #48–#53)

You create rapport with the salesperson by mirroring body language and vocal tone only to a degree that does not interfere with your businesslike and no-nonsense attitude. You determine the salesperson's perceptual mode; this will come in handy later.

Once you are shown the car you want, you open the deal making with your offer: "I am interested in buying this car, and I'll give you $X (the low end of what you consider an acceptable price range for this car) for it." Then you are quiet and stay perfectly still. The salesperson proceeds to sputter, laugh, plead, and generally give you a remarkable and very entertaining performance, which all comes down to "That's too low." Once the salesperson has finished and only then, you start to pace: "It must be really rough [you've determined the salesperson is kinesthetic] to have people offer what you think is such a low amount for this terrific vehicle." The salesperson is nodding away; he/she couldn't agree with you more. "And it is awful that the price tag on this car is already so low it barely comes up to factory cost of the car," you say.

Step #5: Creative Listening (Techniques #54–#68)

Although you are, as always, mindful of another's body language when you speak to him/her, in this case, your creative listening is primarily devoted to listening attentively to what the salesperson says so as to be able to pace accurately. The emphasis in this situation is on credibility, being confident, and holding firm to your $ commitment to yourself, less so on listening to body language.

Step #6: Logic and Reason (Techniques #69–#81)

"I'll increase my offer by $X," you say. "That's my final offer. I'm ready to buy the car right here, right now at $X [theme: 'Do it right, do it now,' umbrella statement, and explicit conclusion]. Let's go see your manager and sign the deal."

Step #7: Emotion (Techniques #82–#110)

You remain calm, self-confident, and unflustered throughout. You are ready to walk out the door if the salesperson doesn't give you what you want. This is only your first targeted dealership. You are treating this like a business transaction, which is what it is in reality, and not like the emotional transaction it feels like. Car salespersons are not used to calm people who have done their research and know what they want. They are used to emotional people who haven't done much research and are either ready to fight or to cry. If you just maintain your confidence (credibility) and cool (appropriate emotion in a business setting), and have done good research (expertness), you'll get the car and the deal you want.

You've used a theme with a powerful emotional hook in it for car dealerships: "ready to buy right here, right now." You've shown your readiness and understanding of the car-buying process by asking to see the manager (who has to sign off on the deal).

When the salesperson once again gives you the inevitable "But I can't sell it so low" with the accompanying pleading, joking, and so forth, listen very carefully, so that you can pace accurately and then lead by simply restating (repetition) your bottom line (theme): "I'm ready to buy the car right here, right now at $X. Let's go see your manager and sign the deal [maintaining a positive focus and positive emotion]." If you have done this three times and the salesperson won't take you over to the manager, be willing to walk out the door.

"Too bad," you say in parting, "I was ready to buy." If the salesperson doesn't come running out after you at some point, even once you're back in your (old) car driving off, then you did indeed offer an amount too low. Recalculate how much you are willing to offer, still staying below your personal limit, and repeat the exercise at the next targeted dealership.

If you make it to the manager's office, then you may have to part with a little more $ in the way of unanticipated "extras," but you should be able to get the car for just about what you said your bottom line was. By the time you finish the deal, you will be an old pro, ready to take on any car salesperson worth his/her salt.

Example #12: Convincing Your Obstinate Soon-to-Be Mother-in-Law to Pay for the Wedding *You* Want

This is your first wedding. You're really hoping it is your one and only wedding, so it's very important to you that it be just the way you want it. You and your beloved are of one mind on this (as on so many other things): You want a small, intimate ceremony with only your nearest and dearest friends. Your future mother-in-law, who so sweetly and generously offered to pay for just about everything for the wedding, is turning into a complete tyrant. You now realize that she offered to pay so that she could take over your wedding. Your future mother-in-law's idea of a "small, intimate gathering" is 500 of her closest and dearest friends. You can't afford to turn away her generosity (you are desperately trying to save enough to move into someplace decent to live together), but the thought of her 500 nearest-and-dearest at *your* wedding sets your teeth on edge. What do you do?

Step #1: Credibility (Techniques #1–#14)

Don't panic. The more panic inducing a situation is, the more important it is to back off, take a deep breath, and start to climb up the steps to success.

Preparedness is important here. You realize if you try to wing it, you'll lose, so you plan your strategy carefully. You respect your future mother-in-law by making an appointment with her to talk, inviting her to Sunday brunch (her favorite meal) at her favorite spot. You verified what her favorite table is and arranged with the hostess to reserve that table. You know image is important to your future mother-in-law (sometimes you think it's everything), so you dress and groom yourself in a way she would approve of.

You are on time (respect) to pick up your future mother-in-law since that's her preference (even remembering as you drove over to her place to throw all the debris out of the passenger side), and you don't even begin to talk about the wedding until after the meal (doing things one thing at a time). When she brings up the subject (there are few things she loves to talk about as much as your wedding) as you are both chomping away, you simply smile and say "Oh, let's not talk about that now. Mmmm, isn't this salad wonderful?" You are outwardly focused toward her, interested in the events of her week; you are positive in your comments and try (OK, so yes, this is asking a lot) to be moderately relaxed, preferably without the aid of a controlled substance. You jogged vigorously this morning to help calm your nerves. It seems to be working. Somewhat.

Step #2: Body Language (Techniques #15–#37)

You let your posture and eye focus reflect a confident self-assurance (whether you feel it or not at this point) and sit on your hands any time you feel the urge to gesticulate wildly or play with your table setting. When you listen to your future mother-in-law, you maintain direct eye focus, and you are still. You let the quiet of your body express the importance you attach to her words.

Step #3: Be Persuasive With Your Voice (Techniques #38–#47)

When you speak, you are clear and direct. You avoid the "I think," "sort of," and "maybe if" that crop up all too often in your usual speech. You take a deep breath before speaking to make sure your voice is settled within your chest. You speak in short sentences, leaving pauses for thoughts to sink in.

Step #4: Rapport (Techniques #48–#53)

In choosing your outfit for the lunch date, you mirror your future mother-in-law's style as well as attending to the credibility factors. You attentively mirror her body language as is appropriate throughout lunch, as well as her energy and vocal tone, again, as is appropriate, meaning you don't stretch past your personal range and you stay within the bounds of common sense. For example, when you were designing your strategy of persuasion prior to the actual meeting, you determined that if your future mother-in-law was totally in a foul mood that day, it would not be wise to mirror her foul mood. You decided you could maintain a tone of compassionate concern that would be a logical partner to her mood without cloning it.

Where you achieve the greatest rapport, however, in this situation, is with your pace.

Step #5: Creative Listening (Techniques #54–#68)

You listen attentively with both eyes and ears as you present your cause to your future mother-in-law. You maintain good eye focus and watch her body language for signs of distress, defensiveness, or upset, which you then defuse.

Step #6: Logic and Reason (Techniques #69–#81)

Lunch over, mouth wiped, napkin down, you take a deep breath (quietly and unobtrusively), engage good eye focus, and begin. "Mom," you say (you know she loves it when you call her that), "I can't thank you enough for what you are doing for us—with the wedding. You are so very special to us." You wait. You hope she will say something like "Well, you're very special to me too, dear." She does! Great. It's safe to continue. "And that's a great feeling, being special," you say, pacing, "and that's why we've been thinking, 'How can we help make this wedding as special as Mom is to us '[rhetorical question with embedded theme of 'specialness,' umbrella statement, maintaining a positive focus]? What we realized is that by inviting hundreds of guests, we're taking away from the specialness of the wedding, we're allowing it to be just a big party, and that's not what this very special moment is all about."

"You mean you don't want a big party? What about all my friends?" Mom asks, looking horribly confused, her face all knotted up in a desperate frown. "Oh, no, Mom, of course we want a big party," you say, watching her body language and facial expression relax once again. "We just don't want it at the same time as the wedding." Mom's face screws up again. "I don't understand," she says. "Mom," you say, "we want the wedding to be as special as you are [repeat of theme]—with just a few select very special people there who will really appreciate what you're doing for us, and then later, after we come back from our honeymoon, we'll throw an afternoon party for absolutely all your friends in Aunt Edna's backyard [explicit conclusion]. That way we can have all the kids and everybody, just like you want (point one of three-point development). And we'll do all the setting up and everything (point two). It'll cost you a lot less (point three) and that way the wedding itself will be really special [repetition of theme]—just like you [repetition; using your warmest, most loving voice]."

Step #7: Emotion (Techniques #82–#110)

"It's like having an *A* list, Mom [an analogy that has meaning for Mom; she reads the movie star magazines avidly]," you continue. "You know, like the celebrities: there's always a very small, select *A* list that gets to go to the really special events, and then a bigger *B* list that goes to the more normal events. You'll have your very own *A* list—just like Faye Dunaway or Anne Bancroft [two of her favorite stars] [maintaining a positive focus, using an emotional hook that makes sense to Mom, rapport]."

The key to this, of course, is your impassioned sincerity and enthusiasm about your plan. Even if you don't totally believe that your future mother-in-law is all that special, surely there is something about her that you can relate to that you do think is special (the fact that she gave birth to your beloved, for example), and from that small reality, your conviction can grow. "Being special" is a money word: Everyone likes to be thought of as being special. It is also a catch phrase in this case that conveniently captures the essence of your theme. "Being appreciated" is another powerful money word, especially to people such as your future mother-in-law who never feels as appreciated as she should be.

You make your voice very warm on the words "special" and "appreciated" to express the essence of those words vocally (color). You have personalized the analogy (and therefore your point) by telling Mom she'll have her very own *A* list, using the word "you" to do so. "Cost you a lot less" is also an emotionally relevant phrase.

You now buttress your argument with either a neatly handwritten or a neatly typed (depending on your future mother-in-law's preference—to some older people, good handwriting is more valuable than typed material) sheet (visual aid) that shows the cost breakdown of a "special wedding" plus reception in Aunt Edna's backyard (you are pretty sure of Aunt Edna; you have a couple of other reasonable possibles you've thought of should Aunt Edna fall through), versus your future mother-in-law's current version of the wedding.

You didn't talk to Aunt Edna about your plan ahead of time, so that when your future mother-in-law objects, "Did you talk to Edna about this already? Was this her idea?" you can say in all honesty, "Oh, no, Mom, I wanted to share making this wedding special with the person who is so special to me in all this—and that's you [repetition of theme]."

"Well, if that's really what you want," Mom says, sighing. "An *A* list, huh?" she says, intrigued. "Well, let's see, that would be . . .." And she starts to name fifty of her nearest and dearest. "Mom?" you say gently. She doesn't hear you. "Mom?" you try again. "Yes, dear?" she replies, somewhat distracted,. "Mom, I've read that Faye Dunaway's *A* list is only ten people" (getting her back on your track with an emotional hook), you say (tabloids read in supermarket lines count, right?). "Ten people!!!" your future mother-in-law exclaims. "Ten," you say, nodding. "It's a real challenge, but if Faye and Anne can do it, you can too [positive focus]." "Mmm," she says, "yes, well—all right. I mean, if Faye and Anne can do it . . ."

EXAMPLE #13: WOOING THE VOTERS AWAY FROM THAT OH-SO-POPULAR INCUMBENT AND GETTING *YOURSELF* ELECTED

You're running for mayor against the popular incumbent, Mayor Bart. You've done well on the city council, but frankly, few people have heard of you. *Everybody*, however, has heard of Mayor Bart, and it seems like *everybody* likes him. You've met the mayor—heck, you've worked during his administration, and you like him too. He's truly a hail-fellow-well-met-type guy, not a sleazy, slick, mean, or otherwise objectionable bone in his body. He just isn't very effective, which is why you're running against him. You can't put the guy down, however, voters would hate you for it, so how in the world do you run successfully against a genuine "nice guy"? What do you say at the rallies to change people's minds?

Step #1: Credibility (Techniques #1–#14)

Credibility is of great importance in politics. Since few of the voters will ever get to know you, 99.9 percent of the electorate will judge you on how you measure up to their stereotyped definitions of credibility. Knowing this, you take special pains to assure that you present a clean, neat, well-groomed, in-shape persona, dressed professionally and conservatively (which is stereotypically associated with power and trustworthiness), and in keeping with the general style of your electorate and community (rapport). You've attended to your hair style so it is conservative yet suits your face, and your glasses are the right prescription so you can see just fine (without squinting, which makes you look shifty), with the frames properly adjusted so the lenses don't fall out like they did when you campaigned for city council.

You've practiced good eye focus and a firm handshake, your ability to do things one at a time is developing nicely, you've finally learned how to stay comfortably in a neutral stance, and you can "be still" on cue.

Your attitude supports your physical credibility. You enjoy people, and therefore it's automatic for you to focus out toward them; you are positive by nature and are dedicated to your cause. You're not exactly what you'd call "moderately relaxed," so you've been listening to some stress-reduction audiotapes at night to help you get there. It seems to be doing some good.

You are well prepared for the rally. You have a good track record on the city council and are well liked among your fellow politicians and professional peers. The only thing that stands in your way is good old lovable Mayor Bart. . . .

Step #2: Body Language (Techniques #15–#37)

You arrive at the rally with an upbeat, energized step, a smile on your face, good posture, and with your head held level. You've eradicated the mannerisms and useless gestures from your body language and have practiced sufficiently with a videocamera that you feel confident your gestures are at least decently expressive. As you stand behind the podium, you remember not to clutch onto it as a drowning person to a lifesaver, but just let your hands rest lightly. You have an outline in front of you with your main points; you've practiced your speech enough so that you can maintain good eye focus with the crowd.

As you greet the crowd, you deliberately look first at one section of the crowd, then at another, then at another, spending a moment or two on each. As you give your speech, you keep focusing for several sentences on one portion of the crowd before you change your gaze to another portion.

You use movement well. You've marked on your outline when you want to move out away from the podium, to the side of it to make a point, and when to move back. You've also marked when you want to take longer pauses, to let your ideas sink in. You've practiced allowing your facial expressions to change as you speak to reflect the different emotions your message seeks to convey. Throughout, you maintain good eye focus.

Step #3: Be Persuasive With Your Voice (Techniques #38–#47)

Your voice is strong and clear; you articulate well. You've practiced putting "color" through words to make your speech warmer; you know you have a tendency to sound cool or "clipped." Your pitch is comfortably placed to convey authority, you phrase for "sound bites," and you have practiced speaking with a microphone so you know how much volume to give and how much you can pull back, for emphasis, yet still be easily heard.

You've practiced your speech with pauses at certain moments to give emphasis. You've included lots of words that engage the senses.

Step #4: Rapport (Techniques #48–#53)

You build rapport with your potential voters in a number of ways. Although you are professionally and conservatively dressed, you mirror by wearing an outfit that reflects the general dress style of your community. Your easy manner and comfortable body language mirror the relatively laid-back, down-home attitude of the electorate. You have made word choices that mirror the habitual vocabulary and vocal style of the community. You are careful to use words from all three perceptual modes, emphasizing especially the visual and kinesthetic, since you know that the vast majority of people fall into those perceptual modes.

The most important way you build rapport, however, is by sharing with your audience your mutually familiar experience of Mayor Bart. It is from this springboard of emotional rapport that you will build your whole campaign.

You greet your audience and then get into your speech: "As you all know, I am running against Mayor Bart. Now that feels like a very strange thing to do, given that I think Bill Bart [removing his title takes him subconsciously off the mayor pedestal] is a terrific guy [people yell and cheer, you nod your head in acknowledgment, rapport]. Heck, I voted for Bill in the last election! But the question I want you to ask yourselves is this: "Could it be that Bill Bart is a great guy, but not a great politician [rhetorical question containing your theme, umbrella statement]? Could it be that Bill, whom we all love, just doesn't have what it takes to get things done on the political front? Could it be, is that possible [reiteration and development of theme in three volleys]? Let's take a look."

You have effectively created rapport with the electorate by admitting to Mayor Bart's huge popularity, making yourself part of his admirers. You've paced their love of Mayor Bart and then started your lead, which is "not a great politician." You have effectively dethroned Mayor Bart without putting him down.

Step #5: Creative Listening (Techniques #54–#68)

As you continue your speech, you listen for the crowd's response. You make room for it, by acknowledging with head nods, smiles (when appropriate), and occasional restating of a point the crowd seems to particularly like. You back off and pace again whenever the crowd seems to be resisting your lead. You pace until you see the crowd's body language become receptive enough for you to attempt a successful lead to your point of view.

Step #6: Logic and Reason (Techniques #69–#81)

You then proceed to show with charts and graphs (visual aid) a comparison between Mayor Bart's promises and the work actually done. It is pathetic (for Mayor Bart, that is—for you, it's great). You keep reiterating your theme throughout, in as many ways as you can think of: "A great guy, but not a great politician."

You admit to weakness in a way that strengthens your cause: "Now, I may not be the greatest politician, but I do have a good track record of accomplishing what I set out to." You then show with charts and graphs your trustworthiness: When you promise something to your voters, 90 percent of the time you deliver. "I'm still working on the other 10 percent" (disclosing weakness in a way that increases trustworthiness), you say, meaning it!

Step #7: Emotion (Techniques #82–#110)

You develop your theme further: "Life is not a popularity contest [catch phrase]. Your interests and well-being should not be at the mercy of a popularity contest [emotional hook]. Let's get back to basics [catch phrase and money words]. Let's get the job done that needs to be done [positive focus and positive emotion]. You may never like me as much as you like Bill Bart, but I'll get the job done [admitting to weakness in a way that increases your trustworthiness]. I'll see to it that what the people of this community want, I'll fight for and do my darndest to get. My goal—is to get for you the benefits and advantages that this community deserves and should have!"

You outline the specifics of what you hope to accomplish for your community. Your slogan becomes "Get the job done! Vote Halaran!"

You have been passionate, enthusiastic, stirring, and uplifting. You have had notes of compassion, caring, humor, and determination in your speech. You have, in short, used emotions vividly and varyingly throughout your speech, sometimes pausing in between to let complete silence provide a change in mood. You have resisted being angry, sarcastic, haranguing, or defensive (negative emotions). Your ability to stay on a positive emotional track has succeeded in rousing the voters to a thunderous ovation at the end of your speech. You did it! It worked! You're thrilled!

One rally down, seventeen to go . . .

CONCLUSION

These examples cover a wide range of situations to show you the variety of ways in which the seven steps to persuasion can be successfully applied. The following checklist will help you use the techniques in specific circumstances.

CHECKLIST OF STEPS AND TECHNIQUES TO USE IN DESIGNING YOUR SPECIFIC PERSUASIVE STRATEGIES

Use the following checklist to help you target those techniques that will be most useful to you in designing your persuasive strategy for any given situation. Be sure to use elements from each step.

The First Step: *Create a Sure Foundation with Credibility*

First Impressions
>Technique #1: Establish credibility with expertness
>Technique #2: Follow through with trustworthiness

Attractiveness
>Technique #3: Cleanliness counts
>Technique #4: Be well groomed
>Technique #5: Choose appropriate accessories
>Technique #6: Be in shape

Self-Assurance
>Technique #7: Do things one thing at a time
>Technique #8: Know when to be still
>Technique #9: Develop direct and steady eye focus

Respect
>Technique #10: Get respect by giving it

Attitude
>Technique #11: Focus out toward people
>Technique #12: Be dedicated and committed
>Technique #13: Have a positive focus
>Technique #14: Be moderately relaxed

The Second Step: *Engage The Power of Your Body*

Body Language
>Technique #15: Your posture: express confidence
>Technique #16: Your stance: create a sure foundation
>Technique #17: Arms and hands
>Technique #18: Head placement
>Technique #19: Power sitting
>Technique #20: Suit your body language to your purpose

Facial Expressions
>Technique #21: Express serious concern to win people's trust
>Technique #22: Convey your disapproval subtly
>Technique #23: Convey your approval subtly

Technique #24: Use your smile judiciously

Technique #25: Communicate interest or distrust with your brows

Technique #26: Give value with your eyes

Technique #27: Let your intent guide your expressions

Gestures and Mannerisms

Technique #28: Weed out irrelevant habitual gestures

Technique #29: Time a gesture to maximize its impact

Technique #30: Get rid of useless mannerisms

Movement

Technique #31: Use movement to establish control of a place or a situation

Technique #32: Use movement to keep people interested and attentive

Technique #33: Use movement to make an effective transition between points

Technique #34: Use movement to drive a point home

Technique #35: Use movement to create special relationships with people or things

Technique #36: Use movement to distract from or discredit a person

Technique #37: Coordinate movement with gestures, facial expressions, and eye focus

Podiums, flip charts and lecterns

The Third Step: Be Persuasive With Your Voice

Vocal Basics

Technique #38: Vary pace

Technique #39: Use authoritative pitch

Technique #40: Project confidence with good articulation

Technique #41: Regulate your volume

Vocal Techniques

Technique #42: Use effective phrasing

Technique #43: Use the pause to highlight important points

Technique #44: Make dull material come to life using color, peaks, and valleys

Technique #45: Use the five senses

Technique #46: Use emotions appropriately

Technique #47: The build-drop

The Fourth Step: *Develop Trust By Developing Relationship*

Establish Common Ground
> Technique #48: Mirror dress and body language
> Technique #49: Mirror vocabulary and vocal style
> Technique #50: Mirror a person's energy

Perceptual Modes
> Technique #51: Recognize perceptual modes (visual, auditory, kinesthetic)
> Technique #52: Use people's perceptual mode to ready them to be convinced by you

Pace and Lead
> Technique #53: Pace and lead

The Fifth Step: *Gain The Advantage With Creative Listening*

Listening for Inconsistencies
> Technique #54: Content that clashes with content
> Technique #55: Content that conflicts with emotional tone
> Technique #56: Content that conflicts with body language
> Technique #57: Variations in vocal tone
> Technique #58: Overly frequent pauses, "uh" sounds, and "I think"
> Technique #59: Inconsistencies in vocabulary

"Listening" to Body Language
> Technique #60: Interpret body language cues
> Technique #61: Use body language cues to evaluate your impact
> Technique #62: Use body language cues to guide you in the successful development of your point

Eye Contact
> Technique #63: Use eye contact to make a person feel listened to and credible

Use Your Body Purposefully
> Technique #64: Use your body to bring a person's attention to a point
> Technique #65: Use your body to distract a person's attention away from a point

Acknowledgment
> Technique #66: Use acknowledgment to gain cooperation

Technique #67: Withhold acknowledgment to make a person uncomfortable

Overheard Conversations

Technique #68: Use "overheard conversations" to get your point across

The Sixth Step: *Persuade With Logic and Reason*

Logic and Reasoning

Technique #69: Use structure to promote people's acceptance of what you have to say

Technique #70: Use a theme

Technique #71: Use the "Rule of Threes"

Technique #72: Follow the "Law of Primacy" and the "Law of Recency"

Technique #73: Use an umbrella statement

Technique #74: Speak everyday language

Technique #75: Use jargon, technical terms, and slang appropriately

Technique #76: Phrase for clarity of thought

Technique #77: Get to the point

Technique #78: Admit weaknesses in a way that strengthens your point

Technique #79: Disclose weaknesses to increase trustworthiness

Technique #80: Use rhetorical questions

Ask for What You Want

Technique #81: Use explicit conclusions

The Seventh Step: *Win With Emotion*

Emotions

Technique #82: Express sincerity

Technique #83: Use positive emotions

Story Telling

Technique #84: Capture people's attention

Technique #85: Organize your facts in an emotionally meaningful way

Technique #86: Facilitate people's vivid vicarious experiencing of an event or situation

Technique #87: Use well-known myths and stories

with built-in emotional appeal as "hooks"
Analogies and Similes
    Technique #88: Use analogies and similes to help people relate
        emotionally to your point
    Technique #89: Use analogies and similes to give focus and impact
        to an issue
    Technique #90: Select analogies and similes that have emotional
        appeal for your specific listener
    Technique #91: Avoid the problems inherent in using analogies
Repetition, Catch Phrases, and "Money Words"
    Technique #92: Use repetition
    Technique #93: Use catch phrases
    Technique #94: Use money words
Personalizations
    Technique #95: Get people directly engaged with the "you" format
    Technique #96: Translate the event or situation into terms taken
        from people's personal experience
Choose a Theme that Sells
    Technique #97: Elevate your theme to a higher cause
Past or Present Tense
    Technique #98: Use the present tense to help people relate
        intensely to an event or situation
    Technique #99: Use the past tense to distance people emotionally
        from an event or situation
The Positive or Negative Forms of Speech
    Technique #100: Keep people on track with you by using the
        positive form of speech
    Technique #101: Sow doubt by using the negative form of speech
Word Choice
    Technique #102: Choose words that hold powerful subconscious
        images
    Technique #103: Choose words that encourage people to think the
        way you want them to
Visual Aids
    Technique #104: Use visual aids to keep people awake and
        interested
    Technique #105: Use visual aids to focus attention
    Technique #106: Use visual aids to access the visual perceptual
        mode

References

Chapter One

1. Spence, Gerry. *How to Argue and Win Every Time*. (New York, NY: St. Martin's Press, 1995), p. 47.
2. Bugliosi, Vincent. *Outrage: The Five Reasons Why O. J. Simpson Got Away with Murder*. (New York, NY: W. W. Norton & Co., Inc., 1996), p. 38.
3. Couric, Emily. *The Trial Lawyers*. (New York, NY: St. Martin's Press, 1988), p. 43.
4. Aron, Roberto, Julius Fast, and Richard B. Klein, *Trial Communication Skills, 1994 Cumulative Supplement* (New York, NY: Shepard's/McGraw-Hill, 1994), p. 4.
5. Ibid., p. 115.
6. Sears, David O., Jonathan L. Freedman, and Letitia A. Peplau, *Social Psychology*. (Englewood Cliffs, NJ: Prentice-Hall, 1985.)
7. Cramer, M. Michael. "A view from the jury box," In *The Litigation Manual*. Section of litigation, American Bar Association (1983), pp. 145–147.
8. Ibid.
9. Spence, Gerry. *With Justice for None*. (New York, NY: Penguin Books, 1989), p. 31.
10. Thornton, Hazel. *Hung Jury: The Diary of a Menendez Juror*. (Philadelphia, PA: Temple University Press, 1995), pp. 46–47.
11. Spence, *How to Argue and Win Every Time*, p. 34.
12. Aron et al., p. 5.
13. Ibid., p. 90.
14. Cooley, Armanda, Carrie Bess, and Marsha Rubin-Jackson. *Madam Foreman*. (Los Angeles, CA: Dove Books, 1995), pp. 88–89.
15. Ibid., p. 106.
16. Aron et al., p. 102.
17. Higginbotham, Patrick E. "How to Try a Jury Case: A Judge's View." In *The Litigation Manual*. Section of litigation, American Bar Association (1983), p. 133.
18. Kerr, Robert L., and Robert M. Bray, (eds.). *Psychology of the Courtroom*. (New York, NY: Academic Press, 1982), p. 175.
19. Doubleday Dictionary (New York, NY: Doubleday, 1975).
20. Aron et al., p. 123.

21. Thornton, p. 33.
22. Cooley et al., p. 88.

Chapter Two

1. Bugliosi, p. 155.
2. Cooley et al., pp. 104–105.
3. Ibid., p. 109.
4. Ibid., p. 97.
5. Ibid.
6. Bugliosi, p. 155.

Chapter Three

1. Gamblee, Joanne D. "What It's Like to Serve on a Jury." *Barrister*, Vol. 6 (3) (1979), pp. 16–20.
2. Bailey, William S. "A Lawyer Looks at Jury Duty." *The Docket*, Winter (1989), pp. 9–15.
3. Bugliosi, p. 208.
4. Ibid., p. 155.
5. Hanley, Robert F. "The importance of being yourself." *The Docket*, Fall (1985), pp. 12–13.
6. Bugliosi, p. 181.
7. Spence, *How to Argue and Win Every Time*, pp. 130–131.
8. Spence, *With Justice for None*, p. 75.

Chapter Four

1. Doubleday Dictionary. (New York, NY: Doubleday, 1975).
2. Sheresky, Norman. *On trial*. (New York, NY: Viking Press, 1977), pp. 12–13.
3. Cooley et al., p. 115.
4. Ibid., p. 114.
5. Allison, William P. "The Environment of the Trial." In D. Lake Rumsey (ed.), *Master Advocates' Handbook*. (St. Paul, MN: National Institute for Trial Advocacy, 1986), p. 24.
6. Aron et al., p. 90.
7. Cooley et al., p. 88.
8. Spence, *How to Argue and Win Every Time*, p. 25.
9. Spence, *With Justice for None*, p. 15.

Chapter Five

1. Strayhorn, Honorable E. (1986). "The importance of watching and listening." In D. Lake Rumsey (ed.), p. 14.
2. Couric, p. 319.
3. Spence, *How to Argue and Win Every Time*, p. 67.
4. Ibid., p. 72.
5. Bugliosi, pp. 113–114.
6. Couric, p. 137.
7. Bugliosi, p. 207.
8. Aron et al., p. 95.

Chapter Six

1. Spence, *With Justice for None*, p. 269.
2. Couric, p. 207.
3. Schuetz, Janice, and Kathryn H. Snedaker. *Communication and Litigation.* (Carbondale and Edwardsville: Southern Illinois University Press, 1988), p. 82.
4. Spence, *How to Argue and Win Every Time*, p. 126.
5. Ibid., p. 127.
6. Bugliosi, p. 194.
7. Couric, pp. 27–28.
8. Adapted from Schuetz and Snedaker, op. cit.
9. Ibid., p. 84.
10. Couric, p. 209.
11. Ibid., pp. 107–108.
12. Thornton, p. 16.
13. Cooley et al., p. 118.
14. Thornton, p. 11.
15. Bugliosi, p. 190.
16. Ibid., p. 155.
17. Schuetz and Snedaker, p. 175.
18. Cooley, pp. 101–102.
19. Aron et al., p. 108.
20. Sheresky, p. 24.
21. Thornton, p. 63.
22. Bugliosi, pp. 221–222.
23. Spence, *With Justice for None*, pp. 81–83.
24. Bugliosi, p. 209.

25. Ibid., p. 28.
26. Ibid., p. 199.
27. Spence, *With Justice for None*, p. 287.

Chapter Seven

1. Bugliosi, pp. 214–215.
2. Musmanno, Michael A. *Verdict.* (Garden City, NY: Doubleday & Company, 1958), p. 244, quoted in Thornton, pp. 145–146.
3. Spence, *With Justice for None*, pp. 43–44.
4. Thornton, pp. 8–9.
5. Couric, pp. 1–39.
6. Bugliosi, pp. 189–190.
7. Cramer, p. 146.
8. Bugliosi, p. 153.
9. Cartwright, Dorwin (ed.). *Studies in Social Power.* (Ann Arbor: University of Michigan, 1959), p. 147.
10. Kerr, Robert L., and Robert M. Bray, (eds.). *Psychology of the Courtroom.* (New York, NY: Academic Press, 1982), p. 203.
11. Cooley, pp. 92–93.
12. Couric, p. 162.
13. Ibid., pp. 243–244.
14. Sheresky, p. 43.
15. Spence, *With Justice for None*, p. 71.
16. Sheresky, pp. 68–76.
17. Couric, pp. 49–54.
18. Ibid., p. 162.
19. Ibid., pp. 180–181.
20. *Newsweek,* July 20, 1987, p. 14.
21. Bugliosi, p. 138.
22. Ibid., p. 196.
23. Ibid., p. 193.
24. Ibid., pp. 39–40.
25. Ibid., p. 45.
26. Ibid., p. 46.
27. Sears, p. 154.
28. Sheresky, pp. 2–3.
29. Spence, *With Justice for None*, p. 310.
30. Klieman, Rikki J. "How To Deliver a Convincing and Winning Opening Statement in a Criminal Defense." In Janine N. Warsaw

(ed.), *Women Trial Lawyers: How They Succeed in Practice and in the Courtroom.* (Englewood Cliffs, NJ: Prentice-Hall, 1987), p. 282.

31. Lambert, Marie. "How to Improve Your Courtroom Appearance." In Janine N. Warsaw (ed.), *Women Trial Lawyers: How They Succeed in Practice and in the Courtroom.* (Englewood Cliffs, NJ: Prentice-Hall, 1987), p. 97.
32. Sheresky, pp. 110–120.
33. Touhy, James. "Effective Final Argument for the Plaintiff." In *The Litigation Manual.* Section of litigation, American Bar Association, (1983), pp. 168–171.
34. Aron et al., p. 105.
35. *Time,* July 20, 1987, p. 16; *Newsweek,* July 20, 1987, p. 15.
36. Couric, p. 143.
37. Loftus, E. "Reconstructing Memory: The Incredible Eyewitness." *Psychology Today,* Vol.8 (1) (1974), p. 116.
38. Thornton, p. 84.
39. Cooley, p. 124.
40. Spence, *How to Argue and Win Every Time,* pp. 130–131.
41. Bugliosi, p. 114.
42. Cooley, p. 127.
43. Aron et al., p. 17.
44. Klieman, pp. 284–285.
45. Couric, p. 140.

Index

6/97